Rural Education Across the World

Simone White · Jayne Downey

Editors

Rural Education Across the World

Models of Innovative Practice and Impact

 Springer

Editors
Simone White ⓘ
Faculty of Education
Queensland University of Technology
Kelvin Grove, QLD, Australia

Jayne Downey ⓘ
Department of Education
Montana State University
Bozeman, MT, USA

ISBN 978-981-33-6115-7   ISBN 978-981-33-6116-4   (eBook)
https://doi.org/10.1007/978-981-33-6116-4

This Springer imprint is published by the registered company Springer Nature Singapore Pte Ltd.
The registered company address is: 152 Beach Road, #21-01/04 Gateway East, Singapore 189721, Singapore

This book was written at the turn of the second decade of the twenty-first century—a time that witnessed increased climate change as evidence in the horrendous bushfires in Australia; the COVID-19 global pandemic; and the world economic downturn. In the midst of these horrific events, we were also moved by the stories of care, generosity and resilience which emerged as nations witnessed the sacrifice, dedication and commitment of all those who stood at the front lines. In particular, the true spirit and value of all those working in the education and teaching profession were revealed. For rural educators and leaders caught at the nexus of 'a perfect storm' this was even more the case. This book is thus dedicated to all those in rural education around the globe, who, every day, in the face of stark adversity, continue to nurture, innovate and work towards a more equitable, hopeful and sustainable future for their students, their families and communities. We stand and applaud to thank you for all you do.

This book is also dedicated to our own families whose support and encouragement makes projects like these possible.

—Simone White and Jayne Downey

Foreword

I write this introduction from inland Australia, 'socially isolated' in the time of the pandemic, on the land of the Wiradjuri people, who are still fighting for the right to control the land taken from them by British settlers to expand the wealth of Empire. I live in a regional city which, though hours from the coastal metropolis, is growing. It's thought of as 'rural' by people on the coast, as very comfortably 'urban' by its inhabitants, and as a significant 'regional' centre by people living in smaller towns further west. It's an educational hub, one site of a multi-campus university dispersed across five rural/regional centres around the state and known for its distance (now online) education. The university is proud of its commitment to the teaching of Wiradjuri language, and attention to Indigenous cultures and histories in every course curriculum. And today as I write, the university's Pro Vice-Chancellor of Indigenous Engagement, Professor Juanita Sherwood, publishes a call for all Australians to reflect on the global Black Lives Matter protests and what we can do to educate ourselves about the 'deep, unfinished business' of the shared history of Indigenous and non-Indigenous Australians. Our connections are global, yet we have work to do locally. The land on which this city grows was once home to a Wiradjuri leader, Windradyne, whose resistance to the invasion of his land and the massacre of his people so convincingly belied the British claim of 'terra nullius' that the military was brought in to control the area. Today, Wiradjuri people, products of invasion, migration and survival, are fighting to keep access to the place their grandmothers used to present boys to male Elders for initiation into manhood. Local government has given this land to a Go-Kart club for use as a racing track.

Several of the chapters in this volume have been written from places with similar histories, more or less 'rural', depending on where we stand: places that have 'made us', shaping our identity and our possibilities. We are all 'occupants of particular places with particular attributes' (Gruenewald, 2003, p. 621, cited by the Editors in Chapter 1). With their focus here on models of innovative practice in rural education across the world, the Editors have conceptualised and curated a set of chapters whose possibilities, as a collection, are strong and powerful. Their focus on innovative practice and resilience opens us up, as readers, to learn *from* each other as we learn *about* each other: raising the possibilities of new forms of education practice in the range of places represented here, and in our own.

Many contributors, like me, are residents of settler nations where land was appropriated, and its meaning altered, through invasion, migration and globalisation. We live on land that has *become* 'rural', not because of its inherent genesis, but in relation to colonial centres of power and commerce. Many of the contributors note this relativity, carefully defining what rurality means in their contexts, and highlighting the important sense that we are always learning, teaching and writing from *somewhere*. Yet there are authors here whose home cultures remain indigenous to the places that have made them, such as those from Scotland, South Africa and China, where the making of rurality, and rural identity, has been slightly different. These pieces highlight the value of an international perspective for the reader: I am struck by the explicit attention to the moral purpose of education in the preparation of teachers for the Highlands and Islands of Scotland; I share the outrage felt by South African teacher educators about the material poverty of the postcolonial legacy they endure; and I am inspired by the challenge of the restorative push to restore the balance of a Taoist duality rather than a Judeo-Christian binary in Chinese sociological thinking. For me, this is the real strength of this collection—the clear sense of difference between places, all of which have been *made* rural, by social practices focused on 'innovation', change and connection. As Corbett writes in his chapter, the problematic binary of rural and urban space 'has been employed in the central narrative of colonial modernity in the story of a movement from the country to the city'. For earlier Wiradjuri people, the concept of 'rurality' was literally non-sense, the word 'rural' simply does not exist in the lexicon: and as Halfacree (2006) reminds us, when European modernity needed it to think with, this binary concept could not be translated into German, either.

In 2006, Richard Teese made an important argument for the necessity of learning from teachers and schools that are, as he put it, 'condemned to innovate' by their socio-economic and locational disadvantage. He argued that '[i]n the end, the quality of a school system can be judged by the experience of the most vulnerable children in it'. Addressing spatial inequity is the challenge that all of the contributors to this volume have taken up in their practice. The focus on teacher identity across the volume is central to this work, as teacher educators like Redmond and Nicol innovate to 'frame rural teaching as a meaningful place-mediated identity' in their chapter here.

Other researchers have argued that the concept of rurality is a project of innovation and change: 'an actively constituted constellation of forces, agencies, and resources that are evident in lived experience and social processes in which teachers and community workers are changed' (Balfour, Mitchell & Moletsane, 2008, p. 102). They argue that, from this perspective, education must be seen as a *placed resource* where ideas, practices and supports that work well in one place can 'become dysfunctional as soon as they are moved into other places'. I am struck by the way the authors here are realistic about the impact and sustainability of their practice. They think critically about the innovations they describe, flagging the need for careful stewardship of place-attentiveness, to combat what Roberts, Bodycott, Li and Qian point to, in their chapter, as 'the mechanisms through which modernity works to erase rurality through the discourse of equity that assumes the values of the city'. This volume makes a strong contribution to the sharing of knowledge and developing a body of knowledge and theory from and of place. Its basis in teacher education here is particularly important, as it is the potential for rural schooling to disrupt and deconstruct the ingrained binary that privileges metropolitan values and places the rural in deficit. We have seen this most strikingly in the time of the pandemic, where city students have had to learn online, at home, in ways that many isolated rural children have been doing for over a century here in Australia. As Teese argued:

> … for innovation—for system-wide change in the fundamental qualities of teaching and learning […] our most likely candidates are going to be the schools where everything depends on relationships between individuals.

As the focus of this volume, these relationships are key to all our futures.

Jo-Anne Reid
Charles Sturt University
Bathurst, Australia

References

Balfour, R. J., Mitchell, C., & Moletsane, R. (2008). Troubling contexts: Toward a generative theory of rurality as education research. *Journal of Rural and Community Development, 3*(3), 95–107.

Halfacree, K. (2006). Rural Space: Constructing a Three-fold Architecture. In P. Cloke, T. Marsden, & P. Mooney (Eds.), *The Handbook of Rural Studies* (pp. 44–62). London: Sage.

Sherwood, J. (2020, June). Black Lives Matter at Charles Sturt University. Retrieved June 29, 2020, from https://news.csu.edu.au/opinion/black-lives-matter-at-charles-sturt-university.

Teese, R. (2006). Condemned to Innovate [online]. *Griffith Review, 11,* 113–125. Retrieved June 25, 2020, from https://www.griffithreview.com/articles/condemned-to-innovate/.

Contents

Editors and Contributors

About the Editors

Simone White is Professor and Associate Dean (International and Engagement) in the Faculty of Education at Queensland University of Technology (QUT). Simone's area of expertise is teacher education and rural education and her publications, research and teaching are all focused on the key question of how to best prepare teachers and leaders for diverse communities (both local and global). Her current research areas focus on rural education, teacher education policy, teacher development, professional experience and building and maintaining university–school/community partnerships. Simone is a past President of the *Australian Teacher Education Association* (ATEA) and had a previous role as Vice President of the *Society for the Provision for Education in Rural Australia* (SPERA). She is the founder and co-leader of the *Rural Education International Research Alliance* (REIRA). Through her collective work, Simone aims to connect research, policy and practice in ways that bring teachers and school and university-based teacher educators together and break down traditional borders between academics, policymakers, communities and practitioners.

Jayne Downey is Professor and Director of the Center for Research on Rural Education at Montana State University. She has worked in the field of educator preparation for over 20 years and her research agenda has focused on strengthening the preparation of prospective educators and improving outcomes of P-20 education across rural contexts. As an Educational Psychologist, she is committed to engaging in research, scholarship and service intentionally attuned to, and respectful of, the complex and unique realities and relationships of rural schools and communities— past, present and future. Jayne serves on the executive committees of the *National Rural Education Association* (NREA) and the *Society for Provision of Education in Rural Australia* (SPERA). In Montana, she serves as the Chair of the Board of Directors for the *Montana Small Schools Alliance* (MSSA) working on behalf of 150 of

Montana's smallest rural and remote schools. She is an editor for the *Australian and International Journal of Rural Education* and a co-leader of the *Rural Education International Research Alliance*, celebrating the importance of learning, teaching and well-being for rural students, their families and communities around the globe.

Contributors

Amy Price Azano School of Education, Virginia Tech, Blacksburg, VA, USA

Peter Bodycott Faculty of Education, University of Canberra, Canberra, ACT, Australia

Ondine Bradbury Faculty of Education, Monash University, Melbourne, VIC, Australia

Carolyn M. Callahan School of Education and Human Development, University of Virginia, Charlottesville, VA, USA

Michael Corbett School of Education, Acadia University, Wolfville, NS, Canada

Jayne Downey Department of Education, Montana State University, Bozeman, MT, USA

Angela Fitzgerald School of Education, University of Southern Queensland, Springfield, QLD, Australia

Dipane Hlalele School of Education, University of KwaZulu-Natal, Durban, KwaZulu-Natal, Republic of South Africa

Margaret Kettle Faculty of Education, Queensland University of Technology, Brisbane, QLD, Australia

Tania Leach School of Education, University of Southern Queensland, Toowoomba, QLD, Australia

Yiting Li School of Education, Shaanxi Normal University, Xian, China

Mosebetsi Mokoena Faculty of Education, University of the Free State, Qwaqwa Campus, Phuthaditjhaba, Free State, Republic of South Africa

Tabitha Grace Mukeredzi School of Education, Durban University of Technology, Midlands/Indumiso Campus, Pietermaritzburg, Republic of South Africa

Lindsay Nicol University of the Highlands and Islands, Scotland, UK

Xuyang Qian School of Education, Hangzhou Normal University, Hangzhou, China

Morag Redford University of the Highlands and Islands, Scotland, UK

Philip Roberts Faculty of Education, University of Canberra, Canberra, ACT, Australia

Simone White Faculty of Education, Queensland University of Technology, Brisbane, QLD, Australia

Part I
Introduction

Chapter 1
International Trends and Patterns in Innovation in Rural Education

Simone White and Jayne Downey

Abstract This chapter explores the interplay between the notions of rurality, innovation and education by analysing the eight chapters in this volume and explores the trends and patterns that emerge by looking at the studies from across multiple global rural places and spaces. The analysis reveals a hopeful and resilient approach to innovative rural education and scholarship, and collectively, important evidence to speak against an often deficit view of rural education. Three patterns are revealed across the studies, namely: the importance of place-attentive strategies, the importance of joined up alliances to maximise resources and networks and finally, the need to utilise alternative methodologies and frameworks that have a starting point of difference rather than deficit for any rural initiative or approach. In short, a tripartite of place, people and power are offered as essential to any effective rural education innovation. And given the highly contextual nature of this tripartite, it is clear that while the specific innovations presented in the current studies can not necessarily be transplanted or adopted wholesale, these three essential elements are a true foundation for future rural education studies and scholars to explore.

Keywords Rurality · Innovation · Education · Place-attentive

1.1 Rural Education Innovation?

Innovation is often defined as the introduction of new things, ideas or ways of doing something. Synonyms for innovation can include words like change, reorganisation, transformation, unconventionality and 'a change of direction'. Occasionally, when we hear a reference to innovation it is used in a deficit context referring to efforts to replace practices that are viewed as old-fashioned, irrelevant or lacking in some way. However, innovation is also used in reference to hopeful, responsive and creative

S. White (✉)
Faculty of Education, Queensland University of Technology, Brisbane, QLD, Australia
e-mail: simone.white@qut.edu.au

J. Downey
Department of Education, Montana State University, Bozeman, MT, USA

© Springer Nature Singapore Pte Ltd. 2021
S. White and J. Downey (eds.), *Rural Education Across the World*,
https://doi.org/10.1007/978-981-33-6116-4_1

efforts to build on the positive outcomes that have occurred and extend those efforts to meet current needs.

When coupled with the word education, a meaning is drawn that is often linked to the development of new ideas, structures, technological advances and various disruptions designed for the purpose of strengthening traditional means of schooling and teaching. In relation to schools, there is often talk of fostering twenty-first century skills for young people such as curiosity, creativity, entrepreneurialism and problem-solving. Sometimes 'innovation' and 'education' combined can be used to refer to programmes, for example, whereby a school is 'going against a particular trend', in a positive direction, in some way addressing an inequity or problem that has been identified. One example is a school that might be retaining more teachers by adopting a unique and different approach.

What then is evoked when the word *rural* is added to the mix? What emerges when the words rural, education *and* innovation are all connected? How do notions of change, transformation, disruption and creativity (as examples) play out when 'rurality' is considered? Are there trends and/or patterns of rural education innovation that emerge if we look at studies from across multiple global rural places and spaces? What can such an investigation offer rural education researchers and the education profession? Such questions were the impetus for this book and a call out to those working globally in rural education to document and discuss their innovations; whether it be through developing new approaches in rural (teacher) education, considering new designs for policy and programmes or applying new theoretical tools. The response to our call was quick and substantive.

Our authors' contributions clearly demonstrate that there is much innovation going on around the world in regard to rural education research, scholarship and policy. The studies shared in this volume highlight examples of transformation and ingenuity enacted by the researchers and their institutions *with* their various rural communities. The work also provides clear, cautionary tales of the perils of any thought of homogenising rural education innovation or wholesale transplanting of any particular idea, concept or practice from one context to another.

This collection draws from a global community of rural researchers writing from a similar stance of deep commitment to rural places but doing their work in dramatically different contexts. The studies include those from vastly different landscapes and cultures: from perspectives from rural China to rural Appalachia in the United States; from the Highlands and Islands of Scotland to the rural towns in South Africa; and from the northern oceanic climate of rural Nova Scotia in Canada to the hot and dry inland rural towns in Queensland, Australia. It is acknowledged that the studies here do not represent *all* rural contexts and places, for example, there are no studies from South America or Continental Europe. The field is however growing and we note a recently published volume exploring the often invisible and adverse consequences of metro-centric educational policies on rural students' and communities' experience of place and space across rural Europe (Gristy, Hargreaves, & Kučerová, 2020).

Throughout this scholarly work, two considerations become clear. First, the fact that the notion of rural cannot be defined simply by geography or distance from a metropolitan city or population density. Rather, around the world, definitions of rural are spatialised, nuanced and scaled relative to particular places and the challenges encountered in those places (White & Corbett, 2014). These definitions are important because they take into account the historical, ecological, economic and politicised understandings of rural communities (Azano et al., 2019), which then guide and shape the nature and implementation of the innovations. Even in comparing the various studies across the collection, each context can be viewed by another as more or less 'rural' considering the perspective and standpoint. As McGrail et al. (2005) neatly notes: "[t]here is no essential rural or metropolitan, but a concept of rural or metropolitan based on a continuum in regard to population numbers, accessibility of services, attitudes and values" (p. 22).

The second aspect that unites the studies is that the authors write from a rural perspective and adopt a researcher position that deeply values the rural community's strengths and voices. These researchers are not writing *about* rural people, nor does their research simply occur *in* rural places. Rather, these authors are demonstrating their commitment to engaging in context-specific educational service, scholarship and research that creates knowledge, insight and understanding as *requested by* and *relevant to* the lives of rural people, schools and communities. This volume also heeds the advice given to the rural education research community about ways to improve the status of research summarised by Hargreaves et al. (2020):

> Avoid unsubstantiated advocacy of the merits of small and/or rural schools, provide better contextual detail (to obviate the angst over dichotomous rural/urban definitions) and increase the criticality, objectivity and empirical work of the research. … rich descriptions of rural deficiency must be replaced with imaginative, constructive ideas and more evidence of community involvement. (p. 340)

This approach to rural education research is intentionally attuned to, respectful of and appreciative of, the complex and unique realities and relationships of rural life—past, present and future. As called for by Greenwood (2013), these researchers are engaged in the important work of remembering, restoring, conserving, changing and creating new, innovative ways to help rural communities thrive. This collection, and this chapter, provide an opportunity to take a 'hopeful' stance to gather insights into building vibrant and resilient rural communities (Halsey, 2018).

1.2 Hope and Resilience in Rural Education

The notions of hope and resilience emerge in the chapters as well as in related literature in rural education innovation. The hope revealed and demonstrated here is not simply wishful thinking or helpless longing for improvement. Rather, the hope depicted by our authors is a steadfast commitment to envisioning possible futures and taking action to bring that vision to reality. In the face of serious challenges, developing a vision that energises action is key to rural education innovation. In these contexts, hope is a vision for what the future can be, accompanied by an effort to create effective pathways to make it so. Throughout this volume, you will encounter examples of rural education innovation empowered by hope—vision and action—and a powerful reminder that how we envision our future together will shape how we live our present together. Hope, when defined as vision and action, is the antidote to despair. The chapters in this volume tell the research stories of enacted hope in rural education innovation and reveal the cultivation of powerful practices leading to resilience.

In the vernacular, the notion of resilience is typically considered as an ability to recover or bounce back and has been used to describe items ranging from cosmetics to agriculture. However, more than 50 years of resilience research has been much more consequential; studies have identified specific factors and mechanisms that can support individuals' and communities' capacity to respond, cope and overcome significant risks, challenges, hardships and traumas (Downey, 2002). These findings have contributed to a nuanced understanding of resilience as a dynamic process of ongoing interactions between an individual and contextual resources that support positive adaptation within the context of adversity (Downey, 2017). Studies have found that this process of positive adaptation for communities and individuals is not a permanent achievement, nor is it the result of a singular trait such as personality. Rather, resilience is a positive trajectory that is sustained by a combination of ongoing protective and supportive interactions between individual, family and local contextual resources that work together to support personal and/or community success (Downey, 2017). This means that we do not ask students and communities to simply be more resilient; rather, we work together to build spaces and processes that can support positive adaptation through interaction.

Throughout the chapters in this volume, the authors provide examples of how rural education innovation energised by hopeful vision has inspired, nurtured and sustained resilience—powerful ongoing interactions producing positive adaptation for rural communities and individuals across the world. Writing from the Australian context, Richard Price (2014) equates rural (education) innovation *and research* as 'adaption' and 'resilience'. Perhaps these two concepts are more important than ever given the global pandemic and what might lie ahead in a post-COVID-19 world for rural and regional communities. He notes:

> In the context of building future resilience in the bush, the role of rural research needs to take into account the nature of resilience. Important elements of resilience are the capacity to self-organise, learn, adapt and cope with nonlinearities and uncertainties (Lebel et al., 2006). These are also important elements in dealing with multiple problem domains (Reynolds, 2001). Most critically, these aspects of resilience support an adaptive management approach to dealing with the growing complexity of rural issues. (Price, 2014, p. 241)

Hope and resilience in light of many of the complex challenges faced by those in rural communities is an important feature of the themes that emerge from the chapters in this book. Some may argue that rural places have always been places of innovation, as the saying goes, 'necessity is the mother of invention' and many rural people and communities have continued to reinvent and renew themselves even in the face of major challenges ranging from experiences of natural disasters to the impact of urbanisation. As Wallin (2007) reminds us: "Rural communities that envision a bright future for themselves and their children have become innovative out of necessity—they learn, and adapt, in order to flourish and to provide opportunities for their children" (p. 1).

Hope and resilience, it can be argued, are traits in which many First Nations people have continued to engage with land and their culture, in the face of constant waves of colonisation and neoliberalism. Drawing from Australian Indigenous research Price (2014) notes:

> Over millennia, Australia's traditional owners found ways to adapt to the harsh and diverse environments of the Australian continent. This adaptation process no doubt involved trial and error, the use of human imagination and creativity to go beyond the bounds of the known, the collaboration of expertise and the sharing of knowledge through stories. (p. 256)

Similar patterns emerge in the ways in which the studies within this collection highlight rural education innovation. In our analysis of the chapters, three particular patterns or themes become clear. The first is the ways in which trial and error and human imagination and creativity are adopted, in particular relation to understanding land and place as sites of renewal. Secondly, the notion of collaboration and connecting expertise (sometimes with unlikely alliances) is a common tool utilised across the studies and thirdly, the sharing of knowledge or developing a body of knowledge and theory *from* and *of* place.

Before a further interrogation of these interconnected patterns and themes are discussed, it is important to look at the studies and how innovation is framed against the current status quo for rural education. In order to understand 'innovation' in light of rural education, it is important to revisit some of the issues faced by rural education and communities to better understand what is 'new' or transformative in this space. In short, we present some of the spaces where the new frontiers or boundaries might be forged from the challenges and opportunities.

1.3 Old Stories and New Frontiers: Innovation Against the Status Quo?

Unfortunately, the challenges for rural education identified in these chapters and more broadly, are not new and continue to be long-standing. For example, the OECD reported that the overall world population living in rural areas has declined (OECD, 2016). This change is one of the factors that has had significant impact on rural school funding (Johnson & Zoeller, 2016; Stelmach, 2011). Funding challenges are connected to difficulties recruiting and retaining rural educators (Sutcher et al., 2016; White & Kline, 2012) and a lack of access to specialised services for learners with special needs and diverse abilities (Cheney & Demachak, 2001; Rude & Miller, 2018). Further, rural schools may have limited access to quality staff development, mentoring and induction supports and university services for their teachers (Berry et al., 2012; Hodges, 2002). Child poverty tends to be higher in rural areas from Kenya (e.g., Okilwa, 2015) to Pakistan (e.g., Gouleta, 2015) to countries in eastern Europe (e.g., Kryst et al., 2015) to the United States (e.g., Biddle & Mette, 2017) and this can have a significant impact on children's learning. Furthermore, families in rural areas may lack geographic access to medical (Kiani et al., 2013), oral (Kaufman et al., 2016), social (Watt et al., 2019) and/or behavioural (Rossiter et al., 2018) health-related services.

Lack of broadband internet connectivity is also a serious challenge for many rural areas, revealed starkly within the current COVID-19 pandemic. While some rural areas have excellent internet connectivity, there are also many places where the connectivity is very poor or absent altogether. For example, in countries of the Global South, only 14% of rural areas have internet access compared to 42% in urban areas (Alliance for Affordable Internet, 2020). In the United States, data indicate that 26% of people in rural areas and 32% of people in Tribal lands lack adequate broadband coverage, while only 1.7% of people in urban areas lack adequate access (FCC, 2019).

The literature is becoming indeed saturated in relation to specific rural education problem identification. Such challenges above, while clearly documented, mask some of the more nuanced social, cultural, political and increasingly environmental forces at play. As Wallin (2007) highlights, these challenges exist within a complex web of global issues. She explains:

> Some of these issues arise from the social, economic, and political differences between urban and rural environments, but at the most fundamental of levels, they stem from the consequences of globalization on trade, labour relations, regulatory control, or governmental rules and guidelines. (Lutz & Neis, 2008) (p. 2)

The studies in this collection are set against such socio-geo-political forces. They have themed themselves in three sections that reflect some of these forces. Namely: the perennial issue of staffing rural schools; the challenge of meeting the needs of all students in a backdrop of schools struggling to staff particular disciplines or where rural communities are ill-prepared for supporting diverse cultural and linguistic student backgrounds and; finally, to the hidden inequities and biases that exist in policy, perspectives and indeed methodologies that are conceived from a largely metro-centric agenda. A brief outline of what the chapters each focus on is provided below to frame the later analysis of emerging innovation patterns and trends.

1.3.1 Staffing Rural Schools

The first theme of this collection focuses on the global issue of addressing teacher shortages for rural schools and their communities and discusses innovations in pre-service teacher education. Three different studies from diverse countries are discussed. The collection begins with a case study in rural South Africa; the next to the Highlands and Islands of Scotland and finally to a comparison study of two locations in rural Australia. Across these vastly different contexts there are many similarities in the stories painted and each highlights the important role universities and teacher educators can play in disrupting deficit thinking in relation to staffing rural school and communities.

In the opening chapter, Angela Fitzgerald, Ondine Bradbury and Tania Leach seek to address rural teacher shortages through two innovative institutional approaches discussed across two different rural locations in initial teacher education in the Australian context. They employed a community of practice approach (Lave & Wenger, 1998) to place pre-service teachers in small groups in rural schools. This was as an intentional programmatic action to further build the pre-service teachers' relationships with their peers and ensure that a localised support network was forming to support the development of professional practice in a rural context.

Morag Redford and Lindsay Nicol also write about addressing rural teaching shortages in Scotland, writing from a rural standpoint (Roberts, 2014) themselves. They document an innovative institutional approach that seeks to embody the very mission statement of the University, "To have a transformational impact on the prospects of our region, its economy, its people and its communities (University of the Highlands and Islands, 2015, p. 8)".

In the third chapter, Tabitha Mukeredzi introduces the South African context firstly through her own childhood experiences and then through her role as a teacher educator in designing innovative initial teacher education programmes to address teacher shortages. As with most countries, rural teacher shortages are a major issue and in South African rural schools it remains the biggest hindrance to meeting Millennium Development Goals (Masinire, 2015). Mukeredzi particularly draws on a study which investigated experiences and interpretations of rurality among 16 Bachelor of Education student teachers in one South African university, during a four-week residential teaching practice (TP) in a rural South African school. The research was part of a larger project, the Rural Teacher Education Project (RTEP) which examined alternative models of TP placement to address rural school needs. This study is similar to those in rural Australia, in particular disrupting the often deficit views of pre-service teachers about rural communities (see White & Reid, 2008). The study highlights the powerful role that *place* can play in welcoming pre-service teachers and when combined with supportive mechanisms, reframing rurality from a strengths-based position.

1.3.2 Addressing All Students' Needs

The second theme of the collection explores innovative responses to meeting the needs of all students and the importance of reframing deficit mindsets often held within policy reforms played out for rural students and their families. Amy Azano and Carolyn Callahan explore the notions of giftedness and rurality as social constructs and highlight the inherent bias that exists within policy and testing regimes when it comes to the relative presence or absence of a set of traits believed to differ across people or geography (for example, low socio-economic status). They specifically explore the challenges of identifying and serving gifted students in places that are labelled 'rural' and 'poor' in America and provide a new set of assessment tools, rather than a one-size-fits-all approach, to better address student learning needs.

Margaret Kettle, writing from the Australian context likewise explores inherent bias within a rural community where increased skilled migration was occurring. She documents the shifts in understanding of all stakeholders when parents, students and teachers learn from and with each other. She describes particular initiatives that included the establishment of a parent advisory group and changed workplace practices allowing parents to attend school meetings to best support students from diverse cultural and linguistic backgrounds.

In the third chapter in this theme, Mosebetsi Mokoena and Dipane Hlalele write from a South African perspective about a successful school enrichment programme set against the backdrop of the many challenges identified within a poor rural community which is geographically isolated, significantly under-resourced and with limited technological access. While they document a range of innovative practices that include forging new entrepreneurial school–community partnerships, they focus on the circumstances of the innovation rather than any one practice. They caution against the uniform application of case study findings and advise instead for the adaptation and tailoring of these conditions to enable thriving school enrichment programmes at rural schools.

1.3.3   Troubling Metro-Centric Policies and New Rural Methodological Tools

The last set of chapters explores and critiques policies largely framed from a metro-centric perspective and rolled out across rural communities. In a volume about innovation and rurality, it is important to explore new theories and perspectives. Philip Roberts, Peter Bodycott, Yiting Li and Xuyang (Karen) Qian bring together Australian and Chinese rural researchers. This collaboration is in itself an example of innovation and a new layer to understanding brought to bear about developing rural methodologies. They provide a fascinating exploration of rural education policy and rural perspectives in China, framed from an Australian viewpoint. The chapter references and compares two nations with similar geographic size and geography, but distinctly different national histories, cultures and populations. It introduces Fei Xiaotong, a famous Chinese sociologist and anthropologist and draws from his 1947 (translated 1992) work, translated as 'From the Soil' with the subtitle 'the foundations of Chinese society', and often regarded as the foundation of Chinese sociology. They explore the current policy and perspectives of building rural China from a philosophical and sociological perspective, broadening their discussion to other contexts.

Michael Corbett bookends the collection with a philosophically oriented chapter highlighting the importance of connecting rural education theory and philosophy to action and innovation and the need for both to grow in concert. Drawing from his

Canadian homeland, his own identity narratives and references to diverse disciplines and contexts, he offers an alternative methodological paradigm for rural education and research as an innovation itself. He discusses a theoretical approach to rural teacher education that imagines schooling as a relational enterprise where stories connect rather than diverge, supporting a movement of the field of rural education into productive conversation with the culturally responsive pedagogy movement and indigenous scholarship.

Across this global collection, what is emerging out of this backdrop are fresh ways to reclaim the rural, just as Stehlik (2001) attempted to reclaim the 'rural' from those analyses that position rurality in terms of deficiency or 'lack'. She argued that: "... 'the rural' as something different to the urban, is a relevant distinction, one which is significant to ('rural') peoples identities". (p. 1) Building from the themes, we now explore the three patterns that emerged across the eight studies. These three form a 'tripartite' set that contributes to the grand narrative as part of a hopeful and resilient stance in rural education. In this collection what surfaces is the essence of an emerging connection of people, place and power. We explore these as keys to rural education innovation.

1.4 Keys to Successful Innovation? Emerging Patterns

In looking across the innovation represented in these studies, three particular patterns emerged. The first, 'place-attentive strategies' was a common approach adopted across many of the studies. This type of approach builds from the earlier work of environmental educators who positioned 'place' in the school curriculum as key to building a sustainable future. Likewise, in relation to rural education, knowing, valuing and learning from 'place' is a key innovation tool that many of the studies used to build greater awareness and care for rural locations. Place in this context, however, extends beyond learning about the land and geography of any one place and includes knowing the diversity of people and the ways in which the place itself functions.

The connection of place to people and people to people—is the second pattern that emerged and involved the key innovation tool of forming alliances which could contribute to new visions of the future and the resources needed to bring those ideas to reality. This was a strategy which required an investment of time to build the relationships which generated the shared understandings, commitments and responsibilities.

These new connections to people and place, in turn brought power in new forms. This third element rounds out the final pattern involved as a key innovation tool of repositioning the state of being rural, adding power to influence policy and practice. The researchers drew from an important set of social and spatial theories to retell rural narratives from a different, but not deficit, perspective. This empowering stance was key to successful innovation. Figure 1.1 highlights these three 'P's' of the connecting

Fig. 1.1 Keys to Rural
Education Innovation: Place,
People and Power

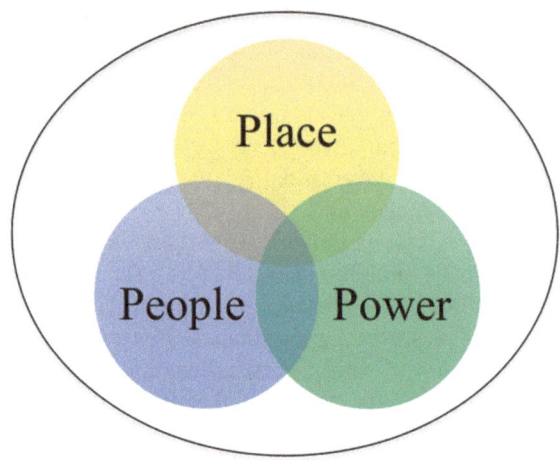

patterns of place, people and power, which are then further discussed in the sections below.

1.4.1 Place-Attentive Strategies

"Places make us: as occupants of particular places with particular attributes, our identity and our possibilities are shaped" (Gruenewald, 2003, p. 621). Place-based education arose at the turn of the twenty-first century as a way to reawaken an interest in and care for, the environment. Gruenewald (2003), coming from an environmental education perspective, raised awareness about the importance of 'place-based' and 'place-conscious' pedagogies as a way for teachers to help children and young people reconnect to nature and care for the sustainability of the world. This involved a re-engagement with the world outside of the classroom as a curriculum, at a time where such activities were viewed as not academically relevant. As Tooth & Renshaw, (2009) noted: "There has been a failure in modern educational discourse to take the 'out-doors', 'place' and 'place identity' seriously, and to see their key relevance and importance for mainstream education" (p. 96).

Place-based education has been designed to help to reposition the natural world and the importance of embodied practice as key tools in ensuring the sustainability of the planet. What some would argue as simple pleasures of going out into the world and discovering and wondering at the seasons, animal lifecycles and learning about human impact can be seen as vital teaching tools. In this way, researchers describe the reconnection of the mind and body as key to place-based education. They explain:

> It is this reconnecting with the world through the body, where knowledge is embodied experientially, physically and sensually over time that is allowing a new kind of pedagogy to emerge that is ideally suited to the age of sustainability. We endorse this focus on the physicality of place as a basis for a new kind of teaching and learning because it offers

us a fresh way of relating to the nature/environment debate that is currently shaping the development of sustainable communities in schools. (Tooth & Renshaw, 2009, p. 96)

This same concept of 'placed-based' emerged as an innovation tool for rural education but with a broader focus on knowing a place. As White and Reid (2008) describe:

> Place-based pedagogies foreground the local and the known. They allow teachers to structure learning opportunities that are framed as meaningful and relevant to their students because they are connected to their own places, to people and to the popular cultures and concerns that engage them (Comber, Reid, & Nixon, 2007). Place-conscious pedagogies are more interested in developing and projecting awareness outward toward places (Gruenewald, 2003) beyond the immediate and the local, with a clear and articulated sense of the relationship of the local to the global, and of the social lifeworld to the natural environment. (p. 6)

Place-attentiveness is a relatively new term in rural education, extending from the notions of place-based and place-conscious but elevating the standpoint of those to pay close attention to all aspects of place using a rural social space model (Reid et al., 2010). It is a term that encompasses a valuing of the physical place, the diversity of people in and connected to the place, and an understanding of how the place itself affords an agentive tool for educators to use as a teaching tool, framing place *with* power. It is the framing of 'place' in this way that many of the chapters refer to as crucial to their innovation. Mokoena and Hlalele, writing from their South African rural perspective in this book note the importance of: "re-presenting rural places as a source of wealth and strength and as delicate environments that require innate stewardship (Corbett, 2015)".

In short, the innovation of place-attentiveness is 'getting to know a place and letting it speak'; letting the place speak to the innovation and the diversity of voices to be heard in and for place. Being immersed in the place appears to be an innovation tool to best know the place. As Fitzgerald, Bradbury and Leach explain in their chapter focusing on the innovation of preparing pre-service teachers for rural contexts:

> … pre-service teachers were immersed in all aspects of teaching and living in a rural community embedded as part of their program requirements. From experiencing the establishment of classrooms at the beginning of a teaching year to exploring extracurricular opportunities and connecting with community, this program provided students with a supported holistic rural experience.

What emerged as a common theme in many of the chapters was the use of place-attentive strategies as a tool of innovation. Valuing 'community' and 'place' thus becomes a way to counteract this issue in 'situated' ways that highlight the importance of local knowledges and diverse perspectives. As the work of Johnson et al. (2005) has shown, getting to know a place often involves seeing, and responding to the people in it, differently. As Azano and Callahan, writing about supporting gifted students in relatively low socio-economic rural United States, highlight:

> Place is also used to consider the diversity of rural places and the affordances for meaning making when students are given the opportunity to connect curricula with places they care about. In this way, we aim to use place as curricular intervention as a means of dialogue about the interactions between environments and education.

Themes from the chapters regarding how innovative efforts in rural education can and have worked, stress the importance of understanding and attending to the land and place. Particular attitudes towards place also emerged, key words such as value, respect, appreciate and honour reflect the particular mind-set required.

Inquiry was another approach to place that was adopted by the various projects. What also emerged as successful innovations were those where the place and the people were connected to others. What emerged were reciprocal relationships and opportunities. The place had a voice and through an open conversation and mentoring offered insights into how to enter and experience place. As Mukeredzi, writing about pre-service teacher education for rural communities in South Africa, also notes: "Mentoring makes an effective vehicle for professional learning through reflection as students learn about the 'self' in context". There appears a growing trend to address issues and challenges in rural education by better attending to place. Innovation lies in place-conscious and attentive practices that can require changes in the physical or embodied places of learning. Kettle, writing in the Australian context about a rural community and the various support mechanisms for refugee students demonstrates the keys to success were where schools recognised, "that engagement with rural-based multilingual immigrant family's needs to be contextualised and differentiated, with foundations in trust and care". This approach enabled "sharing of responsibility at the individual level, irrespective of privilege, to come together as agents in collective action for change".

However, as Corbett in this text also cautions:

> The challenge at this stage is not to retreat into some form of placed based educational practices that celebrate the insularity, particularity and even exceptionalism of particularly rural places. Rather what is needed is a clear and honest recognition of the politics, histories of violence and exploitation and uneven development that have characterised the development of settler societies particularly, but also the development of the global concentration of power and privilege in the equally unevenly resourced and structured global cities. (Sassen, 1991)

1.4.2 Joined Up Alliances and New Vision of Community

One of the common patterns that emerged from the studies was the powerful tool of forming alliances—not always those most likely. This strategy is difficult in many ways as it requires the investment of time to build shared understandings and develop shared responsibilities, but the efforts can reap rich rewards. For example, Mokoena and Hlalele detail the key to their innovation through the formation of various partnerships, for example, between schools and businesses, as well as between schools in the same district that might have traditionally been perceived as competitive. They note:

> The conversations that made rounds in the community resulted in one of the co-researchers convincing one local business person to sponsor the program. This had a snowball effect because other local businesses made donations to the school. Another factor that contributed to the successful formation of positive partnership was the close working relationships which the HoDs (co-researchers) and teachers (co-researchers) had with other teachers and HoDs

from the nearby school. This resulted in these schools sharing resources such as discs and books, and in learners exchanging information with learners from the other school. In addition, the positive working relationship between the principals of the two schools facilitated the success of the partnership.

In other studies, the partnerships were formed between the community and the school. For example, Kettle documents the growing awareness through the research study itself of the needs of migrant workers and their students. Once all parties understood and were focused on a shared endeavour, the partnership gained more meaning. She explains:

> the emerging connections between the school and migrant families appear built on tentative but growing trust forged out of contact and communication. There is a shared responsibility by all stakeholders to participate in the forums directed at improving the students' outcomes at school.

Throughout many of the chapters, the important role that a University can play in a partnership becomes clear. While some of the universities were in regional locations, many were in urban settings. The case studies highlight that when university resources can be harnessed for rural communities, these communities can flourish. The University of the Highlands and Islands is an example of a whole institution putting its focus on rural communities. As noted by Redford and Nicol, this phenomenon came about due to the alliance of the government, education institutions and teaching unions. They refer specifically to the Scottish Government policy:

> The Commission report to Government in 2013 included the following recommendation in relation to ITE, 'Local authorities, the Scottish Government, teaching institutions and trade unions should work together to explore innovative solutions to reduce the barriers to teaching in remote areas'. (Scottish Government, 2013, p. 7)

In many ways committing to stewardship of the wealth and strength of rural places also requires a tipping of power bases to new models of partnership and away from a metro-centric power base. In many of the chapters, the positioning of the researcher and the researched is based on equality and partnership between these stakeholders in the quest to construct knowledge. While aimed at striking a balance between roles played by the researcher and the researched, this kind of relationship further enhances self-liberation and emancipation by the marginalised people (Mahlomaholo and Nkoane, 2002). As noted by Mokoena and Hlalele:

> such positioning removes from the researcher the sole responsibility of emancipating the marginalised communities (Cohen, Manion & Morrison, 2013). As a result, the researched are recognised as co-researchers with meaningful participation rather than objects at the researcher's disposal to *use* and construct knowledge *for*.

1.4.3 **Repositioning Policy and Practice** *as* **Power**

While the previous two patterns highlight the importance of place and people in rural education theory and practice innovation, the third pattern that emerged from these chapters is in the ways the studies approached and positioned the state of being rural as powerful and authoritative. These chapters connect and illuminate how a set of social and spatial theories can be employed as a powerful collective to afford a different (not deficit) retelling of rural narratives. The power demonstrated in these chapters is not an external force or authority to control and direct others. Rather, the power and leadership revealed here extends beyond the reach of a formal hierarchical structure. Rather, this power and leadership is the influence, direction and creativity derived from deep rural identity and knowledge, and enacted to inform and interpret policy and practice in alignment with the vision, commitment and values of rural stakeholders.

While previous policies and practices have often "evolved in response to an assumed rural deficit" (Roberts, et al., this volume), these chapters demonstrate the power and authority inherent in the state of being rural through an *agentic* stance (Bandura, 2001)—a position from which rural residents and researchers engage in deliberate, proactive efforts to develop and test innovative approaches to address current inequities. From this standpoint, individual and community agency is power. This power is enacted when rural residents and researchers, who recognise and appreciate the complex realities, strengths and inequities in their communities, work together to develop cohesive and coordinated practices attuned to the context and goals of the local rural community. Through this process, power can be used to build community capacity to design a course of action to reduce inequity and recalibrate programmes to better meet the complex demands of our times.

Connected to this is the notion of identity within community, Roberts, et al. explicate Fei Xiaotong's philosophy and identity of people and place and introduce us to the foundational values that rural represents as 'from the soil'. They explain:

> Fei creates a description of social relations on various planes about kinship and social obligations to those closest to oneself. In this understanding, social relations are grounded on respect, tradition, and self-management. That is, values and good character comes from inside an individual, not external regulation. Indeed, in many ways, the individual does not exist; they only exist in relation to others to whom they have an obligation. Power exists in, and through, the community through observing these values.

This notion of identity connected to community and the power shifts that occur between the two in rural communities is consistent with this position and are approaches that recognise and elevate the voice (and thus power) of the participants. Many of the studies utilised particular methodologies and research approaches that involved a participatory approach to either the research or the innovation itself. For example, in the case study provided by Kettle, the community is brought together to better understand and align students, their families and the school communication. She notes the use of: "a participatory approach to make visible the experiences of a rural high school community experiencing considerable social and cultural change as a result of growing migrant enrolments".

Likewise, Mokoena and Hlalele explain a particular methodological approach appropriate to positioning the rural community. They utilise Participatory Action Research as it places collaborative and mutual relationships at its centre as a way to enhance participation in the construction of knowledge. They further outline:

> Participatory Action Research (PAR) as a methodology anchors this chapter due to its participatory nature. PAR operationalises Critical Emancipatory Research (CER) as a theoretical lens to ensure partnership and equal participation all stakeholders such as parents, teachers, learners and other officials in the Department of Basic Education (DBE) investigating circumstances under which School Enrichment Programs (SEP) may thrive with the ultimate aim of enhancing these programs for sustainable learning at rural schools.

Fitzgerald, Bradbury and Leach also draw on a particular approach that connects community. They use a Community of Practice approach that centralises Community as a willingness to be an active and contributing member required from all stakeholders and an understanding that, in this context specifically, this stretches beyond the classroom to relationships with peers, school colleagues and the broader rural community.

Consistent with this approach are the types of practices whereby pre-service teachers are positioned within the community and given a range of informal opportunities and more formally designed experiences to support learning and growth with a particular focus on developing not only capacity in the classroom, but also the development of social competencies. Likewise, Mukeredzi explains how structured collaborative conversations were intended to offer students an additional supportive layer to their discussions and individual reflections on their rural TP experiences.

The power and influence demonstrated throughout these chapters are the result of a deep commitment by all stakeholders to taking steps towards more equitable rural futures. This power is the result of developing a shared vision, not of what is easy or convenient, but rather a vision of what is possible, of what can be, undistorted by cynicism.

1.5   Conclusion

As we conclude this chapter, we return to the urgent questions that were the impetus for this book: What emerges when the words rural, education *and* innovation are all connected? Are there trends and/or patterns of rural education innovation that emerge looking at studies from across multiple global rural places and spaces? What can such an investigation offer rural education researchers and the education profession?

We believe that across the world, "rural researchers should challenge those who speak about the rural disparagingly or only in terms of despair" (Reid et al., 2010, p. 262). We offer the chapters in this book as examples of a hopeful and resilient approach to innovative rural education, theory and scholarship, and important evidence to speak against an often deficit view of rural education. The collection has been presented in three themes that showcase examples of innovative approaches to addressing rural staffing challenges, addressing diverse student needs in rural contexts and reframing policy that positions rural at the heart of community. It also highlights the three patterns that emerged across the studies, namely: the importance of place-attentive strategies; the importance of joined up alliances to maximise resources and networks; and finally, the need for any rural initiative or approach to utilise alternative methodologies and frameworks that start with appreciation of difference, rather than deficit.

As we work to upend the status quo in rural education across the world through the development of innovation responsive to place and context, we believe the tripartite of place, people and power can be distilled as essential to any rural education innovation. While the specific studies can not necessarily be transplanted or adopted wholesale, these three essential elements are a true foundation for future rural studies and scholars to explore. And finally, we believe that there is great value in learning from one another. Indeed, in the words of the poet Wendell Berry, "it is not from ourselves that we will learn to be better than we are" (Berry, 2003, p. 29). This highlights the importance of continuing to learn from more countries, contexts and scholars (e.g. Corbett and Gereluck 2020) and to connect with one another across the global rural education community through scholarly initiatives such as ISFIRE (International Symposium for Innovation in Rural Education) and REIRA (Rural Education International Research Alliance). Through these international examples of innovative approaches to rural education, we hope you will be inspired to continue to contribute to the hope and resilience of the future of your rural places.

References

Alliance for Affordable Internet (2020). *Rural broadband policy framework: Connecting the unconnected.* https://a4ai.org/rural-broadband-policy-framework-connecting-the-unconnected/.

Azano, A., Downey, J., & Brenner, D. (2019). *Preparing pre-service teachers for rural schools.* Oxford Research Encyclopedia of Education: Oxford University Press. https://doi.org/10.1093/acrefore/9780190264093.013.274.

Bandura, A. (2001). Social cognitive theory: An agentic perspective. *Annual Review of Psychology, 52*(1), 1–26.

Berry, W. (2003). *The art of the commonplace: The agrarian essays of Wendell Berry.* Berkley, CA: Counterpoint.

Berry, A. B., Petrin, R. A., Gravelle, M. L., & Farmer, T. W. (2012). Issues in special education teacher recruitment, retention, and professional development: Considerations in supporting rural teachers. *Rural Special Education Quarterly, 30*(4), 3–11.

Biddle, C., & Mette, I. (2017). Education and information. In A. Tickmayer, J. Sherman, & H. Warlick (Eds.), *Rural poverty in the United States.* New York, NY: Columbia University Press.

Cheney, C. O., & Demachak, M. L. (2001). Inclusion of students with disabilities in rural classrooms: recommendations and case study. *Rural Educator, 23*(2), 40–46.

Corbett, M. & Gereluck, D. (Eds). (2020). *Rural teacher education: Connecting land and People.* Springer.

Downey, J. (2002). *Perspectives on educational resilience from children facing adversity*. Doctoral Dissertation. University of Northern Colorado. https://search-proquest-com.proxybz.lib.mon tana.edu/docview/305544287/8C5536D2248B4730PQ/1?accountid=28148.

Downey, J. (2017). *Resilience in rural education: Continuity and change across 80 years* [Paper presentation]. Annual meeting of the Society for Provision of Education in Rural Australia, Canberra, Australia.

Federal Communications Commission (FCC, 2019). *Broadband deployment report: Inquiry concerning deployment of advanced telecommunications capability to all Americans in a reasonable and timely fashion*. https://docs.fcc.gov/public/attachments/FCC-19-44A1.pdf.

Gouleta, E. (2015). Educational assessment in Khyber Pakhtunkhwa Pakistan's north-west frontier province: Practices, issues, and challenges for educating culturally linguistically diverse and exceptional children. *Global Education Review, 2*(4), 19–39.

Greenwood, D. A. (2013). A critical theory of place-conscious education. In R. B. Stevenson, M. Brody, J. Dillon, & A. E. J. Wals (Eds.), *International handbook of research on environmental education* (pp. 93–100). New York: Routledge.

Gristy, C., Hargreaves, L., & Kučerová, S. R. (2020). Schools and their communities in rural Europe: Patterns of change. In L. Hargreaves, C. Gristy, & S. Kučerová (Eds.), *Educational research and schooling in rural Europe: An engagement with changing patterns of education, space and place* (pp. 323-338). Information Age Publishing.

Gruenewald, D. A. (2003). Foundations of place: A multidisciplinary framework for place conscious education. *American Educational Research Journal, 40*(3), 619–654.

Halsey, J. (2018). *Independent review into regional, rural and remote education—Final report*. Canberra, ACT: Department of Education and Training.

Hargreaves, L., Gristy, C., & Kučerová, S. R. (2020). Educational research in rural Europe: State, status and the road ahead. In L. Hargreaves, C. Gristy, & S. Kučerová (Eds.), *Educational research and schooling in rural Europe: An engagement with changing patterns of education, space and place*, (pp. 339–356). Information Age Publishing.

Hodges, V.P. (2002, Winter). High stakes testing and its impact on rural schools. *The Rural Educator, 24*(2), 3–7.

Johnson, L., Finn, M. J., & Lewis, R. (Eds.). (2005). *Urban education with an attitude*. New York: SUNY Press.

Johnson, J., & Zoeller, B. (2016). School funding and rural districts. In S. Williams & A. Grooms (Eds.), *Educational opportunity in rural contexts: The politics of place*. Charlotte, NC: Information Age Publishing.

Kaufman, B., Thomas, S., Randolph, R., Perry, J., Thompson, K., Holmes, G., et al. (2016). The rising rate of rural hospital closures. *The Journal of Rural Health, 32*, 35–43.

Kiani, R., Tyrer, F., Hodgson, A., Berkin, N. & Bhaumik, S. (2013). Urban-rural differences in the nature and prevalence of mental ill-health in adults with intellectual disabilities. *Journal of Intellectual Disability Research, 57*(2), 119–127. https://10.1111/j.1365-2788.2011.01523.

Kryst, E., Kotok, S., & Bodovski, K. (2015). Rural/urban disparities in science achievement in post-socialist countries: The evolving influence of socioeconomic status. *Global Education Review, 2*(4), 60–77.

Lave, J., & Wenger, E. (1998). *Communities of practice: Learning, meaning, and identity*. New York, NY: Cambridge University Press.

Mahlomaholo, M. G., & Nkoane, M. M. (2002). The case for an emancipatory qualitative research: Reflection on assessment of quality. *Education as Change, 6*(1), 89–105.

Masinire, A. (2015). Recruiting and retaining teachers in rural schools in South Africa: Insights from a rural teaching experience programme. *Australian & International Journal of Rural Education, 25*(1), 2–14.

McGrail, M. R., Jones, R., Robinson, A., Rickard, C.M., Burley, M. & Drysdale, M. (2005). The planning of rural health research: rurality and rural population issues. *Rural and Remote Health, 5*. http://www.rrh.org.au/publishedarticles/article_print_426.pdf.

Okilwa, N. (2015). Educational marginalization: Examining challenges and possibilities for improving educational outcomes in Northeastern Kenya. *Global Education Review, 2*(4), 5–18.

Organisation for Economic Co-operation and Development (OECD) (2016). Country Roads: Education and Rural Life Trends Shaping Education, OECD Publishing. http://www.oecd.org/educat ion/ceri/spotlight9-CountryRoads.pdf.

Price, R. (2014). Rural research and regional innovation: Are past and present research funding policies building future resilience in the bush?. In A. Hogan and M. Young (Eds.) *Rural and regional futures* (pp. 246–266). Routledge.

Reid, J., Green, B., Cooper, M., Hastings, W., Lock, G., & White, S. (2010). Regenerating rural social space? *Teacher education for rural-regional sustainability, Australian Journal of Education, 54*(3), 262.

Roberts, P. (2014). Researching from the standpoint of the rural. In S. White and M. Corbett (Eds.). *Doing educational research in rural settings. Methodological issues, international perspectives and practical solutions*, 135–148. Routledge.

Rossiter, R., Clarke, D., & Shields, L. (2018). Supporting young people's emotional wellbeing during the transition to secondary school in regional Australia. *Australian and International Journal of Rural Education, 28*(1), 73–86.

Rude, H., & Miller, K. J. (2018). Policy challenges and opportunities for rural special education. *Rural Special Education Quarterly, 37*(1), 21–29. https://doi.org/10.1177/8756870517748662.

Stehlik, D. (2001). "Out there": Spaces, places and border crossings. In S. Lockie & L. Bourke (Eds.), *Rurality bites: The social and environmental transformation of rural Australia* (pp. 30–41). Annandale, VA: Pluto Press.

Stelmach, B. (2011). A synthesis of international rural education issues and responses. *The Rural Educator, 32*(2), 32–42.

Sutcher, L., Darling-Hammond, L., Carver-Thomas, D. (2016). *A coming crisis in teaching? Teacher supply, demand, and shortages in the U.S.* Palo Alto, CA: Learning Policy Institute.

Tooth, R., & Renshaw, P. (2009). Reflections on pedagogy and place: A journey into learning for sustainability through environmental narrative and deep attentive reflection. *Australian Journal of Environmental Education, 25*, 95–104.

Wallin, D. (2007). Policy window or hazy dream? Policy and practice innovations for creating effective learning environments in rural schools. *Canadian Journal of Educational Administration and Policy, 63*, 1–22.

Watt, R., Daly, B., Allison, P., Macpherson, L., Venturelli, R., Listl, S., et al. (2019). Ending the neglect of global oral health: time for radical action. *The Lancet, 394*(10194), 261–272.

White, S. & Corbett, M. (Eds.) (2014). *Doing educational research in rural settings.* New York: NY: Routledge.

White, S., & Kline, J. (2012). Developing a rural teacher education curriculum package. *The Rural Educator, 33*(2), 36–42.

White, S., & Reid, J. (2008). Placing teachers? Sustaining rural schooling through place consciousness in teacher education. *Journal for Research in Rural Education, 23*(7), 1–11.

Simone White is Professor and Associate Dean (International and Engagement) in the Faculty of Education at Queensland University of Technology (QUT). Simone's area of expertise is teacher education and rural education and her publications, research and teaching are all focused on the key question of how to best prepare teachers and leaders for diverse communities (both local and global). Her current research areas focus on rural education, teacher education policy, teacher development, professional experience and building and maintaining university-school/community partnerships. Simone is a past President of the Australian Teacher Education Association (ATEA) and had a previous role as Vice President of the Society for the Provision for Education in Rural Australia (SPERA). She is the founder and co-leader of the Rural Education International Research Alliance (REIRA). Through her collective work, Simone aims to connect research, policy and practice in ways that bring teachers and school and university based teacher educators together and break down traditional borders between academics, policy makers, communities and practitioners.

Jayne Downey is Professor and Director of the Center for Research on Rural Education at Montana State University. She has worked in the field of educator preparation for over 20 years and her research agenda has focused on strengthening the preparation of prospective educators and improving outcomes of P-20 education across rural contexts. As an Educational Psychologist, she is committed to engaging in research, scholarship, and service intentionally attuned to, and respectful of, the complex and unique realities and relationships of rural schools and communities -- past, present, and future. Jayne serves on the executive committees of the National Rural Education Association (NREA) and the Society for Provision of Education in Rural Australia (SPERA). In Montana, she serves as the Chair of the Board of Directors for the Montana Small Schools Alliance (MSSA) working on behalf of 150 of Montana's smallest rural and remote schools. She is an editor for the Australian and International Journal of Rural Education and a co-leader of the Rural Education International Research Alliance, celebrating the importance of learning, teaching and wellbeing for rural students, their families and communities around the globe.

Part II
Place-Attentive Rural Teacher Preparation

Chapter 2
It Takes a Village: Using Communities of Practice as a Framework for Reflecting on Rural and Regional Professional Experience Opportunities

Angela Fitzgerald, Ondine Bradbury, and Tania Leach

Abstract In the Australian context, while the population is largely clustered in metropolitan areas, much of the country can be defined as regional, rural and remote. This reality means that significant numbers of students are experiencing their schooling across these locations. This raises questions around how universities are preparing pre-service teachers to live and work in these contexts where work is readily available and quality educational opportunities are much sought after. This chapter uses case study methodology to tell the stories of two rural and regional professional experience programs supported by different Australian universities. Using Community of Practice (CoP) as a framework for sense-making, these two cases are unpacked to reveal the embedded structures and processes that supported pre-service teachers to engage in a quality rural professional experience. Key learnings relating to the three components of a CoP are shared—domain, community, and practice—before considerations and implications for other contexts and initial teacher education providers are discussed.

Keywords Professional experience · Community of Practice · School · Community

2.1 Introduction

Rural contexts provide numerous opportunities for graduate and early career teachers both in terms of employment prospects, for example securing ongoing rather than contract positions, and career growth, such as gaining positions of responsibility. Sitting alongside this is the reality that the retention of graduate teachers, within the

A. Fitzgerald (✉)
School of Education, University of Southern Queensland, Springfield, QLD, Australia
e-mail: angela.fitzgerald@usq.edu.au

O. Bradbury
Faculty of Education, Monash University, Melbourne, VIC, Australia

T. Leach
School of Education, University of Southern Queensland, Toowoomba, QLD, Australia

first five years of their career in the classroom, is becoming increasingly problematic. This issue, however, becomes even more pronounced when considering graduate attrition from rural and remote contexts (Kline & Walker-Gibbs, 2015). Often these experiences do not turn out to be as positive, productive or sustainable as hoped—from the perspectives of both the teacher and the school community—due to a lack of understanding of what it means to live and work in a rural setting (Green & Reid, 2004; Kline, White, & Lock, 2013; Roberts, 2004).

Australia (the context for this chapter) is a large country, which is heavily populated around the coastlines, but less so in the interior. The Halsey Report (Halsey, 2018), a significant independent review into regional, rural and remote education in Australia, estimated that 47% of schools (from both governmental and non-governmental sectors) are situated in rural and remote communities. This reality gap poses initial teacher education providers with an interesting challenge in terms of preparing pre-service teachers to teach in a range of contexts. Across the country, initial teacher education providers are leveraging professional experience in rural schools as a possible solution. Professional experience enables pre-service teachers to gain teaching experience and skills in a supported environment, which is typically in a classroom setting close to where they live (e.g. usually a metropolitan context).

In the Australian context, pre-service teachers are required to complete 60 (for a postgraduate student) or 80 (for an undergraduate student) days as part of their initial teacher education program in an educational context with the supervision of a registerable teacher. Currently, most professional experiences placements take place in urban settings as this is where most initial teacher education providers and participating pre-service teachers are located. However, the Teacher Education Ministerial Action Group (TEMAG) reforms outlined in the *Action Now: Classroom Ready Teachers* report (Craven et al., 2014) are leading to policy pressure on initial teacher education providers to strengthen the partnerships between schools and teacher education programs. This means that increasingly programs are being devised to enable pre-service teachers to complete part of their mandatory professional experience in alternate contexts, such as in rural Australia and even abroad. Broadly, the intention of these programs is to build and enhance pre-service teachers' skills set as well as increase their confidence in moving outside their comfort zone in relation to possible employment opportunities (Fitzgerald, Parr, & Williams, 2017; Hudson & Hudson, 2008).

This chapter focuses on the rural professional experience programs supported by two Australian universities—one based in regional Queensland (University of Southern Queensland) and the other in metropolitan Victoria (Monash University). The two programs that form the focus of this work both had a number of support mechanisms built into their design, including academic support in situ and remotely, financial support for accommodation and professional staff coordinators to assist with experiencing success. These supports were informed by a move towards a rural-based professional experience grounded in what we believe to be a construct of Lave and Wenger's (1998) theory of communities of practice (CoP). CoP is used as a lens, in this instance, as a way of understanding what is required to ensure a meaningful and valuable rural experience that exposes pre-service teachers to the realities of this context, while deepening their understandings and identities in terms of what it means for them personally to be a teacher. The question explored through this chapter is: What types of structures and processes support pre-service teachers in undertaking a rural placement experience?

2.2 Positioning Community of Practice as a Lens for Sense-Making

The phrase 'community of practice' emerged from Lave and Wenger's (1998) work nearly two decades ago, which examined the formation of groups of people engaged in a process of shared learning around an area of common interest. While they did not specifically focus on teachers as part of this research, it is a concept that is nonetheless fitting for the work that teachers engage in and has been used widely in teacher education as a theoretical framework. Broadly, Wenger-Traynor and Wenger-Traynor (2015) define CoP as 'groups of people who share a concern or a passion for something they do and learn how to do it better as they interact regularly' (p. 1). They also determined that three characteristics must be evident for a CoP to exist:

1. Domain;
2. Community and
3. Practice.

The term 'domain' relates to the field of interest and expertise in a particular area and defines the identity of those involved in a CoP. In pursuing their interest in a particular domain and strengthening that 'community', Lave and Wenger (1998) suggest that participants actively engage in activities and discussions to help each other, share information and develop relationships that promote learning. Over time and through sustained interactions, participants in the CoP develop a shared 'practice', realised as experiences, stories, tools or ways of addressing issues. It is a combination of these elements, domain, community and practice that constitute a CoP. In school settings, it is relatively easy to identify what would constitute a domain (e.g. improvement of learning and teaching) and a community (e.g. teachers). However, less obvious, or perhaps more often the missing link in an education-focused CoP, is the practice or activities that brings it all together (e.g. what do teachers do to improve learning and teaching?). In the context of this chapter, the focus is shifted to pre-service teachers and the practices or activities that support their emerging practice and identity as a teacher. While Lave and Wenger's CoP work is not without critique (see Hodkinson & Hodkinson, 2004; Jewson, 2007), it does provide a useful lens for making sense of what, in practical terms, might be meaningful ways to develop practice through professional experience set in rural and regional areas.

In an education context, teachers participating in a CoP are encouraged to think about their broader purpose and practice in ways that support longer term goals associated with learning and teaching rather than being solely concerned with the specifics of day-to-day lessons (Vangrieken, Meredith, & Kyndt, 2017). Lieberman and Pointer Mace (2009) state that this may be due to 'participat[ion] in a learning community allowing teachers to develop or confirm a teacher identity that includes meeting the needs of students and learning from other teachers in order to do so' (p. 4). This approach to developing teacher identity and practice enables those participating in a CoP to be more innovative as they are continually rethinking their practice based on how their students perform and how their own learning evolves (Vescio, Ross, & Adams, 2008). These findings are potentially no different for pre-service teachers in some ways, but this research starts to highlight some of the specific needs of this cohort and provides insights into how these needs can be appropriately met.

2.3   Context: Understanding Programs and Place

In better understanding the nature of the structures and processes enacted to support pre-service teachers both professionally and personally, an overview of the context is required and is detailed below. These insights are important because the location for these rural professional experiences—Bass Coast region in Victoria and Charleville in Queensland—and the format of their subsequent placement programs are critical to what this experience was and why it worked. In understanding our definition of 'rural' for this chapter, it is noteworthy that both the Bass Coast region and Charleville are defined under the Australian Statistical Geography Standard (ASGS) as being Statistical area level 2 (SA2) (Australian Bureau of Statistics, 2016). SA2 regions are designed to represent a community, that vary in size from about 3,000 to 25,000 permanent residents. For the purposes of this chapter, we will continue to refer to both locations as rural in nature.

2.3.1   Bass Coast Region (Case Study 1)

The Bass Coast *Teaching Academy of Professional Practice* (TAPP) was formed through a Victorian Department of Education and Training (DET) funded initiative that strives to establish strong school–university partnerships to enhance initial teacher education preparation. Funded over two-year periods, partnered universities and schools develop a Committee of Management and work towards achieving a set of objectives that aim to:

- deliver an immersive preparation experience for pre-service teachers;
- test innovative approaches to ITE and
- strengthen the links between theory, research and practice to enhance course effectiveness (Department of Education and Training https://www.education.vic. gov.au/about/educationstate/Pages/tapp.aspx).

The Bass Coast TAPP is a partnership between Monash University and 12 schools in the Bass Coast region, which is about 150 km south-east of Melbourne. This region is positioned within the Australian state of Victoria, which, while it is the second most populous state (after New South Wales), it is the smallest mainland state in terms of land area, located in the south-east corner of the continent. The schools involved in this collaboration are located across a 50 km stretch, taking in coastal and inland regions, and range in size from 39 to 1300 students. One early years centre, 10 primary schools and a secondary school participated in this professional experience program; all with the vision of providing pre-service teachers with the opportunity to experience living and working in a rural context. This program began in 2017 with 34 applicants and has risen to 150 applications received in 2019 for 50 places.

To participate in the Bass Coast TAPP Professional Experience program, pre-service teachers are required to complete a formal application process, which includes citing reasons why they believe they would be a suitable candidate for this opportunity. The placement duration ranges from 10 to 15 days depending on the requirements of the pre-service teacher's program and includes participants from Bachelor of Education and Master of Teaching across early years, primary and secondary programs. A particular feature of this program is the support provided by a Professional Practice Consultant (PPC) employed by the university and a Project Coordinator (PC) funded through the TAPPs initiative. Additionally, the cost of the pre-service teachers' accommodation was provided through Monash University's received funding from the *Student Teacher Rural Professional Practice* (STRPP) grant, which is also a DET initiative.

State-wide acknowledgement of the growing need to employ and retain teachers in rural areas was a significant driving force in the development of the Bass Coast TAPP program. This opportunity provides pre-service teachers with an alternative to the usual metropolitan-based professional experience. It is intended to spark an interest in pre-service teachers seeking future employment in rural contexts as well as assisting pre-service teachers who may have originally grown up in a rural area, to return.

2.3.2 Charleville (Case Study 2)

Queensland is the second largest state in Australia and is positioned in the northeast of the country. Half of Queensland's schools are located in rural and remote (geographically isolated) locations with approximately one-quarter of state school students enrolled in these schools. To address the particular needs this reality brings, the Queensland Government (2018) developed the *Advancing rural and remote education in Queensland State schools action plan*. This plan acknowledges the importance of ensuring every student has access to high-quality education along with the need to attract and retain teachers within these contexts. Alongside this, the Federally funded independent review of regional, rural and remote education

(Halsey, 2018) identified that collaboratively optimising pre-service teacher opportunities to engage and reflect upon teaching in rural and remote communities has the potential to increase the placement and retention of quality early career teachers.

In 2018, the University Of Southern Queensland (USQ), a regionally located University, decided to leverage their existing relationship with the Queensland Department of Education (DoE) Darling Downs South West region (DDSWR) to collaboratively address projected future teacher shortages in rural locations. While graduate teachers were being employed in these areas, the team noted that there was an increasing number of early career teachers who did not have the personal capacity or confidence to move outside their comfort zones to embark on a career away from their social support networks.

As a result of this problem, the *Alternate Context Professional Experience* program was developed and offered to third year pre-service teacher students as a placement option. The University team decided to link this opportunity to a three-week establishment phase (e.g. beginning of the school year) professional experience within the Bachelor of Education primary program. The timing of this opportunity was aimed at ensuring students had successfully completed half of their program and demonstrated professional practice competencies within four previous school placements.

Through this program, pre-service teachers were immersed in all aspects of teaching and living in a rural community embedded as part of their program requirements. From experiencing the establishment of classrooms at the beginning of a teaching year to exploring extracurricular opportunities and connecting with community, this program provided students with a supported holistic rural experience. As part of the pilot offering of this program, a university academic accompanied the small group of six primary Bachelor of Education pre-service teachers to provide contextualised support and connections within the community. Another critical aspect of the program was the provision of face-to-face support for early career teacher mentors in the placement schools. These parallel mentoring opportunities were provided to build the capacity of teacher mentors in utilising the *Australian Professional Graduate Standards* to provide targeted feedback to pre-service teachers.

To ensure the pre-service teachers were engaged in a rural experience, the community of Charleville was selected. Situated in the Darling Downs South West Region of Education Queensland, the Charleville cluster is located nearly 700 km west of Brisbane (capital city for the state) and is accessible by road and regional planes. With a population of approximately 3335, Charleville hosts four primary and secondary schools, but through this program the pre-service teachers were placed at either Charleville State School or Charleville School of Distance Education. Community services in Charleville include a small independent supermarket, coffee shops, bakeries, community pool and multiple hotels.

2.4   Storying Professional Experience in Rural Contexts

As previously mentioned, this chapter draws upon the two cases, with their context described in detail above, to represent the possibilities and challenges inherent in supporting pre-service teachers in rural professional contexts. The insights now shared in the stories below have been shaped by discussions with key stakeholders in each context: school-based educators, university-based educators, regional support staff and participating pre-service teachers. The intention in sharing these cases is to provide insights into the ways in which these two programs enabled pre-service teachers to experience living and working in a rural setting. The two case studies are presented differently to reflect the specific educational contexts and design features of the professional experience programs. By maintaining this diversity, the intention is to highlight that while initial teacher education providers may take a variety of approaches to this notion of preparing pre-service teachers for working and living in rural settings, there are still some key shared features that support productive and positive outcomes.

Storying through narrative is a methodological approach, which draws on narrative inquiry as a way of thinking about and making sense of lived experiences (Clandinin & Huber, 2010). This research method draws upon a reflexive and recursive approach to move from the field, which captures the living or telling of stories, to the field text, which references the collected data to share emergent stories. In this chapter, two of the authors—Ondine and Tania—developed the case studies based on their significant involvement in the focal programs. Ondine, in her role as a Professional Practice Consultant, developed Case Study 1, while Tania, in her role as academic lead, developed Case Study 2. Case Study 1 was informed by Ondine's experiences leading the Bass Coast TAPP in 2017 and 2018 along with semi-structured interviews with the Project Coordinator and a participating pre-service teacher. Case Study 2 grew from responses to an online questionnaire following the first Alternate Context Professional Experience placement at the beginning of 2019 and captures the voices of the six participating pre-service teachers, their supervising teachers, and members of the local leadership teams at the two schools.

The following 'boxes' present the collated reflections of two professional experience programs to highlight the types of structures and processes used to support the participating pre-service teachers in undertaking a rural placement experience. Following these stories, the theoretical construct of CoP is used as a framework to make sense of the support provided and its subsequent influence on a future workforce of graduate teachers who have the confidence and competence to consider a teaching career in a rural setting.

Case Study 1
Rural Professional Experience Program
Bass Coast Region, Victoria

The induction into the Bass Coast TAPP rural professional experience and the expectations associated with this experience begins with the application process. As part of this process, which directly informs selection into the program, pre-service teachers identify the ways in which they contribute to their local community. The intention behind this line of questioning is to highlight to the pre-service teachers their suitability for the program and the nature of their responsibilities during their time on the Bass Coast, which includes a strong emphasis on participating and 'giving back' to the school and wider community.

Following selection into the program, a series of 'meet and greet' sessions were initiated by Ondine, the university-based Professional Practice Consultant (PPC) and second author of this chapter, and Greg, the Project Coordinator (PC), a retired assistant principal and local resident of the Bass Coast region. One of the participating pre-service teachers, Christina, reflected on the value of these sessions in terms of showing her the level of 'support in place' prior to beginning their school placement. This included outlining the context, arranging the living arrangements, detailing safety considerations and finalising logistics of travel to the region. Also as part of these sessions, time was allocated to the pre-service teachers for creating videos to introduce themselves to their mentor teachers. In these videos, Christina and the other pre-service teachers outline their teaching goals and explain why they are dedicated to participating in a rural placement. While not necessarily the original intention, these videos were also showed to the school students as a way of connecting them with this experience and increasing the excitement of having a pre-service teacher from Melbourne in their classroom.

On reflection, both Ondine and Christina highlighted the importance of having someone like Greg involved in this professional experience program. Greg coordinated this project, lived locally and was respected as a retired teacher. For Christina, 'it was really good to have that inside knowledge' in terms of meaningful linking between the school community, the pre-service teachers and their mentor teachers. A key aspect of Greg's role was building and maintaining relationships, trust and rapport between the schools and the University. From Ondine's perspective, having a locally known and respected PC participating in the program greatly assisted all stakeholders in having the 'hard discussions' around assessment as well as mediating any difficult conversations between the mentors and the pre-service teachers. She also noted that when she conducted visits to the Bass Coast TAPP schools with Greg that she felt a sense of comfort in being with a member of the community. Reflective conversations between Greg and Ondine identified that the PC role was much more than a conduit between the university and the schools, it was key connective element to rural education more generally. In working alongside the pre-service teachers and Bass Coast TAPP schools, Greg was able to bring an extensive knowledge of the region, his vast experience of teaching in rural schools, and his passion for preparing pre-service teachers for the profession to offer valuable, relevant and authentic support.

Through DET funding, the university arranged accommodation in the Bass Coast in the form of holiday rental houses that were either a short drive or walking distance from the placement schools. This was an approach that Christina celebrated because she was living alongside other pre-service teachers, and together they were able to provide each other with significant levels of support. This support ranged from assistance with lesson planning to emotional and social support in managing professional experience in an unfamiliar context, to collegiate discussions of 'how the day had gone' over dinner. In many ways, the provision of shared accommodation served as a community within a community. However, not all aspects of shared living were positive and for some pre-service teachers living in a house without the support of family and friends was challenging due to factors like the unfamiliar setting, personality differences between housemates, the expansive nature of the rural landscape and being away from home for the first time. Both the PC and PPC became alternate points of contact for pre-service teachers to debrief when space was needed from peers or if it had been a particularly difficult day in the classroom. Regardless of the challenges, Christina viewed her housemates as 'like-minded peers' and enjoyed learning from their trials and successes in the classroom. While this might not seem different from any other student-shared housing experience, increasingly the pre-service teachers participating in this program are living in their family home while they attend university. This means sharing accommodation with people who are not their family is not a common experience. From another perspective, Christina appreciated the approach taken to housing as it afforded her proximity to her placement school and the broader community, which allowed an immersive experience of what it might be like to live and work in a rural context longer term.

Another important component of the Bass Coast TAPP professional experience program was the significant support from the mentor teachers and participating schools. Christina noted that the rural placement provided her with a sense of inclusiveness and feeling like a valued member of the teaching community. For example, prompt responses to her emails and being included in staffroom conversations were experiences that Christina identified 'you wouldn't have this back in Melbourne' meaning that these experiences were not commonplace in her usual metropolitan-based placements. While this difference may not be entirely attributable to rurality and instead speaks to school culture, anecdotally this kind of response is common from participants in rural professional experiences. Part of feeling included was the level of out-of-school activities that Christina and the other pre-service teachers were invited to be part of, such as local trivia nights, surfing after school on Fridays and dinner with their mentor and their families. This safe and trusting environment was a highlight for Christina and further iterated to her that community was a central component of feeling supported during a rural placement.

Case Study 2
Alternate Context Professional Experience Program
Charleville, Queensland
The University-based team worked closely with the DDSWR Human Resource team to identify a suitable rural community and strategies to overcome potential barriers to student participation. An authentic rural experience, the cost of travel, accommodation

and loss of income over the three weeks were highlighted as possible sticking points. To address these needs and concerns the DoE enabled the University to apply for State Government-funded rural grants (e.g. Beyond the Range funding) on behalf of the collective student group. With the funding secured, the Charleville cluster was selected to host the students. A key reason for this decision was that the cluster's lead principal was a strong active advocate for the provision of quality education in rural and remote locations. She became the community link (in a similar vein to the PC role in Case Study 1) and was fundamental in the sourcing of appropriate accommodation and planning of community events prior to the placement.

Selecting and grouping suitable candidates was the first intentional support mechanism implemented into the program. Each candidate was required to submit an expression of interest to showcase their personal attributes and capabilities. Once the group was shortlisted, a panel with DoE and University representatives interviewed each candidate using case-based questions. This process, which is quite different to Case Study 1, was implemented to explore candidates' social and problem-solving skills and was utilised to group the candidates into school and accommodation groups. Candidates' personality traits, communication styles and background experiences were considered with the aim of promoting positive relationships through the balancing of group dynamics across living and work arrangements.

The development of a positive group dynamic and rural experience was further supported through the allocation of an in situ university academic (for the first 10 days of the placement), Tania (the third author of this chapter), who had significant experience teaching in rural and remote locations. The formal role of this person was to provide liaison support to each student during their formal placement, assisting the students and mentor teachers to clarify the placement expectations against the Australian Professional Standards for Teachers. However, as the experience unfolded, they became a 'more knowledgeable other' (Vygotsky, 1978), parent figure, mentor and coach. With this support, the richness of the rural placement, from the pre-service teacher perspective became more about the community experience than the teaching experience. The students relished the opportunity to explore what living in these communities would be like and noted that 'without your (Tania's) mentorship we would never have had the experiences connecting with community and exploring the rural context'. This insight was also supported by the teachers within the community as they continually highlighted that the provision of an academic enabled the pre-service teachers to 'experience and understand teaching and life in rural and remote areas'.

Underpinning the inclusion of this support was the explicit provision of group and individual reflection and coaching sessions. These sessions provided a structured safe space where the group could learn to respectfully raise and resolve issues related to their living experiences. Individual coaching sessions empowered the students to problem solve, building their confidence in addressing the distance from family, lack of usual resources and the emotions of living in extreme heat.

Within the structure of the first ten days, the implementation of an explicit transition strategy enabled the students to identify group and community connections that could support them over the remainder of their experience. Personnel identified by the students included the hotel manager, the support teacher and her husband (who was the local head nurse) and the school's social group members. This approach potentially enabled the group to reduce their dependence on the academic 'as they had been supported to connect with the school and community while the academic support was there and transition to a balance of formal and informal support'.

The transition to the identified school and community support personnel was an organic process that encouraged the students to make authentic connections. Teachers stated that the power of these formal and informal supports in the subsequent weeks was to assist in debriefing about the formal teaching experience and listening when the impacts of location were felt. The power of the community and group support structures were highlighted by the students when they stated: 'after the first week the novelty wore off and you felt what teaching in the community would be like with everyday routines and being away from family…it was really important to have a pseudo "mum" like Karen to go to'.

In addition to the on-the-ground support, the University academic continued to provide virtual group and individual reflections that were gradually reduced over the duration of the experience. This model was welcomed and recognised by the students and as one student outlined 'the support during the experience and the gradual release of responsibility that has been provided will ensure we are all independent for the remainder of our placement'.

Through the case study it became evident that the triumvirate of support from the University, school and community was formally and informally provided to the students. Some of these structures were strategic and planned and other connections grew organically. The student and community perception of these various structures were consistently positive and attributed to the development of authentic, trusting relationships.

2.5 Sense-Making: What the Cases Tell Us

We now move towards bringing meaning to these two cases and in doing so, further understanding the role and value of CoPs in supporting pre-service teachers in rural professional contexts by using Wenger-Traynor and Wenger-Traynor's (2015) three characteristics (i) Domain, (ii) Community and (iii) Practices. These characteristics provide a framework to understand the structures and processes embedded in the two programs/locations that supported pre-service teachers to engage in a quality rural professional experience. Each characteristic is explored in detail below.

2.5.1 Domain: Improving Professional Practice in Rural and Regional Contexts

As discussed earlier in this chapter, the notion of 'domain' in Lave and Wenger's (1998) CoP interpretation focuses on shared interest and expertise in a particular area that defines the identity of those involved. Pyrko, Dorfler, and Eden (2017) simply describe this as 'real-life problems or hot topics' (p. 390) that bring people together. In the context of this work, the domain could be defined as improving professional practice in rural and regional contexts. To make sense of this aspect of CoP, this section explores what it is about the domain that influenced the types of supportive structures and processes for the pre-service teachers in the Bass Coast area and Charleville. This analysis identified three emergent themes: systemic approach, localised support and strategic alignment.

2.5.1.1 Systemic Approach

Systemic backing plays an important role when attempting to initiate educational change. As Wagner (1993) puts it, 'systemic reflection, not reflexive reaction, is fundamental to long-term improvement' (p. 24). Similarly, this sentiment is reflected in the research of those who have explored reflection in teacher education, such as Schon (1982) and Ghaye and Lillyman (2019). In the context of this research, both rural professional experience programs had support—financially and structurally— from their respective state-based Governments and Departments of Education. The Victorian Department of Education provides support to 10 TAPPs, which are partnerships between clusters of state schools and universities with the explicit purpose of improving initial teacher education. This level of investment has a significant influence on the feasibility and longevity of these two programs. For the Bass Coast region, this initiative resulted in the formation of a TAPP involving 12 schools (early years, primary and secondary) with the specific intent to develop pre-service teachers' professional practice in a rural context.

The Bass Coast TAPP is one of only two rural-focused partnerships. The Charleville partnership with the Queensland Department of Education is unique in that it is the only rural-focused professional experience program of its kind currently operating in the state. In a state like Queensland, which is largely classified as regional, rural and remote, this initiative is particularly important due to a policy focus on ensuring that all schools regardless of location have equity of access to quality teachers. The *Beyond the Range* funding initiative speaks directly to this policy with targeted support for Queensland-based pre-service teachers to undertake a regional, rural and/or remote professional experience.

2.5.1.2 Localised Support

Through their research on rural and regional professional experience, Kline and colleagues (2013) considered the critical role that communities play in preparing pre-service teachers for this context. Community connections were important in both initiatives with locally based liaison playing a significant role as a conduit between the pre-service teachers, university, schools and wider community. This was largely due to their extensive experience and expertise as a teacher, previous or current, committed to living, working and strongly advocating for rural education. In the

Bass Coast, a retired deputy principal was employed through the teaching academy funding to foster school–university connections and support the seamless operation of the program in the region. The Charleville program was supported in situ by a lead principal.

The key difference between the initiatives was voluntary participation over a paid position. The pre-service teachers in Charleville were additionally supported by a university-based support person who had intimate knowledge and experience of this particular setting. Alongside this localised support, the importance of community was reiterated through the application processes and pre-placement briefings for both programs with the onus placed on the pre-service teachers to make a commitment to contribute to their placement communities. This emphasis on giving back and being part of the community was enacted through the pre-service teachers living in the community and actively engaging in a range of activities for the period of their two- or three-week placement block, including over the weekends.

2.5.1.3   Strategic Alignment

While partnership development can be achieved in a number of ways, these programs showcased some possibilities that were manageable and relevant for the rural context. In both instances, a close collaboration was formed between a school-focused professional and a university-based liaison. These relationships combined understandings of university requirements and local knowledge to help successfully navigate and negotiate the expectations of all stakeholders. The relevant Departments of Education also fostered the formation of these school–university partnerships in both locations as a way to achieve their own strategic goals of promoting and valuing rural education. Equally important was the way in which the two universities strategically positioned themselves to enhance their reach into rural communities as a higher education provider of choice.

For Monash University, the Bass Coast TAPP opportunity aligned with their focus on providing their pre-service teachers with a range of professional experience opportunities to broader their horizons, skillsets and, ultimately, employability. The focus for USQ was more about the institution's positioning as a regional university and the way in which this program enhanced its reach into rural communities as a higher education provider of choice. This section highlights how formalised rural professional experience programs in the Bass Coast region in Victoria and in Charleville, Queensland assisted in bringing together pre-service teachers interested in further honing professional practice and defining their teacher identity in a rural context. In terms of defining the domain of these respective CoPs, the pre-service teachers were significantly supported in forming a shared interest through program alignment with state-based systemic drivers, the support of professional's in situ and strong connections with the strategic goals of the two universities.

2.5.2 Community: The People Involved in Improving Professional Practice

Communities of practice by their nature are multi-faceted and multi-dimensional. In considering 'community' in the contexts explored through the two cases, there are a number of relationships and connections at play. Lave and Wenger (1998) consider community as a group of participants engaged in shared activities, discussions and meaning making. Importantly, they emphasise co-constructed learning and collegial support. At the core of these cases, the pre-service teachers were the principal members in the CoP and were required to forge relationships between themselves and those around them, which included mentor teachers, school staff, community members, university staff and other supporters of the rural placement initiatives. This complex system of relationships is defined by Wenger (2010) as a 'social learning system' (p. 179) and this definition captures the dynamic and ongoing formation of identity and meaning making happening for the pre-service teachers within these two communities. In making sense of this aspect of the CoP, what became apparent was that three components influenced how structures and processes were enacted within the communities to support pre-service teachers in both the Bass Coast region and Charleville: selection processes, structural considerations and strategic connections.

2.5.2.1 Selection Processes

While nearly three decades old, Lave and Wenger's (1991) construct of situated learning is still a useful way to make sense of learning. Learning, using this lens, happens through being with other learners and is therefore ultimately considered as a social act or interaction. There is a somewhat informal element to this definition which runs counterintuitive to the more unified and bounded approach that seems to characterise CoPs. Lave and Wenger (1991), however, dismiss this as a shallow interpretation of what is meant by community in a CoP. Rather than viewing community as a well-defined group, they instead consider community as 'participation in an activity system about which participants share understandings concerning what they are doing and what that means for their lives' (Lave & Wenger, 1991, p. 98).

The Bass Coast TAPP and Charleville professional experience programs were grounded in this notion of learning from other learners and were essentially communities formed around a shared interest of constructing and reconstructing teacher identity as a rural teacher. These two cases illustrate that instead of being structured or rigid, it is possible to put in place intentional mechanisms to guide and support the formation of meaningful and productive communities. In both instances, the selection processes that were enacted played a critical role in identifying pre-service teachers who had the skills, attributes and interest to engage in the improvement of their own as well as others professional practice in a rural context.

2.5.2.2   Structural Considerations

In considering the creation of a community, Wenger (2010) likens this to the forma-tion of a 'social history' (p. 180). This construct refers to the active and dynamic processes that characterise the lived experience of participating in a community. Through this social history, criteria and expectations are generated that underpin what it means to belong, which draw on both individual and collective elements. In the context of the two case studies, an influential factor acting on the development of 'social histories' was the way in which both universities structured their rural profes-sional experience programs. This was particularly evident in two key ways for both the Bass Coast TAPP and Charleville contexts: shared accommodation arrangements and placing small groups of pre-service teachers in each school. Although concerted efforts were undertaken in both settings to ensure group dynamics were a key consid-eration in the decision-making around living arrangements, the experience of living with unfamiliar people in an unfamiliar context often resulted in varying levels of discomfort.

Despite these challenges, the pre-service teachers were supported by the programs to navigate and negotiate their way through these situations with participants citing that, conversely, this experience resulted in significant levels of shared learning and peer bonding. Placing the pre-service teachers in small groups in the Bass Coast and Charleville schools was also an intentional programmatic action to further build the pre-service teachers' relationships with their peers and ensure that a localised support network was forming to support the development of professional practice in a rural context. Although this structural consideration does not replicate how graduates are likely to be employed (e.g. as individuals rather than collectively), it does provide a scaffolded approach to forming partnerships with colleagues.

2.5.2.3   Strategic Connections

Relationships are fundamental to the formation of community with Pyrko and colleagues (2017) arguing that CoPs cannot exist without the collaborative element. In relation to the Bass Coast TAPP and Charleville cases, different types of rela-tionships emerged from these communities that acted to serve and support the pre-service teachers in a number of ways. While some productive relationships formed organically (e.g. between peers sharing accommodation, pre-service teachers and their mentors), it is evident that some deliberate programmatic decisions were made to ensure the establishment of a formalised support network. From the outset, both contexts had Government backing for the initiative (e.g. DoE in Queensland and DET in Victoria), largely through financial contributions, which made a significant differ-ence to pre-service teachers' access and participation in the program. More localised connections were also established to nurture the establishment of strong community links. In Charleville, this was with principals and the broader teacher network, both socially and professionally. The support provided through this mechanism was not only about the personal and professional well-being of the pre-service teachers, but about advocating for the importance of equitable access to quality education in rural contexts. For the Bass Coast TAPP, the program coordinator (Greg) was the lynchpin in terms of building strong connections between the university and the schools. Greg worked to build and maintain trust between both parties, though ultimately his extensive knowledge of the region enabled him to enact strategies to overcome potential barriers to pre-service teachers' participation and growth through the program.

This section captures the range of people, individuals and collectives, involved in the formation of communities that promote and value rural-based professional practice. In terms of harnessing these insights to encourage pre-service teachers to consider their professional practice and identity in a rural context, a number of formal mechanisms were identified. These mechanisms included carefully considered selection processes, the structural design of the professional experience programs and strategic connections with key community members.

2.5.3 Practices: The Actions and Strategies Involved in Improving Professional Practice

As this chapter unfolds, it is becoming more evident that rural professional experience programs have the potential to build pre-service teachers' confidence, knowledge and skills related to living and working in an unfamiliar and sometimes complex rural community context (Hudson & Hudson, 2008). Using the lens of CoP, pre-service teachers in both contexts had opportunities to engage in formal and informal 'practices' that were targeted at moving them beyond the traditional placement norms and boundaries of developing their teacher identity within a school or classroom context to include the social context of the community. In better understanding the structure and processes adopted and implemented to support the pre-service teachers in their learning in the Bass Coast region and Charleville, this section examines three emergent practices: navigating context, interpersonal awareness and reflective practice.

2.5.3.1   Navigating Context

The placement of pre-service teachers into rural contexts can pose well-documented unique personal and professional challenges (e.g. Mukeredzi, 2016). A number of physical and psychological structural features including the geographical location, access to resources, school and community demographics and community values can impact on pre-service teachers' self-esteem, confidence, levels of anxiety and feelings of isolation, all of which can be compounded by the blurring of boundaries between professional and personal roles. While this is not necessarily unique to rural contexts, the two case studies showcased in this chapter highlight that this is certainly heightened when the placement context is located away from the pre-service teachers' home and their usual support mechanisms. These potential challenges can be proactively addressed through the implementation of a comprehensive pre-placement program that is co-designed with key stakeholders to meet the pre-service teacher and communities' identified needs.

Both settings established unique pre-placement programs that incorporated a series of formalised activities to: (i) unpack the professional role of a teacher within the school and community context; (ii) discuss university and school organisational requirements; (iii) outline placement logistics—including travel, accommodation and access to resources; (iv) explore school and community demographics and (v) beginning the establishment of their professional profile. These programs were implemented through a series of group face-to-face and/or virtual sessions that were primarily facilitated by the university contacts with introductions to school and community-based support personnel. Another key aspect of this practice was to establish peer relationships and with the person responsible for in situ support to support the initial phase of the placement.

2.5.3.2 Reflective Practice

It is well documented that group dynamics can have a significant impact on the quality of knowledge sharing (Cyr & Choo, 2010). This highlights the importance of planning for and implementing formal practices including meeting structures, communication protocols and reflective practices. Utilising the in situ community support person (Greg in Case Study 1 and Lead Principal in Case Study 2), both cases incorporated practices that supported the individual and provided reflective opportunities with peers and experienced practitioners. Both cases also provided formal professional reflective opportunities, through the provision of face-to-face site visits aimed at clarifying placement expectations and where necessary provide support. This type of support is typically provided to all pre-service teachers regardless of their placement context. Where the support practices within these cases differ from traditional placements are in the provision of knowledge sharing practices within the social context of the placement (Hanson-Smith, 2006). This was essentially to assist the pre-service teachers in managing potential issues themselves and with others from within the intense group experience created by these programs. Within the Bass Coast case, individual reflection opportunities were provided on a needs basis with most of the reflective opportunities occurring within informal social settings, such as at community events and through individual conversations with the Professional Practice Consultant and Project Coordinator. The Charleville case implemented a more formalised approach through the inclusion of timetabled group sessions that included negotiating and establishing group norms and communication processes, explicitly developing strategies for collaboration and establishing a coaching relationship with the in situ support academic.

2.5.3.3 Interpersonal Awareness

Research highlights that individuals' personal dispositions and group thinking within a CoP can impact on an individual's ability to engage in practices aimed at building personal and professional awareness (Malm, 2009). To counteract this, the CoP structure within both case studies informally and formally supported the development of practices aimed at building such awareness. The Bass Coast case fore-fronted the need for collaborative and conflict resolution skills through the inclusion of practices within their pre-placement sessions. These included outlining professional expectations, engaging in group conversations around what this means within the rural and remote context and the development of social competence by formally unpacking what it means to give back to a community.

Within the Charleville case, the pre-service teachers' individual dispositions were utilised to balance time spent with each other within and outside of school hours. Students who shared accommodation were placed in different school sites providing opportunities for diversity within informal conversations and the reduction of perception-based group thinking. Both case studies provided group and individual reflection opportunities to address the potential for this group thinking. Within these reflective opportunities, conversations were structured the university-based support people typically following an observed lesson or a critical moment experienced in the classroom to reflect upon their personal attributes and what this means for teaching within a rural and remote context. These conversations supported pre-service teachers to explore their career adaptability and career planning. Within the Charleville case, pre-service teachers connected with education system human resource personnel to position the importance of using the placement as an opportunity to develop their personal awareness of living and teaching in a rural community.

This section explores the possible actions and strategies that can be enacted to improve pre-service teachers' professional practice in a rural context. What emerged from this sense-making is that there is a range of specific practices that differentiate preparing for a traditional school placement experience from getting ready to engage with living and teaching in a rural context. These practices include spending time understanding the contextual landscape, being supported to develop reflective practice, and enhancing awareness of interpersonal skills to better manage the community contexts.

2.6 Conclusion: Key Learnings

The use of CoP as a framework for analysis and sense-making of the case studies allowed for characteristics and conditions to emerge. This assisted in defining the types of structures and processes that supported pre-service teachers in undertaking a quality rural placement experience. In response to the original literature to better articulate the relationship to the work shared through this chapter and demonstrate a level of criticality, the key learnings in relation to the three components of a CoP are as follows.

- *Domain*: Macro (big picture) and micro (specific details) factors need to align to foster the right conditions for a CoP to thrive, which can be aided thinking carefully about the selection processes used to best identify an appropriate cohort.
- *Community*: A willingness to be an active and contributing member of a CoP is required from all stakeholders and an understanding that, in this context specifically, this stretches beyond the classroom to relationships with peers, school colleagues and the broader rural community.
- *Practices*: A range of informal opportunities and more formally designed experiences support learning and growth with a particular focus on developing not only capacity in the classroom, but in the development of social competencies.

This approach to supporting pre-service teachers in rural contexts, while fulfilling and impactful, is resource intensive, and with numerous complexities to negotiate. This raises a number of considerations for future programming and for others wanting to work in this space, which are detailed below.

- *Sustainability*: Sustainability in these programs can appear problematic due to the structure's resource intensive nature. Linking into this is the personnel-dependent nature of the program, which can impact succession planning, and in turn, the sustainability of the program.
- *Scalability*: These two CoPs supported relatively small numbers of stakeholders within a single location at one time, which raises questions about the potential reach of such programs. Drawing on CoP as a framework assists in understanding the conditions required to provide a structure for replication and involving larger cohorts across multiple locations.
- *Influence on professional experience more broadly*: All pre-service teachers complete a significant amount of professional experience across their initial teacher education programs, but very few receive the level of support and additional resourcing evident in these two cases. To address this inequity, aspects of this CoP format, such as fostering intentional reflective practice and focusing on the development of interpersonal skills, could be adapted and applied.

The learnings from this chapter matter in two key ways. Firstly, the cases speak to creative responses to the problems faced in attracting and retaining quality teachers in rural schools across Australia. Secondly, this work through using a CoP framework draws out the conditions that support the successful induction of pre-service teachers into rural contexts. In combination, these learnings provide hope that there are ways to ensure that the teaching profession flourishes in rural communities and that pre-service teachers placed into these contexts have access to a quality educational experiences and opportunities. While further resourcing, both human and material, is required, this chapter starts to draw out what is possible and how it might be achieved.

References

Australian Bureau of Statistics. (2016). *Australian Statistical Geography Standard (ASGS): Volume 1—Main structure and greater capital city statistical areas, July 2016.* https://www.abs.gov.au/ausstats/abs@.nsf/Lookup/by%20Subject/1270.0.55.001~July%202016~Main%20Features~Statistical%20Area%20Level%202%20(SA2)~10014. Accessed 9 May 2020.

Clandinin, D. J., & Huber, J. (2010). Narrative inquiry. In B. McGraw, E. Baker, & P. Perterso (Eds.), *International encyclopedia of education* (3rd ed., pp. 436–441). New York, NY: Elsevier.

Craven, G., Beswick, K., Fleming, J., Fletcher, T., Green, M., Jensen, B., … Rickards, F. (2014). *Action now: Classroom ready teachers.* Canberra, Australia: Teacher Education Ministerial Advisory Group.

Cyr, S., & Choo, C. W. (2010). The individual and social dynamics of knowledge sharing: An exploratory study. *Journal of Documentation, 66*(1), 824–846.

Fitzgerald, A., Parr, G., & Williams, J. (Eds.). (2017). *Narratives of learning through international professional experience.* The Netherlands: Springer.

Ghaye, T., & Lillyman, S. (2019). *Reflective leadership: A practical guide for positive action.* London, UK: Mark Allen Group.

Green, B., & Reid, J.-A. (2004). Teacher education for rural and regional sustainability: Changing agendas, challenging futures, chasing chimeras? *Asia-Pacific Journal of Teacher Education, 32*(3), 255–273.

Halsey, J. (2018). *Independent review into regional, rural and remote education—Final report.* Canberra, ACT: Department of Education and Training.

Hanson-Smith, E. (2006). Communities of practice for pre- and in-service teacher education. In P. Hubbard & M. Levy (Eds.), *Teacher education in CALL* (pp. 301–316). Amsterdam, The Netherlands: John Benjamins Publishing Company.

Hodkinson, P., & Hodkinson, H. (2004). *A constructive critique of communities of practice: Moving beyond Lave and Wenger* (Oval Research Working Paper 04-02). Sydney, VIC: OVAL Research.

Hudson, P., & Hudson, S. (2008). Changing preservice teachers' attitudes for teaching in rural schools. *Australian Journal of Teacher Education, 33*(4), 67–77.

Jewson, N. (2007). Cultivating network analysis: rethinking the concept of "community" within communities of practice. In J. Hughes, N. Jewson, & L. Unwin (Eds.), *Communities of practice: Critical perspectives* (pp. 68–82). London: Routledge.

Kline, J., & Walker-Gibbs, B. (2015). Graduate teacher preparation for rural schools in Victoria and Queensland. *Australian Journal of Teacher Education, 40*(3), 68–88.

Kline, J., White, S., & Lock, G. (2013). The rural practicum: Preparing a quality teacher workforce for rural and regional Australia. *Journal of Research in Rural Education, 28*(3), 1–13.

Lave, J., & Wenger, E. (1991). *Situated learning: Legitimate peripheral participation (Learning in doing: Social, cognitive and computational perspectives).* New York, NY: Cambridge University Press.

Lave, J., & Wenger, E. (1998). *Communities of practice: Learning, meaning, and identity.* New York, NY: Cambridge University Press.

Lieberman, A., & Pointer Mace, D. H. (2009). The role of 'accomplished teachers' in professional learning communities: Uncovering practice and enabling leadership. *Teachers and Teaching: Theory and Practice, 15*(4), 459–470.

Malm, B. (2009). Towards a new professionalism: Enhancing personal and professional development in teacher education. *Journal of Education for Teaching, 35*(1), 77–91.

Mukeredzi, T. G. (2016). The nature of professional learning needs of rural secondary school teachers: Voices of professional unqualified teachers in rural Zimbabwe. *SAGE Open, 6*(2), 1–12.

Pyrko, I., Dorfler, V., & Eden, C. (2017). Thinking together: What makes communities of practice work? *Human Relations, 70*(4), 389–409.

Queensland Government. (2018). *Advancing rural and remote education in Queensland state schools.* https://education.qld.gov.au/schools-and-educators/other-education/Documents/advancing-rural-education-qld-state-schools-action-plan.pdf. Accessed 9 May 2020.

Roberts, P. (2004). *Staffing an empty schoolhouse: Attracting and retaining teachers in rural, remote and isolated communities.* Surry Hills, NSW: New South Wales Teachers Federation.

Schon, D. A. (1982). *The reflective practitioner: How professionals think in action.* New York, NY: Basic Books.

Vangrieken, K., Meredith, C., & Kyndt, E. (2017). Teacher communities as a context for professional development: A systematic review. *Teaching and Teacher Education, 61,* 47–59.

Vescio, V., Ross, D., & Adams, A. (2008). A review of research on the impact of professional learning communities on teaching practices and student learning. *Teaching and Teacher Education, 24*(1), 80–91.

Vygotsky, L. S. (1978). Interaction between learning and development. In M. Cole, V. John-Steiner, S. Scribner, & E. Souberman (Eds.), *Mind in society: The development of higher psychological processes* (pp. 79–91). Cambridge, MA: Harvard University Press.

Wagner, T. (1993). Systemic change: Rethinking the purpose of school. *Educational Leadership, 51*(1), 24–28.

Wenger, E. (2010). Communities of practice and social learning systems: The career of a concept. In C. Blackmore (Ed.), *Social learning systems and communities of practice* (pp. 179–198). London, UK: Springer.

Wenger-Traynor, E., & Wenger-Traynor, B. (2015). *Introduction to communities of practice: A brief overview of the concept and its uses.* https://wenger-trayner.com/introduction-to-communities-of-practice/. Accessed 9 May 2020.

Angela Fitzgerald is an adjunct Associate Professor at the University of Southern Queensland. She has a decade-long association with supporting and growing professional experience opportunities for pre-service teachers across two Australian initial teacher education providers. Regardless of location, the key driver for Ange's energy and passion for these spaces is the professional and personal growth these opportunities activate in pre-service teachers and the avenue it provides to connect with burgeoning teacher identity in a very different way. Additionally, as someone born and raised in a rural location, she highly values quality educational experiences for students and teachers in these contexts.

Ondine Bradbury is currently in the role of a Site Director at Deakin University, Burwood Campus. She has over a decade of experience in mainstream classrooms, has been a Senior Project Manager at the Victorian Department of Education and Training overseeing the Teaching Academies of Professional Practice (TAPP), and has held roles in the professional experience space in two Victorian universities. During her time at Monash University, Ondine was an integral part in the development and delivery of the Bass Coast Teaching Academy of Professional Practice (TAPP). Ondine holds a strong desire to connect teaching and learning communities, and to build and grow collaborative networks across a range of educational settings.

Tania Leach is currently the Director of Professional Experience at the University of Southern Queensland with 20 years' teaching and leadership experience across regional and rural contexts. During her time at the University of Southern Queensland, Tania collaborated with systems and key stakeholders within rural communities to develop the contextualised Alternative Context Placement Program. Driven by her personal experience of raising and educating her family in rural Queensland, and her desire to ensure every student has a quality education, Tania continues to connect with communities and professional organisations to grow Communities of Practice focused on developing the next generation of rural and regional teachers.

Chapter 3
Knowing Myself as a Teacher: Transforming the Place of Rurality in Scottish Initial Teacher Education

Morag Redford and Lindsay Nicol

Abstract This chapter challenges the view that preparation for rural teaching is a specialist provision. We explore rural teaching as a meaningful place-mediated identity through analysis of a one-year Initial Teacher Education programme, delivered partly through a digital infrastructure. The programme is framed around a trajectory of learning and experience that supports the development of teacher agency, and we use constructs of Activity Theory and place to analyse student engagement with the programme. We reflect on the ways collaborative programme activities and relationships empower students to work out their emerging teacher identity as it is shaped by their experiences of living in a rural area while becoming a teacher. In particular, we focus on how existing rural identities in the student community generate and use the resource of collaborative intentionality capital to facilitate the development of their teacher identities. From this we conclude that programmes preparing students for entry to the teaching profession should work with rural teaching as a place-attentive, self-expressive and embodied identity, and that rurality is important for emerging teachers as a shaping influence within their professional community. We present this as a critical pedagogy of place, nurturing the emergence of a collaborative, agentive teacher self, situated willingly as a school community inhabitant.

Keywords Activity Theory · Ecological agency · Initial teacher education · Place-attentive

3.1 Rurality in Scottish Initial Teacher Education

> I am beginning to understand myself as a teacher and I can't wait to try that out in school.

The University of the Highlands and Islands (UHI) is the only Scottish University to offer Initial Teacher Education (ITE) in rural regions of Scotland. UHI is locally based in nine colleges and four research centres across the north and west of Scotland and uses an established digital infrastructure to connect virtually between and

M. Redford (✉) · L. Nicol
University of the Highlands and Islands, Scotland, UK
e-mail: morag.redford@uhi.ac.uk

© Springer Nature Singapore Pte Ltd. 2021
S. White and J. Downey (eds.), *Rural Education Across the World*,
https://doi.org/10.1007/978-981-33-6116-4_3

across all of the study locations. ITE is strategically important to UHI and to the geographical, cultural and linguistic communities it serves. The University offers one-year postgraduate programmes for primary and secondary teaching, in English and Gaelic Medium, in partnership with local education authorities. The provision of ITE across the region provides local access to teaching qualifications and newly qualified teachers for local schools, meeting the needs of individuals and communities. This enacts through ITE the mission statement of the University, "To have a transformational impact on the prospects of our region, its economy, its people and its communities" (University of the Highlands and Islands, 2015, p. 8).

Rurality is defined by the Scottish Government (2018a) through an *Urban/Rural Classification* based on population and accessibility to urban centres. As experienced in other countries (e.g. Roberts & Green, 2013; Greenough & Nelson, 2015), the Scottish policymakers define rural as *not urban* and through distance from urban centres. This classifies the regions supported by UHI on the continuum from "very remote rural, with a drive time of over 60 min to a settlement of 10,000 or more" to "other urban areas, as settlements of 10,000 to 124,999 people" (Scottish Government, 2018a, p. 2). In a physically small country like Scotland, it is the distribution of population rather than distance that is a key part of the definition of rurality. UHI serves a region that covers 58% of the Scottish landmass but has only 17% of the population (Scottish Government, 2018b). The same *Urban/Rural Classification* is used to determine which schools in Scotland are rural. This is identification was established by an *Act of the Scottish Parliament* in 2010 in order to protect rural schools from closure (Redford, 2013). The legislation, and the *Commission on the Delivery of Rural Education* in 2011 that proceeded it, were introduced in response to community action to retain schools and to address national difficulties in recruiting teachers to posts in rural schools. The Commission report to Government in 2013 included the following recommendation in relation to ITE, "Local authorities, the Scottish Government, teaching institutions and trade unions should work together to explore innovative solutions to reduce the barriers to teaching in remote areas" (Scottish Government, 2013, p. 7).

In Scotland, schools, teachers and ITE are managed through local and central government, with all teachers required to pass a recognised initial teaching qualification, undergraduate or postgraduate, and register with the General Teaching Council for Scotland (GTCS). There is a two-part qualification structure with graduates evidencing the Standard for Provisional Registration (SPR) by the end of their university programme and then the Standard for Full Registration (SFR) at the end of an induction year, their first year of employment as a teacher (GTCS, 2012). The Scottish Government oversees the number of student enrolments in ITE programmes each year and the recommendation above led to an expansion of Teacher Education provision for rural areas. While the 2013 Commission report reiterated the *Urban/Rural* divide in Scottish education policy, it also provided an opportunity for UHI to introduce ITE programmes that were designed to work with the rural and local place of the University. UHI first offered a one-year *Professional Graduate Diploma in Education* (PGDE) for Primary teaching in the 2013–14 academic year. This chapter will focus on the 2018–2019 Primary programme.

All ITE programmes offered by Scottish Universities must be GTCS accredited (GTCS, 2019) to enable programme graduates to progress into their induction year post. At the time of writing, we are working towards the first GTCS reaccreditation of our programmes and engaging with a new, national self-evaluation structure for ITE (Education Scotland, 2019). In both situations we are struggling to find a vocabulary to answer set questions about our digitally connected model in a way that demonstrates what we know ourselves to be: a successful rural ITE provider whose graduates are teaching in schools across all of our partner local authorities and beyond. We use this chapter to evidence rural ITE provision as a "dwelt-in place" (Mannion et al., 2013, p. 794) and to claim our deepened understanding of the foundational significance of place (as rural, local and digitally connected) in our Scottish PGDE Primary programme as transformative.

3.2   How Rural and Local Place Informs the PDGE Primary Programme

The PGDE Primary programme is offered in nine of the University colleges and two learning centres, each based in a village, small town or one city in the region (University of the Highlands and Islands, 2019), and in partnership with each local education authority as school placement (or practicum) hosts. The majority of our students are recruited from, and live near, one of the University colleges, with some who have chosen to move to that area. In offering a programme and placements locally, our PGDE students are, in the main, intrinsically motivated to become a teacher *here,* ether capitalising on our programme as the means to study within an established local home life, or accepting the requirement to have an address in the vicinity of the college they enrol with for the duration of the programme.

They are supported and taught by a tutor in that college, who also observes them on school placement. Each college cohort has a minimum of three students and connects into a programme cohort and wider tutor team via a blend of digital tools already constituent to the university infrastructure. Therefore, as in UHI as an institution, each annual iteration of the PGDE community—students, tutors and host schools— can be situated somewhere on the continuum of rurality framed in Scottish policy (Scottish Government, 2013, 2017). Thomson (2011) allows this rurality to be viewed as a multivocal embodiment of a foundational identity, while Kerkham and Comber (2013) allow for an ontological conceptualisation of our local and digitally connected model through the lens of place. The writers are part of that rurality, living and teaching in two different regions serviced by UHI. The first author, Morag Redford, joined UHI in 2014 to lead the development of ITE, a role which allows her to retain a narrative overview (Kearney, 2003) of the programme. The second author, Lindsay Nicol, has worked with the PGDE Primary programme from the start, and now enacts the programme leadership role for UHI, while teaching locally and digitally as a tutor.

As the University of, for and in the Highlands and Islands of Scotland (University of the Highlands and Islands, 2015), and as an ITE provider working through partnerships with rural local education authorities, we are inherently rural, located *here,* not *there.* This means our understanding of rural lies with our already "rural lives" (Howley et al., 2005, p. 1) and for all of us in the programme community in any given year, this is "real" not imagined (Green & Reid, 2014, p. 28). Cloke (2006, p. 18) defines rural as encompassing "space, place and society", and we utilise a digital dimension (Hibbert, 2013) to socially construct and connect spaces that support the development of individual teacher identity across UHI and in what education policy defines as rural schools (Scottish Government, 2017). In this understanding we acknowledge the work of Gruenwald (2003) in raising awareness of place conscious education and recognise that the programme works with a pedagogy of place (Wattchow & Brown, 2011; Mannion et al., 2013). As this chapter will show, the students, tutors and programme exemplify Heidegger's idea of relationship to place by "dwelling authentically in place" and "taking responsibility for place" (Wattchow & Brown, 2011, p. 54).

In this chapter we used the theoretical framework of Engestrom's (2008) Activity Theory to analyse the structure and integrated activities of the PGDE Primary programme in 2018–2019, to illustrate how our programme deploys its continuum of rural identities as a means to enable collaborative student engagement in ITE. The chapter demonstrates that our students draw on their concurrent lived experiences of being rural and becoming a teacher, generating their own place-attentive (White & Reid, 2008) embodiment of the teacher identity expressed in the SPR (GTCS, 2012). We conclude that our UHI PGDE programme frames rural teaching as a meaningful place-mediated identity, rather than as a specialist material provision and resists the Scottish policy construct for rurality as "distance from an urban centre" (Scottish Government, 2017: 4).

We present our analysis from the perspective of an individual engaged student teacher in the following steps

- Establishing the metaphor used with students of journeying on an agency trajectory (Priestley et al., 2015) into the Scottish teaching profession.
- Construing our programme ethos of teacher identity construction and participation through Engestrom's (2008) Activity Theory as the collaborative working out of a possible self (Markus & Nurius, 1986).
- Exploring programme activities as local, digital and rural through Wildy's (2010) detailed rural framework of place, system, people and self.
- Critically reflecting on a systemic analysis of collaborative activity within PGDE to deepen our understanding of how the rural place of students informs their identity as a teacher.

3.3   Establishing the PGDE Primary Programme as a Trajectory into Teaching

The structural design of the PGDE programme is based on the theoretical constructs of the ecological framework for teacher agency (Priestley et al., 2015). This framework emphasises agency as an emergent quality of dynamic engagement with iterative, projective and practical-evaluative contexts as shown in Fig. 3.1.

The students enter the programme with their life and professional history (Iterational) which establishes their starting point as an emergent teacher. The programme content and contexts address the cultural, structural and material aspects of becoming a teacher (Practical-evaluative) and enable each student to enact the individual agency that mediates their emergent understanding of what it means to be a teacher. This supports the students as they work towards a short-term aim of passing the PGDE programme at the end of the academic year, and the majority towards the longer-term aim of employment as a teacher in their locality (Projective). Students are introduced to the ecological framework (Fig. 3.1) at the beginning of the programme and are actively encouraged to develop their capacity, "to act reflexively … to effect change" (Priestley, 2011 p. 16), to act with moral purpose (Begley, 2010) and to engage directly with the SPR (GTCS, 2012) as they construct their own professional identity. The programme is taught and experienced cumulatively in college and school blocks, with 18 weeks of study in college interspersed with four blocks of school

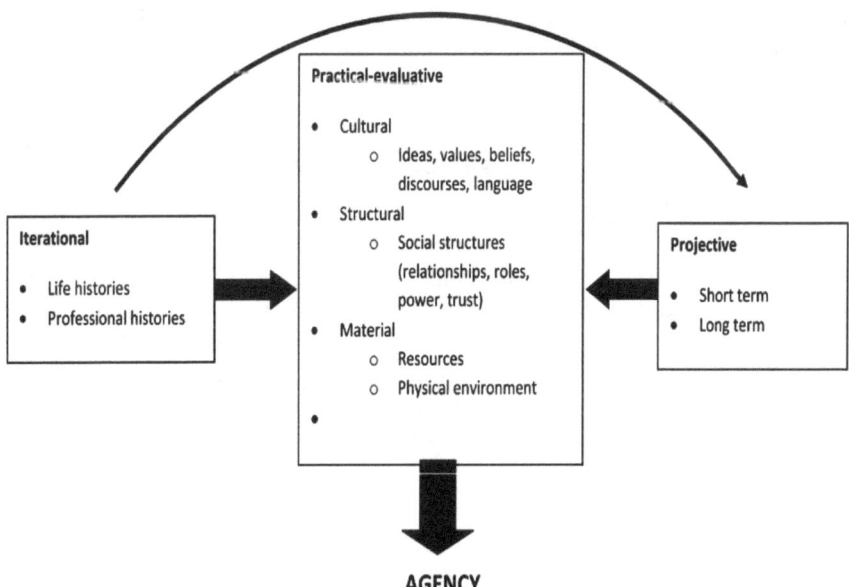

Fig. 3.1 Ecological framework for teacher agency (Priestley et al., 2015, p. 30)

placement providing 19 weeks of experience in up to three schools. These alternate periods of time structure a student journey of repeating short-term cycles of the ecological framework (Fig. 3.1) as interim opportunities for assessing progress towards meeting the SPR (GTCS, 2012).

Programme engagement in a typical college week uses the University technologies to establish different peer groupings, enabling participation through synchronous and asynchronous digital tools from college, online or personal (home) learning spaces. The PGDE community of students and tutors use the digital interface to cross the spatial and temporal boundaries of each college and create a virtually connected partnership of local groups, founded on individual starting identities. Each of these peer groups is a different collection of students, sometimes located in the same college, sometimes between colleges, all of them, "located somewhere" on our rural continuum, "but nowhere in particular" (Dee, 2018, p. 6).

Coker (2017) examined the student teacher agency development in the college-based weeks on the programme and characterised this trajectory as "inward" (p. 61), guiding the individual from a peripheral position in teaching through registration into the profession. Through independent study, collaborative dialogue within and between college-based groups, and structured discussions with school-based mentor teachers and placement-supporting tutors, students are required to collate and self-report evidence of their journey through an e-portfolio, presentations and written assignments. In their final placement they take full responsibility, as a member of the school staff team, for pupil learning and well-being over ten consecutive days. The programme design as a journey supports each student teacher to acquire individual knowledge and skills, but also to foster and develop collaborative working practices, which are a key policy focus of Scottish education (GTCS, n.d).

3.4   Construing the PGDE Primary Programme Using Activity Theory

Students are selected onto the PGDE Primary programme as *possible teachers*, having demonstrated the potential to engage in a collaborative pursuit of this future *local-self-as-teacher* that they, and all programme participants, can only initially envisage in very generic terms. This fits well with Engestrom's (2008) construct of a "runaway object" (p. 227), which he proposes embeds "interagency" (p. 225), as the capacity and motivation for work across all contextual interfaces. These alignments enabled us to engage with his concept of "knotworking" (p. 196), where collaboration is "a partially improvised orchestration" (p. 194) with an evolving "locus of initiative" (p. 194). Our programme requires collaboration to be increasingly student-led and involves different groupings and varying modes of participation, both locally based and digitally connected. Engestrom, (2008, p. 194) refers to this as an "unstable knot", worthy of being analysed to understand the contributory activities.

PGDE Knotworking: transforming the self into a teacher through collaborative learning

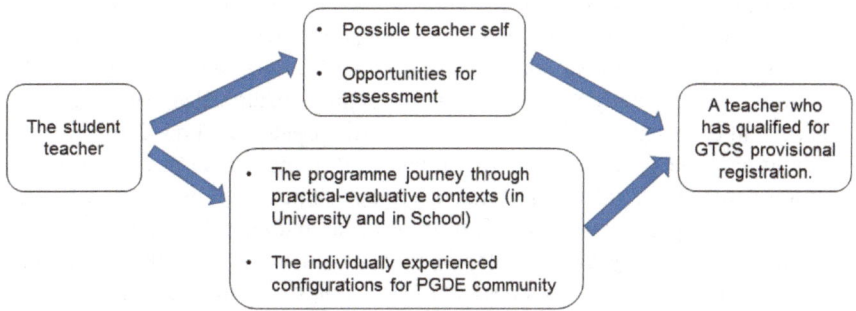

Fig. 3.2 PGDE primary programme activities as agentive identity construction

We used these definitions to characterise how programme engagement operates as student teachers gradually take ownership of the responsibilities of being a teacher by collaborating through learning activities with different programme actors. Engestrom (2008) locates knotworking within these changing "co-configurations" (p. 195) as gathering necessary intelligence from those who are impacted by the outcome of the work being undertaken. He also models that we can create a framework for analysing programme activity by construing it as "systemic activity" (Engestrom, 2008, p. 27) for becoming a teacher. We illustrate this systemic provision of our inherent rural multivocality (Thomson 2011) and the ecological contexts for achievement (Priestley et al., 2015) as mediating resources to draw on, in Fig. 3.2.

3.5 Exploring Programme Activity as Local, Digital and Rural

To undertake our analysis of programme functionality and progress towards demonstrating that our student teachers are transformed into place-attentive selves (White and Reid 2008), we worked from the starting points of place established in Figs. 3.1 and 3.2 above. We explored the unstable continuum of rural identities that is available to students across the University and the programme through:

- Our system of alternating practical-evaluative contexts in college and school as salient co-configurations of local.
- The affordances for collaborative relationships.
- Assessment artefacts requiring students' expression of their current possible self.

This encouraged us to draw on Wildy's (2010) detailed consideration of rural encompassing place, people, system, and self to allow us to understand the programme actors and the activities contributing to identity construction as collaborative and at least partly facilitated by our integral digital connectivity.

In a focus on system (Wildy, 2010), our programme journey metaphor alternates the provision of Practical-evaluative contexts in college and in school contexts as a systemic cycle of agency-generating activity which shapes, and is shaped by, each individual student's iterative and projective identities as emergent (Fig. 3.1). The necessity for us, as for any Scottish PGDE programme, to embed at least ninety days of placement experience (GTCS, 2019), establishes contextual boundaries between University and placement schools which are local to the student, as organisers for becoming a teacher. Student engagement through digital tools in a typical college week, allows for participation in and from physical and virtual learning spaces. At any point in their journey, the student is positioned within a collaborative professional community of student teachers, or teachers in school, with a mandate to evolve their current teacher identity based on the situated knowledge and learning made possible. This interplay is conceptualised for Teacher Education by Knight et al. (2018) as being attentive to their current place.

Engestrom (2008) construes the agency developed as "interagency" (p. 225), an intrinsically motivated capacity to transition between available learning spaces. Our students achieve this by alternately transcending the spatial and temporal boundaries for studying *here* by digital means, and grounding themselves in role enactment and identity evidence-gathering in schools. By working with partner staff in schools and across the University PGDE tutor team, the students access a multivocal continuum of rural identities throughout the programme, which provides each of them with a meaningful co-configuration of local. We effect a trajectory of interagency development orientated inwards (Coker, 2017) through the programme ethos of becoming a teacher who meets the SPR (GTCS, 2012). The shifting positionality and community configurations render such interagency as inherently collaborative (Engestrom, 2008) and place conscious (Gruenwald, 2003). This is further nuanced by the time-bounded liminality of each Practical-evaluative block of place-based identity work (Green & Reid, 2014).

For the developing interagency to be individually transformative, it must be mediated by dialogue-based relationships (Lipponen & Kumpulainen, 2011). The programme provides such dialogue by focussing the relationships onto a narration of the emerging self (Lumby & English, 2009) to achieve a sense of coherence and worth. This is supported by the range of local influences we configure as students articulate their developing sense of self as teacher *here*. The people (Wildy, 2010) providing these influences, validate the individual, which is central to constructive formative self-assessment (Coker, 2017).

Two key programme relationships which facilitate identity rehearsal as a co-construction of meaning and sense of self (Thomson, 2011) are the placement mentor–student relationship and the college seminar peer-group relationships. It is through engagement with mentor teachers and seminar tutors that we build a capacity for collaboration during each phase of the PGDE journey and enable students to inhabit our expectations for becoming a teacher. Over the course of the three school placements comprising the professional practicum component, each student works closely with four volunteer mentors. This affords access to place-based (Green & Reid, 2014) expertise, and to pupils and classrooms as constituents and mediators of *teacher-identity-being-locally-enacted*. As their role responsibility builds over the year, from taking individual discrete lessons, to acting-in-lieu of the mentor teacher to showcase their teaching as meeting the SPR (GTCS, 2012), the situated intelligence needed by students for role efficacy increases. As role model and performance observer, the mentor is the key enabler for rehearsal, through debrief and feedforward, as dialogue in school with the student effectively generates a script (Lumby & English, 2009) for how to teach *here*.

In the college-based weeks, programme activity is organised thematically, with an engagement structure which builds pedagogic content knowledge and orientates it towards individual experiential use during the next placement. Tutors facilitate weekly seminar discussion between student peers, within groups engineered as cross-university, via a synchronous digital tool. This gives students access to examples of emerging possible teacher selves (Fig. 3.2), and a tutor with PGDE journeying expertise who works with an awareness of place across the programme. It facilitates practice focussed dialogue between multi-located peers as "site specific work for what can be recognised as site-specific lives" (Dee, 2018, p. 12). Engestrom (2008) allows for this digitally engineered social context to creatively co-construct a meaning for each student as *the teacher I know I am becoming*, which is inherently multiply influenced by the collective experience and knowledge base.

The programme engages the students in discussing how they understand their emerging teacher self through their local identity. They then collaborate digitally as a group of emergent teachers to learn about different situated teacher identities. Being "nowhere in particular, but somewhere" (Dee, 2018, p. 6) activates Knight et al.'s (2018) intentional noticing as an imperative to rework self by an "allegiance to perspectives and practices" (Dinkelman, 2011, p. 321, in Knight et al. p. 10) that feel most immediately salient. The structured journey of alternating college and school blocks keeps the next enactment of that emerging teacher self in clearer focus than the end of PGDE teacher-self. Engestrom (2008) models that the interagency will similarly be intelligent and adapting.

To focus our analysis through self (Wildy, 2010), we then worked with two central programme artefacts, the PGDE residential and the student e-portfolio. These artefacts value local enactment as an expression of the emergent teacher self, and so contribute to the knotworking (Engestrom, 2008) to ground it. In the first of these artefacts, the PGDE residential, the whole PGDE community of staff and students meet in person on two occasions in the programme year, staying together away from home for three days off-campus in the rural Scottish Highlands. In Induction week, we build and enculture our community through social and participatory activities which mirror indicative programme engagement, establishing relationships within groups who will work together in our digital learning environment. At the end of the college block just prior to the final placement, we return to the same location for student-led learning planned with particular habitat affordances in mind. This culminates in an assessed collaborative group presentation, framing a creative professional response to experiential learning outdoors, as a justification for, and a commitment to a place-based (Green & Reid, 2014) disposition. Such activity aligns fully with

Wattchow and Brown's (2011) signposts for a pedagogy of place, and both residential experiences centre on locating the self, intentionally and for positive affect, on the journey as it is currently understood.

Engestrom (2008) allows for activity system artefacts to be used in different ways and our programme orientates the use of residentials by the student towards making sense of the *teacher-I-am-becoming*. The first builds vocal capacity as participatory presence, while the second legitimises the teacher self presented as a hybrid of leader, learner and performance artist. Each generate confidence to express that self from within the multi-local "patterned ground" (Dee, 2018, p. 1) we uniquely call into being as this year's PGDE community. Each serve to affirm an already credible possible future self (Markus & Nurius, 1986), by affording a coherence from being expressive together, which Mabey (2018) suggests moves the self beyond its own envisioning.

The second artefact we used to examine the dimension of self is an e-portfolio the student completes throughout the programme to practise a narration of *self-as-local-actor* in which the seminar tutor becomes their invited audience. Lipponen & Kumpulainen (2011) show that this digitally interactive space is potentially transformative, when owned by the student as primary "accountable author" (p. 813), and while distributing the agency work of becoming a teacher. In presenting examples from practice and reflection in their own words as episodes in the "flow of situated practice" (Lipponen & Kumpulainen, 2011, p. 818) they experience on placement, students prompt dialogue with the tutor to interpret them as a situation of self.

3.6 Deepening Our Understanding of How Rural Place Informs Teacher Identity for Our Students

Our exploratory analysis of local, digital and rural demonstrated that students on the programme typically participate as collaborative agents within an evolving professional community. In order to understand rurality as a place dimension of the programme, we returned to Engestrom's (2008) studies of systemic activity and his concept of "collaborative intentionality capital" (p. 200). Collaborative intentionality capital (CIC) is generated in collaborative activity where the intentionality for success is collective and agency is distributed across organisational interfaces, as in our ecological and inward trajectory knotworking model (Engestrom, 2008). Acknowledging the value in simplifying the complex knot of variables involved for the purposes of critical analysis, we followed the advice offered by Yamagata-Lynch (2010) to identify microcosmic systems of activity within the boundaries of very specific settings. The analysis could then focus on the impact on constituents, or tensions, from any contradictions introduced by changes in the bounded system. The contradictions provided a starting point for working with our expectation that the rural continuum of each PGDE community functions as a generator of CIC as a critical place-attentive resource.

To analyse the use of existing student rural identity we brought together three bounded activity sets: the work by seminar groups at the second Residential, the mentor–student relationship over all three school placements, and student work from the final placement which is self-reported in the e-portfolio at the point of completing the programme. Table 3.1 shows the contradictions involved from introducing the following changes:

- Being digitally connected
- The rural continuum as a given
- Work happening ecologically

Two further contradictions emerged from considering our ontology overall in terms of the raison d'etre for the programme as place-based in a rural setting: that we are not only a provider for entrants who already live in one of our rural areas, or for those who wish to teach here as an a priori decision; and that the journey is mediated holistically by the individual students surrounding personal ecology, by influences whose negative affect cannot necessarily be fully mitigated by people in the programme. These are shown in Table 3.2.

The reality of our integrated programme is that activities do not happen discretely and the impact from contradictions becomes an overall programme dynamic, experienced by anyone in the programme albeit to a different extent, and in a different way. So, we also reflected on the tensions commonly felt by students which centre on accountability, identity, presence and role efficacy as potential system contradictions.

Table 3.1 Contradictions from changes to the use of our rural continuum as a place-attentive resource

Bounded activity set	Contradictions
Seminar Groups presenting at Residential 2	• Participation is not mediated by the usual technology • Group function is visible to all • Group work is centred on response to, and is subject to, a particular rural habitat • Multivocal dialogue has to reach consensus
Identity work with mentors in each of the three school placements (as an inward trajectory of agency)	• Digital connectivity is not needed • Each placement configures "rural teacher" as a short-term situated enactment (a continuum location) • Mentor relationships are not a match to current trajectory location • Each experience of trajectory is different
Final placement work	• Embodiment of self (as evidence) is needed and becomes subject to a sufficiency judgement by others • Teaching in this place has to become teaching in any place • Achievement has a national construct (not an ecological one)

Table 3.2 Contradictions from our place-based setting as rural

The programme as a setting	Contradictions
Becoming a teacher through the UHI PGDE	• *Being rural* is not part of what motivates
Staying on the intended journey	• The outcome of *becoming a teacher* (the trajectory as designed) is not solely a programme construct

Our analysis of systems of activity (Yamagata-Lynch, 2010) revealed that:

- CIC is available as a resource in the programme, and can be further generated in situ, by place-based activities.
- CIC is an emergent dynamic of relationship and individual affordance sometimes subject to conditions set by others.
- Programme-based outcomes confront individual actors with a place conscious sense of self as a collaborative agent and an explicit power differential positions the student as responsible for enough CIC.
- Place-based activity which affords socialising in a professional context supports CIC continuing beyond the programme.
- The use of, and requirement for, CIC surfaces the affective and cultural dimensions of how the programme is currently configured as a PGDE community.

Engestrom (2008) models production, distribution and exchange as constituent work processes which contribute to the impact of CIC in systemic activity. He shows that we can claim to have resolved the tensions resulting from these contradictions if the CIC generated in programme activity facilitates our object work of producing teachers in, of and for, our rural localities. To arrive at a deeper understanding of these CIC processes as contributory to place-attentiveness as a programme resource, we considered the use of CIC, how it involved other people and the flow of CIC. This analysis demonstrated that:

- The net effect of agentive collaboration within programme relationships for the student is empowering.
- These relationships safeguard the student journeying as an inward (transformative) trajectory to teaching (Coker, 2017).
- The rural continuum is kept available in all programme contexts.

White and Reid (2008) model that empowerment comes from being admitted into the school as a participant in the life there and being enabled to draw on the insider expertise as a capacity for being successfully place-based in future. We promote this by according the school-based actors foundational respect as consciousness expanders and allowing the students to rehearse what it takes to join in a school community as a successful collaborative agent. Sometimes an individual journey has to be extended into extra placement, but so far in our six-year history, all who stay on the journey have been sufficiently empowered to complete it. Engestrom (2008) aligns this with successful improvisation, worked out collectively through interagency, and the PGDE frames the student as the locus for the initiative and responsibility needed. In the programme, the seminars and e-portfolio foreground the sense of self the student chooses to present to the tutor and seminar peers, and their skill in articulating that. These supporting programme actors work with an enacted teacher self at face value, but also develop the capacity for individuals to ground themselves by being part of the collective dynamic for engaging with an increasing experiential evidence base within the SPR (GTCS, 2012). As current and future members of the professional teaching community, themselves influenced by real teaching in predominantly rural schools, they offer the intelligence to be "adaptive" which Engestrom, (2008, p. 195) models as a key knotworking resource. The activity system outcome of the end-of-programme teacher accepted into the profession, embeds student motivation in that envisaged possible self, and it is the affective dimension of community participation that has the most impact on this.

Our analysis revealed the salience of the university and programme digital infrastructure as affording access to rehearsal opportunities (journeying expertise) and building a capacity to have and use a professional voice. By varying the configurations and purposes of connecting virtually with other UHI programme actors on our rural continuum, different rural influences are accessible by the transcending self without particular reference to local or school contexts as scripts to effect identity rehearsal (Thomson, 2011). Digital tools render voices temporarily disembodied and location ambiguous, which foregrounds individual style and creative authorship (Thomson, 2011), but also requires a deepening commitment to individual development, as in Lumby and English's (2009) communicative performance. The programme assessments are timed and designed as integral to the journey, but the logic and relevance will only be perceived in hindsight once the intended capacity building has taken place. Our activity systems thinking designs this as Engestrom's (2008, p. 129) "how, why and where to" artefactual uses, allowing students to merge all the intelligence they have gathered collaboratively to date as an expressed construct for their current teacher self. Professional autonomy and confidence are built discursively (Ajayi, 2013) through programme engagement with many voices. As the group assignment at the second Residential reveals each year, this can also afford very creative expression of what we have come to characterise as the community spirit of the PGDE. It is a permission for self-expression as a rural disposition shaped by collaboration with other members.

As a programme located in rural Scotland, we include two days each week of individual study as spaces to personalise work on the possible teacher self and to enable realistic grounding within ongoing personal lives. While the net effect is empowering enough, we have to accept that by standardising efficacy through an overall orientation towards meeting the SPR, we have to let the student control their own programme of study, and it will not be transformative in every case. Engestrom (2008) models it as potentially "emancipatory" (p. 227), but students report it as feeling inconsistent at times. A relational trajectory, construed as we have shown in Fig. 3.1 as multiply mediated, can only ever be effected by agency as a negotiated communicative engagement (Engestrom, 2008) and it is the student as future *teacher-as-collaborative-agent* who has to own the logic for how best to use our infrastructure affordances. This is a collective intention for empowerment which we safeguard on our part as keeping a rural continuum and CIC available in all contexts, but it imposes a dynamic of accountability which positions each student as the individual author for any use of it to story themselves (Lipponen & Kumpulainen, 2011).

There is a discernible shift in the flow patterns of CIC as the programme year unfolds and students establish their own networks of support from peers, mentors and school-based colleagues. This analysis highlighted mentor willingness as pivotal to trajectory and empowerment. Positive affect for students came from sensing fit and acceptance: feeling like a teacher and being observed as a credible embodiment of that in the particular placement school. Lumby & English (2009) discuss identity fit in terms of "having learned the script" (p. 107) and presenting themselves as expected, so individuals choose an enactment that is contextually relevant. This emerged as a delicate balance between the place-based emphasis on the context as local (expected by mentors), and the shorter term place conscious sense making of inhabiting an aspirational possible self in situ (expected for this stage of the programme journey). Where place-based activities also allowed for socialising, role boundaries became less reified as *for the programme* and successful students established a professional network they can continue to access. However, when the rural context blurs the boundaries between school and community (Eppley, 2015) uncertainty is introduced, most notably when there is doubt about a student's current progress or envisaged suitability. This connects overall positive affect with valued intelligence and meaningful progress, and a proactive placing of self (Markus & Nurius, 1986) within the available rural community.

3.7   Knowing Myself as a Teacher: Transforming the Place of Rurality in Scottish Initial Teacher Education

The analysis revealed, perhaps surprisingly, that the majority of the tensions that we have resolved are not primarily about rurality at all, because we are always rural without actually trying to be or needing to self-identify as such within the liminal timeframe of the programme journey. Rurality only became salient when:

- We explicitly emphasised ourselves as a specific configured local place.
- Individual students joined the programme without an *iterative* or *projective* (Fig. 3.1) driver for their student teacher identity as rural and so only made *practical-evaluative* (Fig. 3.1) use of this year's continuum of rural identities to shape their teacher identity enough to complete the programme.
- The situated and shaping expectations for agentive participation in identity construction introduced negative affect.

In the wider contested landscapes of rural teaching as a potential deficit construct for specialised content or practicum contexts, we concluded that we voice an ecological salience for rurality as a pedagogy for engagement on individual terms, and that this engagement is with a continuum of lived experiences through an intrinsically motivated attention to place which is meaningful to the possible self (Markus & Nurius, 1986). This is a place-attentive (White & Reid, 2008) construct which is a blend of place-based (Green & Reid, 2014) and place conscious (Gruenwald, 2003) identity work orchestrated by programme affordances. However, crucially, it is led and gradually owned entirely by the student through knotworking (Engestrom, 2008), as an accountable and collaborative programme role. Our conclusion is that the programme does facilitate individual knotworking with a *"runaway" teacher identity* (Engestrom, 2008, p. 227) because we work with rural teaching as a situated, place-attentive (White & Reid, 2008) and self-expressed identity.

We contend that an ITE programme should work with rurality as a practical-evaluative (Fig. 3.1) context, because students do not yet know the projective context where they will be employed as a teacher. Part of the remit in any ITE programme is to build capacity, to establish teacher identity through becoming rather than of being. This needs to be transformative over the agreed programme timeframe, as a liminal period for working on the current self with the projected *self-as-teacher* in mind, but not yet as a placed enactment. Where rurality is a characteristic of that practical-evaluative (Fig. 3.1) context, it must effect the transformation of foundational identity to teacher identity, as in Mannion et al.'s (2013) collaborative "learning to dwell or inhabit places differently" (p. 804). Our programme offers rurality ontologically as a multivocal (Thomson, 2011) embodiment, a continuum of lived experiences, which can shape the consciousness of the emerging teacher self and model fit for purpose as an attribution by those in professional relationships with future teacher in role. The salience for rurality belongs within those interactions. This is offering Knight et al.'s (2018) deep engagement in *being a rural teacher* as an integral part of the present lived reality of being a student teacher, respecting it as a situated identity: expressed by the individual in relation to the other members who matter to them, as they will be the key influences who shape who they need to be and actually can be. This acknowledges the community for and in which the teacher role will be enacted, as integral to the possible teacher self (Markus & Nurius, 1986; Goodnough & Mulcahy, 2011).

Rurality derives its salience from the everyday lives of the inhabitants of any rural place. The meaning for any embodiment of that, including being a teacher, can only be negotiated as a live dynamic of being in role, in situ, and it will be expressed as an informed and achieved animation of the individual (Lumby & English, 2009). As such, we contend that the ethical stance on any mandated use of rurality for ITE, is one which accommodates the full community of voices as intrinsically valid influences (Anderson & Lonsdale, 2014). We resist the meaning for rurality as distance from urban in Scottish policy (Scottish Government, 2017), and challenge policymakers to rethink the measures on which they define rural as disadvantaged (Roberts & Green, 2013). We question any pre-determination or quantifying of rurality as a normative construct to characterise rural teacher or rural school or rural community as a bigger picture to feel positive about (White & Reid, 2008). However, we embrace White and Reid's (2008) conceptualisation of attention to place and the use of "place conscious pedagogies" (p. 2) to develop place conscious teachers. Like Eppley (2015) we question the value of a short-term ITE placement in a rural school driven by a mandate to prepare for subsequent employment in a different rural school, or de-contextualised engagement in university with rural content and discourses, but we draw a different overall conclusion. We acknowledge that material provision has learning value but contend that to be transformative, it must nurture the possible future teacher self as a projective individual life being lived, as both personal and professional. To do this we advocate that ITE provision should acknowledge rurality as inherently place-attentive, rural teaching as inherently school mediated, and *being a rural teacher* as an individual community shaped embodiment.

We frame this for consideration by others through Engestrom's (2008) "mental landscape" and "material infrastructure" (p. 229) as:

- A commitment to individual student teacher ecological transformation and a respect for any embodiment of teacher as inherently multivocal (a knowing of self as teacher).
- Material provision as practical-evaluative (Fig. 3.1) attention to place which builds the capacity to self-identify as a teacher as an intrinsically motivated enactment within professional community (a supporting infrastructure for rural teacher identity construction).

This is a pedagogy of place-attentiveness (White & Reid, 2008) aimed at nurturing the emergence of a collaborative, agentive teacher self, aspiring to embody their own ideals for being a teacher colleague and a teacher of pupils, and to willingly situate themselves within a school community as a fellow inhabitant of everyday life there. We present this as a critical pedagogy for empowering student teachers to construct themselves first as a teacher (Ajayi, 2013), and then to know their place in school where they become the teacher they have come to know they can, and must, be there.

References

Anderson, M., & Lonsdale, M. (2014). Three Rs for rural research: Respect, responsibility and reciprocity. In S. White & M. Corbett (Eds.), *Doing educational research in rural settings* (pp. 193–205). London: Routledge.

Ajayi, L. (2013). Exploring how the school context mediates intern learning in underserved rural border schools. *Asia Pacific Journal of Education, 33*(4), 444–460.

Begley, P. (2010). Leading with moral purpose: The place of ethics. In T. Bush, L. Bell, & D. Middlewood (Eds.), *The principles of educational leadership and management* (pp. 31–54). London: Sage Publications Ltd.

Cloke, P. (2006). Conceptualizing rurality. In P. Cloke, T. Marsden, & P. Mooney (Eds.), *Handbook of rural studies* (pp. 18–28). London: Sage.

Coker, H. (2017). Developing understanding of Student-Teacher Agency: Implications for programme development. *Teacher Education Advancement Network Journal, 9*(2), 51–63.

Dee, T. (2018). *Ground work: Writings on people and places.* London: Vintage.

Dinkelman, T. (2011). Forming a teacher educator identity: Uncertain standards, practices and relationships [Special issue]. *Journal of Education for Teaching: International Research and Pedagogy, 37,* 309–323.

Education Scotland. (2019). Self-evaluation framework for Initial Teacher Education. https://edu cation.gov.scot/improvement/self-evaluation/Self-evaluation/framework/for/Initial/Teacher/Edu cation. Accessed 21 May 2020.

Engestrom, Y. (2008). *From teams to knots: Activity-theoretical studies of collaboration and learning at work*. New York: Cambridge University Press.

Eppley, K. (2015). "Hey, I saw your grandparents at Walmart": Teacher education for rural schools and communities. *The Teacher Educator, 50*(1), 67–86.

Goodnough, K., & Mulcahy, D. (2011). Developing teacher candidate identity in the context of a rural internship. *Teaching Education, 22*(2), 199–216.

Green, B., & Reid, J. (2014). Researching space(s) and place(s). In S. White & M. Corbett (Eds.), *Doing education research in rural settings* (pp. 26–40). Abingdon: Routledge.

Greenough, R., & Nelson, S. R. (2015). Recognizing the variety of rural schools. *Peabody Journal of Education, 90*(2), 322–332.

Gruenwald, D. (2003). Foundations of place: A multidisciplinary framework for place conscious education. *American Educational Research Journal, 40*(3), 619–654.

GTCS. (2012). Standards for registration. https://www.gtcs.org.uk/professional-standards/standa rds-for-registration.aspx. Accessed 21 May 2020

GTCS. (2019). Guidelines for Accreditation of Initial Teacher Education Programmes in Scotland. http://www.gtcs.org.uk/web/FILES/intitial-teacher-education/ITE-Programme-Acc reditation-Guidelines.pdf. Accessed 21 May 2020.

GTCS. (n.d.) Collaboration is key. https://www.gtcs.org.uk/News/teaching-scotland/75-collabora tion-is-key.aspx. Accessed 21 May 2020.

Hibbert, K. (2013). Reconfiguring the communicational landscape: Implications for rural literacy. In B. Green & M. Corbett (Eds.), *Rethinking rural literacies: Transnational perspectives* (pp. 155–175). Basingstoke: Palgrave Macmillan.

Howley, C. B., Theobald, P., & Howley, A. (2005). What rural education research is of most worth? A reply to Arnold, Newman, Gaddy And Dean. *Journal of Research in Rural Education, 20*, 1–6.

Kearney, C. (2003). *The monkey's mask: Identity, memory, narrative and voice*. Stoke on Trent: Trentham Books Ltd.

Kerkham, L., & Comber, B. (2013). Literacy, place-based pedagogies, and social justice. In B. Green & M. Corbett (Eds.), *Rethinking rural literacies: Transnational perspectives* (pp. 197–218). Basingstoke: Palgrave Macmillan.

Knight, S., McLeman, L., Salvador, K., De La Mare, D. M., & Hiramatsu, K. (2018). Building the house while we're living in it: Conceptualizing place-based teacher education. *National Teacher Education Journal, 11*(2), 5–4.

Lipponen, L., & Kumpulainen, K. (2011). Acting as accountable authors: creating interactional spaces for agency work in teacher education. *Teaching and Teacher Education, 27*(5), 812–819.

Lumby, J., & English, F. (2009). From simplicism to complexity in leadership identity and preparation: Exploring the lineage and dark secrets. *International Journal of Leadership in Education, 12*(2), 95–114.

Mabey, R. (2018). A Wood Over One's Head. In T. Dee (Ed.), *Ground work: Writings on people and places* (pp. 140–147). London: Vintage.

Mannion, G., Fenwick, A., & Lynch, J. (2013). Place-responsive pedagogy: Learning from teachers' experiences of excursions in nature. *Environmental Education Research, 19*(6), 792–809.

Markus, H., & Nurius, P. (1986). Possible selves. *American Psychologist, 41*(9), 954–969.

Priestley, M. (2011). Schools, teachers and curriculum change: A balancing act? *Journal of Educational Change, 12*(1), 1–23.

Priestley, M., Biesta, G., & Robinson, S. (2015). *Teacher agency: An ecological approach*. London: Bloomsbury Publishing plc.

Redford, M. (2013). The political administration of Scottish education, 2007-12. In T. G. K. Bryce, W. M. Humes, D. Gillies, & A. Kennedy (Eds.), *Scottish education fourth edition: Referendum* (pp. 175–183). Edinburgh: Edinburgh University Press.

Roberts, P., & Green, B. (2013). Researching rural places: On social justice and rural education. *Qualitative Inquiry, 19*(10), 765–774.

Scottish Government. (2013) Commission on the delivery of rural education. https://www.gov.scot/publications/commission-delivery-rural-education-report/. Accessed 21 May 2020.

Scottish Government. (2017) *Rural schools in Scotland.* https://www.gov.scot/publications/rural-schools/. Accessed 21 May 2020.

Scottish Government. (2018a). *Scottish government urban rural classification.* https://www.gov.scot/publications/scottish-government-urban-rural-classification-2016/pages/2/. Accessed 21 May 2020.

Scottish Government. (2018b) *Rural Scotland: Key facts 2018.* https://www.gov.scot/publications/rural-schools/. Accessed 21 May 2020.

Thomson, P. (2011). Coming to terms with voice. In G. Czerniawski & W. Kidd (Eds.), *Student voice handbook: Bridging the academic/practitioner divide* (pp. 19–30). London: Emerald Group Publishing.

University of the Highlands and Islands. (2015), *Strategic vision and plan 2015–2020.* https://www.uhi.ac.uk/en/about-uhi/strategic-plan/. Accessed 21 May 2020.

University of the Highlands and Islands. (2019). *Campuses.* https://www.uhi.ac.uk/en/campuses/. Accessed 21 May 2020.

Wattchow, B., & Brown, M. (2011). *A pedagogy of place.* Clayton: Victoria AU, Monash University Publishing.

White, S., & Reid, J. A. (2008). Placing teachers? Sustaining rural schooling through place consciousness in Teacher Education. *Journal of Research in Rural Education, 23*(7), 1–1.

Wildy, H. (2010). Foreword. In M. Anderson, M. Davis, P. Douglas, D. Lloyd, B. Niven, & H. Thiele (Eds.), *A collective act: Leading a small school.* Victoria, Australian Council for Educational Research: ACER Press.

Yamagata-Lynch, L. C. (2010). *Activity systems analysis methods: Understanding complex learning environments.* New York: Springer.

Morag Redford is Professor of Teacher Education in the University of the Highlands and Islands, Scotland. Her teaching and research interests are focused on Initial Teacher Education and career-long professional learning for practising teachers, inter-professional practice and the history and politics of education in Scotland. Since 2006 she has been writing a regular review of Education in the Scottish Parliament for the Scottish Education Review. Appointed as Head of Teacher Education for the University in 2014, Morag has led the development of teacher education in the University, working closing with local authority partners and specializing in blended provision accessible to aspiring and practising teachers across the north and west of Scotland.

Lindsay Nicol is the Programme Leader for the Professional Graduate Diploma in Primary Education in the University of the Highlands and Islands, Scotland. Her teaching interests and expertise in digital delivery have emerged from a commitment to teachers in rural areas, and focus on the foundations for professional identity construction, student teacher agency, school placement experience, and fostering meaningful virtual collaboration between dispersed professional groups. More recently, Lindsay's scholarship interests have centered on resilient professionalism and educational leadership, and she has worked with colleagues and external partners to develop online masters-level professional learning for practising teachers and aspiring school leaders.

Chapter 4
Teacher Preparation for Rurality: A Cohort Model of Teaching Practice in a Rural South African School

Tabitha Grace Mukeredzi

Abstract Rural schools the world over are generally beleaguered by pressures of "hard to staff, harder to stay" quality than urban schools. In South African rural schools, teacher shortage remains the biggest hindrance to meeting Millennium Development Goals, developed during United Nations Millennium Summit declaration. Together with measurable targets and deadlines, goals were intended to improve lives of poor people throughout the world. This chapter reports findings from a study which investigated experiences and interpretations of rurality, of 16 Bachelor of Education pre-service teachers from a South African university, during a four-week residential Teaching Practicum in a rural school. Data suggests that students encountered "ruralisation" of minds and developed sense of rurality which dissipated some of their fallacies, seemingly increasing their employment possibilities in rural settings which might ultimately stimulate interest for teaching in rural schools. While teacher preparation for rurality during ITE could be an avenue for investing in youth who choose teaching, this may be a starting point for supporting rural teachers, learners, and communities. Given the South African education sector diversity, teacher education should focus on quality education for varied contexts, with particular attention to rural contexts.

Keywords South africa · Rural teacher education project · Student teachers · Rural school

4.1 Introduction

A brief chronicle of my experiences as a rural school child may provide first-hand insights into challenges related to teacher shortage in rural schools.

T. G. Mukeredzi (✉)
School of Education, Durban University of Technology, Midlands/Indumiso Campus, Pietermaritzburg, Republic of South Africa
e-mail: tabitham@dut.ac.za

© Springer Nature Singapore Pte Ltd. 2021
S. White and J. Downey (eds.), *Rural Education Across the World*,
https://doi.org/10.1007/978-981-33-6116-4_4

I attended a rural school more than 350 km from Harare in Zimbabwe. My school was 12 km on a rugged road off the public road. There was no transport on this rumble-strip to the school which forced teachers to walk. Piped water and electricity were non-existent. We fetched water for teachers from a pond near a small stream. Health services were only available in town 350 km away. Teachers would come and go, sometimes we had three different teachers in a year.

Rural schools globally face pressures of *"hard to staff, harder to stay"* quality teachers than urban schools (Islam, 2012; Kline, White, & Lock, 2013; Miller, 2012; Mukeredzi, 2013; Pennefather, 2011). Teacher shortage in South African rural schools remains the biggest hindrance to meeting Millennium Development Goals (Masinire, 2015). Millennium Development Goals (MDGs) are part of goals developed, with their set measurable targets and deadlines for improving lives of poor people throughout the world. The goals were set up to eradicate poverty by leaders of 189 countries from different parts of the world who signed the historic millennium declaration at the United Nations Millennium Summit in 2000 (Statistics South Africa, 2017).

The low uptake o f teaching posts by competent qualified and experienced teachers in rural contexts is due inter alia to: geographical, social, professional, collegial and cultural isolation; socio-economic conditions; multiple grade/multiple subject teaching assignments; lack of familiarity with rural schools and communities; and notions of disadvantage that consider rural school teaching as inferior and loathsome (Arnold, Newman, Gaddy, & Dean, 2005; Greenough and Nelson, 2015; Mahlangu and Pitsoe, 2013; Miller, 2012; Pennefather, 2011). Some of the qualified teachers who accept rural school posts do not stay, and new graduates with modern individualistic outlooks shun rural postings arguing that too much time teaching in a rural village school, causes one to become "a village man" (Monk, 2007). In addition, rural areas in South Africa are affected by social problems like disease, poverty, low literacy levels, low learner achievement, poor/inadequate facilities and services, and, low self-efficacy of those living and working there (du Plessis, 2017; Greenough & Nelson, 2015; Hlalele, 2014; Johnson & Strange, 2009; Myende & Chikoko, 2014).

This chapter draws on a study which investigated the experiences and interpretations of rurality of 16 Bachelor of Education student teachers (herein called students) in one South African university, during a four-week residential teaching practice (TP) in a rural South African school. The research was part of a bigger project, the Rural Teacher Education Project (RTEP) which examined alternative models of pre-service placement to address rural school needs. By contrast to other pre-service teacher rural school TP placement, in this model, these student teachers were placed at one school as a cohort, lived alongside the rural community nearby the school, shared residential facilities living in a community of teacher educators and their peers.

This article explores the students' experiences of their professional learning journeys and their understandings and interpretations of rurality within this collaborative cohort model. This model reinforces Coles (2012) conception that such professional learning is not isolated, nor individualistic, but a communal activity which involves a range of participants including peers, university programme facilitators, tutors and assessors, their school-based mentors, learners and potentially their parents. The model was intended to encourage student collaboration to develop a community in which they would be empowered to resolve TP challenges, problems, and difficulties thereby professionally learning (Mukeredzi, 2015).

Without a supportive environment for professional learning, higher levels of reflective thinking and self-evaluation of TP are unlikely to happen by themselves. My argument here is that rural offers much more than a research setting or a site that provides residential differences to justify research publication, rather it should be generative for and or relevant to the research purpose (Hamm, 2014). The conception is made that there is quality inherent in rural schools and communities which should be preserved such as the desire for learning in learners and teachers and the contextual "situativity" from where student teachers could learn.

The study addresses one question: How do pre-service teachers experience and interpret their experiences as they journey towards becoming teaching professionals in rural school TP? This model is thus unique as it entailed a group of students experiencing and interpreting their TP experiences in one rural school, living alongside a rural community, and in commune with peers and teacher educators (Mukeredzi, 2016).

The chapter provides some highlights on South African rurality and Teacher Education. A discussion on the Rural Teacher Education Project follows. The research site and data production and analysis strategies employed constitute the subsequent section. The findings, discussion and conclusion conclude the chapter.

4.2 Rurality and Teacher Education in South Africa

There appears to be no consensus on the definition of "rural" in South Africa due to its elusive nature. This may emanate from the subjective nature of distinctions between rural and urban given the similar school curricular and practices which overlook idiosyncrasies of rural settings. Hlalele (2014) reports that the South African government regards "rurality" as: a life style; mind-set and cultures around land, livestock and community living; peri-urban areas; informal settlements; and small towns. Further, rurality in South Africa is also tantamount to isolation, poverty, disease, neglect, backwardness, marginalization, depopulation, traditionalism, conservatism, corruption, low adult literacy levels and low quality education in schools, entropy and exclusion (Balfour, 2012; Masinire, 2015). Such distressing notions of deficiency and disadvantage are disempowering for teachers who may want to teach in rural schools (Moletsane, 2012). In this chapter, rurality is understood as synonymous to remote. *Remote area* generally connotes underclass models that signify notions of rurality in social development where the people concerned are socially deficient, and more often than not, overlooked fully or partly from mainstream socio-political engagements.

Residing in rural South Africa has links to apartheid colonial policies of deprivation, resettlement and deliberate, systematic exclusion from opportunities, which forced all black South Africans to live in rural areas—called *"homelands"* (Wedekind, 2005). *Homelands* are generally depicted by poor services/facilities, either jam-packed homesteads or village-style settlements. The least developed and poorest South African *homeland* areas are in Eastern Cape, Limpopo and KwaZulu-Natal (KZN) provinces (Gardiner, 2008). KZN is the site for this research. Under-development and poverty in these *homelands* are reflected by poor education quality available. Most South African rural schools are wanting in resources, basic services and facilities. Hugo, Jack, Wedekind, and Wilson (2010) discovered lack of on-site toilets at many rural schools, for example, with numbers exceeding 50 sharing one toilet. Electricity and piped water were non-existent and schools depended on bore-hole or rainwater harvesting. Some areas had been discounted for development for decades, compounded by the under supply of human, material and other provisions; many of these South African rural schools have depreciated to an extent that the picture portrayed is not enticing for a teaching career or for living (du Plessis, 2017; Mitchell, de Lange, Balfour & Islam, 2011).

Many policy initiatives have been instituted and a Rural Education Directorate established (Mitchell et al., 2011). The South African Rural Education Directorate is a section of the Department of Basic Education (DBE) set up broadly to dress the challenges associated with rural schools and rural education (Gardiner, 2008). The Directorate was established in 2006 and disbanded in 2010 and then re-established in 2014 with a core mandate to create a forum to build intra- and inter-sectoral collaboration between the DBE, its provincial departments, and relevant stakeholders "in identifying, developing and implementing the context-specific and sustainable strategies and solutions for the provision of quality rural education and rural school education improvement". (Pasensie, 2015, p. 2). However, notwithstanding, South African rural education remains beleaguered by extensive challenges (du Plessis, 2017; Gustafsson, 2016; Moletsane, 2012). Mukeredzi and Mandrona (2013) ascribe this to implementation challenges and connections between rural realities and govern-ment responses, yet to be unresolved. This compromises the many school-age chil-dren residing in rural districts. 40% of the South African population resides in rural areas (World Bank, 2013) and of a total of 25,720 government (public) schools in South Africa, 11,252 schools (almost half) are located in rural areas (Savides, 2017). The majority of these rural schools are situated in three provinces: KwaZulu-Natal (KZN) (4,040), Limpopo (3,342) and the Eastern Cape (1,832). In KZN 54% of the population resides in rural communities with approximately 3,000 schools that accommodated about 1,097,499 learners out of the provincial total of 2,798,570 learners and 5,937 schools (Statistics South Africa, 2017). Clearly, more than half the schools in KZN are rural-based and about half the learners attend these rural schools, with severe shortages of qualified teachers. The Education Department admitted that of the 5,139 unqualified or underqualified rural school teachers nation-ally, 2,875 (57%) were in rural KZN (Mahlangu & Pitsoe, 2013; Rural Education Policy, 2018; Savides, 2017). Further, the schools were under-resourced which often forced teachers to "make-do" with limited resources unlike the qualified teachers in urban well-resourced schools (Mukeredzi, 2016).

This begs several questions: How can South African teacher education institutions contribute to rural school teacher provision? Many university pre-service teachers come from rural communities (Masinire, 2015). How can they be persuaded to return home to teach following graduation? Developing more and better teachers is not the panacea for rural school teacher shortage given the apparent teacher oversupply in urban schools. What is critical is expansion and reorientation of teacher education curricula towards teacher preparation for rurality, and reorientation of students' perceptions to appreciate likelihoods of rural school teaching (Masinire, 2015). Research (for example Adie & Barton, 2012; Balfour, 2012; Islam, 2012; Lingam, 2012; Moletsane, 2012) confirms that tools and strategies for rural teacher development and rural school postings are in teacher education. The assertion is corroborated by many rural education researchers (for example Lingam, 2012; Mitchell, de Lange et al. 2011; Pennefather, 2011; Sullivan, McConney, & Perry, 2018) who blame teacher education institutions for paying little or no attention to teacher development for rurality. However, while teacher education institutions may be unable to address structural challenges like toilets, they are neither empowering students with skills and knowledge for rural and remote school teaching nor proactive in addressing this problem given their essentially "metro-centric mind-set" (Masinire, 2015). Countries like Australia, which recognised the central role of teacher education institutions in rural school teacher preparation have supported research funding towards programmes like the Rural Teacher Education Project (Green, 2008), the Renewing Rural Teacher Education and others (Masinire, 2015; White & Kline, 2012) that in turn have informed teacher education.

Notwithstanding the fundamental role South African teacher education can play in turning-around the rural education terrain, students are not exposed to opportunities for rural school teaching during preparation (Islam, 2012). As well, curricula overlook components on rural education and teaching. Lack of teacher knowledge and skills for rural school teaching negatively impact education of rural children who are already at risk (Lingam, 2012). Effective teacher preparation for rurality requires appropriate professional preparation during initial teacher education (ITE) (Lingam, 2012; Mitchell et al., 2011). White and Kline (2012) add that during ITE, students need exposure to: issues pertinent to rural education; a broad representation of rural, regional and remote contexts so that they become familiar with diverse rural, and remote locations and communities. Such exposure to realities of living and teaching in rural schools for students anticipating rural school employment, may expand their job prospects in these areas and eventually boost their interest in countryside teaching (Mukeredzi, 2016).

Formation of rural school-university partnerships is a good starting point for enabling students' direct personal experiences of rural education in context, through practicum in rural schools. Globally, there is consensus that teacher development institutions should develop strong partnerships for effective student teacher preparation for promoting rural school teaching appointments (Balfour, 2012; Brady, 2002; Haugalokken & Ramberg, 2007; Islam, 2012; Mitchell et al., 2011; White & Kline, 2012). The RTEP was one example of rural school-university partnership models launched by one South African university.

4.3 The Rural Teacher Education Project (RTEP)

Each year the RTEP exposed cohorts of 15–20 students to working side by side with teachers in rural schools, promoting understanding and appreciation of rural issues and ultimately fostering interest in rural school teaching. This chapter reports on experiences of such students during 2014 rural TP and their interpretations of those experiences.

The RTEP, a rural school–university partnership project was launched in 2007 by the Faculty of Education, collaborating with rural schools 200 km north-west of Durban in South Africa's KZN province. While university teacher education programmes did not discriminate against rural school TP placements, it was not mandatory that students undertake practicum in such schools, although it was expected that they would experience TP in resourced and under-resourced settings. Thus, students sought placements in urban schools where transportation and accommodation were easily available. The RTEP was developed partly to counter this urban bias.

Contrary to traditional TP placements where single students are attached to a school during practicum, RTEP explored alternative models of placement where students were attached to one school as a cohort. The RTEP brought together an amalgam of research, intervention, and teacher education strategies (Balfour, 2012) to investigate how partnership between in-service rural school-based teachers and students' cohorts could promote students' professional development and eventually persuade them to consider postings in rural schools. Specifically, the RTEP wanted to offer trainees opportunities to: observe and experience first-hand realities of life, teaching/learning in a rural school; work with experienced rural school teachers, while living alongside the community (RTEP Recruitment Brochure, 2012). With this approach the RTEP was gently reorientating teacher education in the university's Education Faculty to rural schools as fundamental sites for cultivation of students' interest in rural school teaching and professional learning.

Student participation was voluntary. After wide project publicity within the Faculty, students formally applied and were interviewed. In their application and interviews, students had to: express interest in rural school teaching; be in second, third or fourth year of study; specializing in Senior Phase or Further Education and Training; and majoring in any two subjects: technology, management studies, English, computer studies, mathematics or science. Foundation Phase students who spoke isiZulu (local language) were also considered.

For effective on-site leadership, and management, the project team appointed two advisors/teacher educators. One had to have a Ph.D. in Teacher Education. This is how I got drawn into the RTEP in 2011. At the time, I was a resident post-doctorate with Ph.D. in Teacher Education. Teacher educators shared residential facilities with students about three kilometres away from the school. The RTEP researchers created this residential arrangement to build a professional community among students and teacher educators while professionalizing the experience through individual and collaborative reflections, and academic mentorship (Mukeredzi &

Mandrona, 2013). Thus, the communal dwelling structure and in-built opportunities for reflections would foster students' reflection on their experiences, interpretations and perceptions of the rural context practicum.

4.4 Methodology

4.4.1 The Research Site

The RTEP was taken to Mziwaxolo (Pseudonym) combined school in Malute (Pseudonym), a harsh, and rather isolated geographical area in 2014. Malute, approximately 139 kilometres from the nearest town Pietermaritzburg, could be viewed as no rural idyll, with many of its inhabitants' in surrounding villages experiencing socio-economic disadvantage, as well as limited access to services as some of the particular problems. Mziwaxolo was a combined school, a school with primary and secondary sectors under one principal, and classes from Grade R to 12. Mziwaxolo had a big enrolment; approximately 1,500 on the roll in 2014, 850 in the primary and 650 in the secondary and 39 staff. Given its central location, amid densely populated multiple, compact village settlements, without another school nearby, Mziwaxolo inevitably serviced a heavily populated catchment area with an entirely Black isiZulu speaking population. It was larger than an average combined school in most South African rural areas at the time.

Its combined structure enticed RTEP as all students would be under one "roof". This was ideal for on-site support as teacher educators remained in one place without splitting time across sites. All the 16 students undertook TP at MziwaXolo. The school displayed a clean and orderly outlook, well-disciplined, respectful, and neatly dressed learners. A calm and business-like atmosphere, where no learners loitered outside during learning time, prevailed. The principal lamented gross under-resourcing and large classes between 70 and 80 learners. Office space was limited consequently, the RTEP team used a school library as their office. While this arrangement was broadly beneficial for enabling interaction among RTEP students, and educators, it created "borders" between students and schoolteachers. This tended to portray doing research "on" which marginalizes rural spaces and undermines their vitality and uniqueness, contrary to the ideal, doing research "for" which is of critical importance (Corbett & White, 2014).

4.4.2 Method

As the sole researcher, I adopted a qualitative research design within an interpretive paradigm for investigating how a cohort of 16 purposively selected B.Ed. students experienced and interpreted those experiences of rural school TP. I also chose research methods that were consistent with reflective approaches to research and used both student's daily individual reflective journals and collaborative reflections dialogues as sources of data. Practicum was from middle of July to first week of August 2014. In the 2014 RTEP, I was the only advisor and I worked closely with the 16 students while the project leaders/researchers would be in and out of the research site to oversee the processes. Six students were in academic year two, five in year three and five in fourth, final year. Their ages were between 19 and 40 years. There were six men and ten women, with diverse backgrounds.

To kick-start the four-week rural school TP, I conducted one-day workshop for students and mentors to: demystify some misconceptions about rural schools, learners and communities; expose students to common challenges confronting rural schools; develop a supportive relationship with the host school; and expose both students and mentors to university mentoring expectations of mentoring.

Each student had one school-appointed mentor for each specialisation for the duration of TP. School management and other staff would support students' TP and integration into school life. I introduced the workshop by requesting students to document their conceptions of rurality. To conclude, after taking the students through reflective questions below, explaining and clarifying each question, I asked them to document their reflections on the workshop answering the questions:

1. What are your understandings/views about TP in a rural school?
2. How did it go? What happened?
3. What did I experience?
4. Why did things happen in that manner? My contributions? Contributions of others?
5. What does all this mean to me personally? Professionally?
6. What could have been done differently to improve? Could be done differently to uphold?

These questions provided the Framework for students' reflections in their daily reflective journals and for collaborative debriefing reflections sessions throughout TP. Each TP day was concluded by individual reflections in daily journals followed by collaborative reflection sessions which lasted approximately two hours from 16hr30 and 19hr00. In these two-and-half hour sessions, students reflected on their teaching, cross-examined and examined, questioned and detailed the day's actions. This promoted self-evaluation of lessons and pedagogies, what worked and did not work and why, what could have been or could be done differently to improve or uphold the performance (Mukeredzi & Mandrona, 2013). Discussions were characterized by lively dialogue which stimulated collaborative reflection, sharing and feedback. Although I had some insights into rural school learning life, from childhood experiences, I now live in an urban setting. Like Hamm (2014) I found myself drawing on my experiences and my background as a rural school child, to connect with student teacher experiences and interpretations. These commonalities probably contributed to building a good relationship, trust and rapport with these student teachers which facilitated intimate discussions. Dialogues with supervisors, peers and colleagues enable identification of appropriate mediational artefacts and clarification of beliefs and dispositions (Kline et al., 2013). This process made for rigorous collaborative reflective learning and self-interrogation of perceptions. Again, similar to what Hamm (2014) experienced, I also kept on asking myself a number of questions: Whether as a qualitative researcher I needed to be presently living in a rural area, or whether I needed a rural background? What would the implications on my research if I did not have any rural background/experiences at all? How would this research compare with one conducted in my own rural home school? These thoughts and insights made me examine my positionality regarding insider/outsider dynamics as they relate to rural education research or research in rural contexts and communities more broadly.

As advisor, I saw my role as both "insider" and "outsider" in terms of the rural context and relationships with the various groups involved in the RTEP. The concept of researcher as insider, outsider or somewhere in between according to Hamm (2014) has been discussed across disciplines. In my case, my identities were flexible and the extent to which I was part of or apart from the groups was fluid and altered dependent on the day or activity. In a way I was "in between" my membership roles as insider and outsider. Current scholarship confirms that a researcher can be in between the roles (Hamm, 2014). Notwithstanding that I was born and bred in a rural context, I was from outside South Africa and had not been part of the original team that conceptualized the RTEP. I arrived as a new addition to the research activities albeit I had previous professional relationships with the RTEP researchers. As advisor, I was accommodated together with students in a guesthouse nearby the school and drove them to and from the school, remaining typically on site with them supporting and attending to their professional issues.

I facilitated collaborative debriefing and reflection sessions daily and offered the students on-going emotional and professional support throughout the TP period. As much as I was an authority in this context, I had some vulnerabilities. This was a new group regarding working together and understanding the complexities of the rural school context where I was supposed to help student teachers navigate. Compounded by this was the fact that I did not speak isiZulu the local language. Although my liminal situation did bring feelings of alienation at times, this was also helpful in revealing contradictions within the research site, not only the potential of TP to reproduce any disjunctures, but also to empower participants.

This position as Hamm (2014) points out enables identification and reflection on biases, and offers insights through observation and experience. Hamm further argues that "the insider/outsider dichotomy is simplistic, and the distinction is unlikely to adequately capture the role of all researchers. Instead, the role of the researcher is better conceptualized on a continuum, rather than as an either/or dichotomy" (p. 6). Consequently, a role as neither an insider-researcher nor outsider-researcher is thus beneficial to the researcher from the advantages which minimize potential barriers of any of the statuses.

Research foregrounds rural communities, rural contexts as well as promoting and sustaining rural education (Hamm, 2014). Before settling on the methodology for this study, I surveyed literature on rural education research, collaborative TP models where trainees live in or alongside rural communities, and examined issues of enhancing rural education. I was interested in methods of facilitating engagements with and among student teachers from diverse backgrounds through individual and collaborative reflection dialogues to understand how they experienced and interpreted their experiences as they journeyed towards becoming teaching professionals in rural school TP while residing alongside a community and in commune with peers and teacher educators.

Designing reflective questions, and facilitating collaborative reflection dialogues served to unpack and explore students' (Hamm, 2014) interpretations of rurality. My objective was to facilitate exploration of student teacher understandings of rurality, their rural school TP experiences and how they understood those experiences. In this study, I had explored the potential for reflective questions as basis for individual reflections as well as for collaborative reflections by testing this process with a group of Post Graduate Certificate students in the educational psychology module that I taught at university and considered how reflections could be applied to understand experiences and interpretations of rurality during TP.

Some of the rural researchers apparently use the rural just as a setting or a convenient context, which consequently does not add to an understanding of the rural or how issues play out in the rural (Hamm, 2014). My view in this study was that this would enhance student teachers' understanding of the rural and/or how issues uniquely play out. Citing Roberts and Green (2013), Hamm further points out that if research does not promote understanding of the rural, this may be enacting symbolic violence against the place it purports to represent. My role was to facilitate students' individual reflections and also lead collaborative reflections to show how these could be applied to promote students reflections, enhance and deepen their understanding of rurality thereby enhance their professional growth during rural school TP. This would probably ultimately generate some interest in rural school teaching.

4.4.3   Data Generation

Throughout TP, pre-service teachers recorded their thoughts, observations and experiences, in daily journals and would share them during collaborative reflection sessions. The collaborative conversations were audio-recorded. Students reflected on teaching/learning in a rural classroom and ruralness itself, and shared views and experiences about rurality and teaching, describing, cross-examining, and interrogating them (Mukeredzi, 2016). These conversations advanced students' verbalizing abilities and corroborated their experiences. Students evaluated their lessons, approaches and language, successes and failures, their learning therefrom, and what they would do differently (Mukeredzi & Mandrona, 2013). The experiences exposed them to challenge-filled actualities of South African rural education context, and from ongoing reflection on classroom and contextual activities, attitudes, and experiences, students developed profound understandings of what being a teacher in a rural school entailed (Mitchell et al., 2011). In retrospect, as students were required to articulate and reflect on their teaching, this could be construed as tugging them into conformity to RTEP requirements. Such strategies are viewed as producing some form of *contrived collegiality* (Hughes, 2013) to fulfil expectations of project participation requirements.

This chapter draws data from students' reflective journals and transcripts of audio-recorded collaborative reflection conversations. The extended fieldwork, research procedures adopted to ensure authentic generation, interpretation and representation of perspectives of these students and inclusion of verbatim quotations to give students a voice, enhanced rigour. Participants were aware that collaborative reflection sessions were being audio-recorded, however, recording was employed discretely with their awareness. The thick descriptions, and data triangulation further enhanced rigour. The concept of thick description originates from interpretive ethnography, and involves deep, profound, exhaustive accounts of a phenomenon of inquiry particularly the context(s) where it occurs. Thick descriptions also establish verisimilitude statements that construct for the reader, feelings of experiencing the events under discussion in a study. Thus, credibility is established through the lens of readers who, in reading the narrative, and are transported into a setting or situation (Lietz & Zayas, 2010).

4.4.4   Data Analysis

The senior researchers were neither directly involved with students' professional learning issues apart from over-seeing, nor participated in the data generation, it was my sole responsibility. Content analysis which involved carefully and systematically examining and interpreting texts to identify patterns, themes, biases and meanings (Plunkett & Dyson, 2011) was followed in analysing data. The approach entailed eight steps. First, I transcribed students' individual reflections and the audio recorded collaborative reflection dialogues. After this, I read through the transcripts over and over, listening to audio tapes several times comparing and contrasting them and making brief notes in the margin when interesting or relevant information was found. Third, going through the notes that I made in the margins and listing the different types of information that I found. This was followed by reading through the list and categorising each item in a way that offered a description of what it was about (an "in vivo" term). I then determined whether or not the categories could be linked in any way and listed them as major categories (or themes) and / or minor categories (or themes) (Erlingsson & Brysiewicz, 2017). Fifth, I compared and contrasted the various major and minor categories and then repeated these stages for all the transcripts. After going through each of the transcripts, I collected all of the categories or themes and examined each one in detail and considered if it fitted in, and also its relevance. Sixth, I then categorised all the transcript data into minor and major categories/themes and reviewed in order to ensure that the information was categorised as it should be. All the categories were then reviewed to ascertain whether some categories could be merged or if some needed to be sub-categorised.

Finally, I returned to the original transcripts checking to ensure that all the information that needed to be categorised had been so. Following this I examined each transcript, scrutinizing data and selecting appropriate quotes that depicted themes, and ensured that all specializations, gender and race were represented. The quotes substantiated participants' stories of their experiences and understandings of TP and learning in a rural school. Given the close relationship that always developed with each student cohort, drawing on Cohen, Manion and Morrison (2012) who emphasize use of independent judges to minimise bias, and verify themes, I thus requested one of the researchers, my Post Doc mentor, to go through the data set to identify errors or omissions and confirm my themes. I was also informed by Mauthner and Doucet (2003) who foreground an "interplay between our multiple social locations and how these intersect with the particularities o f our own personal biographies need to be considered at analysis stage" (p. 419). While students discussed deep-rooted and deep-seated self-critical experiences, the personal reflections and audio records were mediated and mandatory items. Consequently, they may not be sincere students' experiences and interpretations because these activities were incorporated into the RTEP model mandates. Further, that teacher educators and peers attended, probably mediated the content of reflections. However, the methical, immersive and investigative strategy that I adopted to comprehend students' written stories, synthesizing the usually inherent TP context tensions, strengthened the analysis and enhanced rigour.

4.5 Findings

From the data, students' experiences and interpretations emerged around: their perceptions of rurality, linkages with rural school setting; the classroom; mentors; and with peers. In discussing findings, participants are identified by Codes (e.g. ST1).

4.5.1 Conceptions About Rural Schools

At the pre-TP workshop, students' views about rural school TP portrayed ambiguous predictions and understandings of teaching and working in a rural school. Three students confirmed lack of understanding of rurality displaying blurred views from the press and word of mouth. Others displayed fantasised dreams of rural school TP making comments like: "welcoming teachers", "helpful staff and students", "university peers empathetic, friendly and caring", "friendly residence", "I don't think I will be lonely". Most of the expectations were generally accurate, they were fulfilled as most teachers and learners were welcoming. Others expressed fears like, "demanding mentors", "overworked by mentors, few teachers there" "unsupportive, cruel mentors", "teaching practice in rural schools scary", "will have difficulties away from home", "dirty environment, broken windows, paper and clatter". These fears were inaccurate, mentors were supportive and the environment was very tidy.

Some were concerned about resource availability far from town: "I am worried about resources, rural schools are under-resourced—you can't teach without resources", "it will be hard without resources, teaching is poor". City dwellers lamented lack of understanding by learners from diverse economic, social, cultural and linguistic backgrounds. They anticipated "learner difficulties communicating in English, who do not understand English", "unfriendly learners", "poorly disciplined and hard to manage", "difficulties motivating and controlling learners", "where you teach multi-grades", "where anything goes, and nobody cares". The negative understandings and fears held by city dwellers before experiencing rurality were obliterated following interactions with and experiences in the rural context. What the students experienced was the opposite of what they had expected. School learners were disciplined and motivated, they understood and spoke English, there was no multi-grade teaching. Further, Mziwaxolo school had effective leadership and the atmosphere was calm and business-like.

4.5.2   Relating with the Rural School

Students were amazed and encouraged by the extent to which learners at Mziwaxolo School comprehended and communicated in English. ST2 exclaimed: "I didn't think they would understand and speak English". This comment portrays discourses of deficit which denote mistaken beliefs that rural learners are lacking or deficient in numerous ways in this context in speaking English. This kind of snobbish discourse of insufficiency views rural school teaching as second-grade and objectionable (Pennefather, 2011). The realization of learners' linguistic capabilities possibly influenced their understandings and attitudes towards rurality, rural learners and rural teaching. Some were impressed by the school context: "This school is clean, there are no broken windows, children respectful, clean uniforms, wearing shoes" (ST16) and "You can only know about teaching/learning in a rural school, by doing TP in a rural school" (ST1). The primarily urban and township dwellers got exposure to concrete introduction to rurality, and first-hand direct observation and interaction with rural-based teachers, learners and the environment about rural life, rural learning and rural teaching practices. There is appreciation of the rural experience.

There was satisfaction with the school organization and the reception students received. "I am happy with how the principal welcomed us, made us feel important. Mentors introduced us to all classes" (ST2). "Yes met with mentors, I am happy here" (ST8). "All of them warmly welcomed us" (ST11). Students in 3rd and 4th academic year of study reported that the warm school welcome gave them the confidence they missed in their previous residential TP.

However, two students reported unfruitful mentor–mentee meetings as exemplified by ST3: "I met with my mentors, but there was confusion. They had not prepared for me". Another three expressed frustrations from not meeting with the allocated mentors that day. ST7 during collaborative reflections lamented: "I didn't meet them. It's annoying, when you don't know your mentors. You feel lost and fearful. No-one knew where they were even management".

It is essential to make students feel welcome particularly on their first day to position them in good stead more in unfamiliar rural contexts (Sharplin 2009). Comments portrayed inadequate preparation by the school. Subsequent to our initial visit to Mziwaxolo, we communicated dates in advance and sent a reminder, days before our arrival. Like on any school day, we expected all staff to attend. The unknown absences may confirm "where anything goes, and nobody cares" made during pre-TP workshop. On reflection, what would subsequently be done differently to improve, would be to arrive on the TP venue after the first day of term.

Students appreciated being viewed as colleagues. ST6 recorded: "I feel confident, you feel like one of them, a professional, member of staff, you get confidence to share your knowledge and also learn from them". ST3 implies that students were valued. When students have some sense of being devalued and lowly regarded, negative emotional feelings may develop. Further, students' situated identities (Putnam & Borko, 2000) were also heightened by taking up out-of-class responsibilities. ST9 commented: "Being assigned netball trainer for a big district match was huge.... You gain confidence, feel good that teachers trust you. In my previous TP no-one ever talked to you or thought you were capable of anything". And ST6 said: "Having a chance to lead assembly was good, you feel like a real teacher, taking control of everything".

Students' involvement in school activities had considerable influence on students and the school. "Fitting in" and a sense of belonging is indispensable as both students and schools often use professional placements as spaces for assessing "fitness" for future employment. Murphy and Angelski (1997) add that the "ideal" rural teacher is able to teach many subjects and/or grade levels, facilitate learning of various skills including, coaching extra-mural activities.

Students also acknowledged the importance of thorough preparation for and commitment to teaching including learner discipline and learning motivation. As stated by ST13, "Discipline is good, they want to learn. There are some smart kids we have to prepare thoroughly for lessons. Very different from what I thought of rural schools. I would teach here".

These experiences helped to clear myths and fallacies about rural education, rural learners and rural schools as the learners were smart and eager to learn. One delusion related to declining moral values, discipline and learning motivation in rural schools (Kiggundu & Nayimuli, 2009). At the pre-TP workshop many students expressed misconceptions about learner discipline and management, learners who did not speak/understand English, were unfriendly, uncontrollable and difficult to motivate, including school cultures with poor teaching/learning, and where anything was possible and nobody cared. These unfounded beliefs were probably due to lack of knowledge/experience in rurality. Interactions with learners and teachers, classroom and co-curricular participation made these students start challenging those misconceptions.

Another generally accepted fallacy that students challenged was around ineffective teaching in under-resourced rural schools. While they understood performance resources (like overhead projector) vital for enhancing/changing how teachers accomplish teaching activities, and pedagogical resources (focusing primarily on transforming the teacher's competencies e.g., reading materials) (Putnam & Borko, 2000) as important for effective curriculum delivery, students realized that under-resourcing was not an excuse for poor teaching. ST12 recorded: "If you are creative, you make good lessons. You improvise, you must stretch your brain and prepare for your lessons. TP here is good preparation for future work in rural schools". Two students who experienced learner indiscipline, understood those experiences as learning opportunities: "A few are naughty, which is expected in a normal classroom. A teacher must be able to control stubborn kids. Yeah!! this is giving me learning" (ST7). Ideal teacher practice calls for skills for in resolving classroom conflicts, evoking strategic knowledge while sustaining conducive classroom environment, focus, and harmony, and displaying readiness to exercise both personal and professional knowledge.

Three second year students however, complained that TP duration was too short for comprehensive understanding of rural setting complexities. ST8 wrote: "four weeks is not long enough to understand rural issues". Such sentiments may have been because this was their first TP.

4.5.3 Relating with the Classroom

Students (11) expressed amazement at the seriousness with which teachers and learners regarded their work, notwithstanding under-resourcing. Some of these students during the pre-TP workshop had envisaged, unmotivated, uncommitted learners and teachers. What they found at Mziwaxolo was contrary to their imaginations as the teachers had a professional and committed approach to their work. ST13 reported: "You get into their staff room, its dead silent they are preparing". The increasing contextual understanding and awareness of learner learning barriers probably prompted students to challenge those assumptions. Seemingly, students now understood that interactions with rural teachers and learners, and rural classroom practice were indispensable opportunities to experience and conceive rurality, rural teaching and rural life. For example, ST8 wrote: "This is the best teacher, experiencing rural teaching, rural learners, working in a rural classroom, with rural teachers. You see their efforts and seriousness. I would not refuse a job here".

Classroom practice was hailed as valuable exposure to the teaching profession and nuances of rural school practice. Other students described rural school TP as good preparation for future work: "The classes are big 9A-72, 9B-80. It's challenging, but that's what is in many schools. I must experience big classes for the future. What if I get such classes after training?" (ST12).

4.5.4 Relating with Mentors

Many students (10) benefitted from mentor support and collaboration. They applauded the mentors' professional knowledge and experience from how they carried out their work, explained and justified issues. ST16, reflected: "these experiences make you question and reflect on your thoughts and attitudes". Some had anticipated demanding, cruel mentors. These concerns were now questioned. Many students considered themselves lucky given the tremendous support they received. ST1 reported: "I am very fortunate; my mentor is supportive. We share, and consult each other. ... feedback is constructive, developmental will help me throughout...", and ST15 stated, "Both mentors are good colleagues, we learn from each other. Mrs X asked me to teach one topic that she wasn't familiar ... after each lesson they say reflect, before giving their feedback. I reflect on their lessons too. There is better mentoring in this rural school than I got at an urban school". Finally, ST3 shared, "We discuss lessons before, mine or hers, what to teach, methods, everything. Then after observation we sit again, they say think about your lesson, how it went, the good, bad and why, what to do next time, before they give comments".

Comments above signal current conceptualization of mentoring as a journey, underpinned by equality and collegiality in the relationship (Shank, 2005). Asking students to reflect on their practice aids self-evaluation and identification of strengths and weaknesses, which promotes learning from own errors and practice by answering what would have done differently. Thus, mentoring does not only guide students in classroom learning management, but helps them explore, interpret and explain the "how" and "why" of what happened leading into the next stage of the teaching cycle, (re)planning of next lesson (du Plessis, 2017). ST3 suggests clinical mentoring and supervision with pre-observation, observation and post lesson observation conference which increases instructional learning quality.

However, five students reported minimal learning from mentoring. Some mentors probably lacked knowledge of "good" mentoring, lacked effective mentoring skills, or were not aware of students' TP learning needs. ST14 commented: "She wants to be our mother, but no beneficial feedback. She always says you are a good teacher but not saying what makes me good".

The evidence suggests ignorance on mentoring roles, portraying a semblance of perceiving mentoring as fundamentality for offering emotional support. Sometimes it is difficult to distinguish between being a mother and a mentor who stimulates a mentee's growth into a teacher they envision. Other mentors did not model lessons for students. For example, ST16 shared, "We agree that I will observe, then before that lesson he gives excuses... and tells me what to teach, content, methods. I want to learn how he teaches those things he asks me to teach".

Students always expect mentors to model lessons as good teachers who they can emulate. Observations are professionally growthful for students, which give them immediate space to familiarize themselves with classroom practice while they prepare for own teaching particularly in unfamiliar rural classrooms. Students often regard mentors' expert knowledge and personal experience as critical components for their practice. However, comments above imply "apprenticeship" mentoring model, where students "act as told", and "as acted by the mentor", contrary to current mentoring conceptualization as collegial partnerships. Mentors should not impose, or dictate content and/or strategies for students' classroom activities (Gershenfeld, 2014).

Some mentors doubted students' abilities, and were reluctant to hand over their classes. ST6 wrote: "She doesn't allow me to teach full lessons alone. She teaches with me every time". (ST13). It is typical for some mentors to be apprehensive about how their learners are taught. Instead of viewing students as knowledgeable partners, with something to offer, they regard them as trespassers without teaching knowledge.

4.5.5 Relating with Peers

TP experiences with built-in collaborative reflections opened students for structured, integrated interactions where they discussed challenges from the rural context. Linking with peers professionally occurred during the debriefing collaborative reflection conversations. These meetings were vital for collective reflections and reflexions on their teaching and, the rural context broadly. ST11 recorded: "They give me ideas about strategies. Even my own suggestions they question me and this gives me confidence knowing that peers approve".

Through cooperative conversations, students shifted from individualistic to collaborative thinking and behaviour, "looking" up to peers to confirm their propositions and provisional solutions to rural classroom challenges. Further, collaborative engagements were particularly valuable for promoting students' re-imaginations of the "self", where they viewed themselves from the broad picture, regarding what that meant to them as individuals and professionals. ST10 wrote: "Encouragement and comments from peers developed me. I am now comfortable discussing teaching issues in the group, confident in the classroom. Have become very open. …Yeah! I wouldn't mind working here".

Rural school TP offered genuine spaces where students directly experienced realities of rural school teaching which prompted consideration of career prospects in rural contexts. Others saw cohort participation as suitable preparation for future classroom challenges in similar contexts. ST16 commented: "They critically question you, want you to think about what you should have done differently. They don't just offer ideas or suggestions, but stretch you. This gives you learning, and confidence to tackle future challenges".

For these students, collaboration fostered confidence development from the comments and teaching ideas. Conversations also seemingly enhanced their teacher dispositions, inclusive of self-consciousness and responsiveness to different viewpoints. Students became able to extract the best in themselves and their peers through sincere interactions (Mukeredzi & Mandrona, 2013). Genuine dialogue calls for compassionate listening while searching for common ground, empathetically probing ideas, being open to new learning, isolating challenges and working as critical friends notwithstanding gender, race, cultural background or social class. Impartiality becomes a key feature (Prince, Snowden, & Mathews, 2010) as discussions occur regardless of the human elements.

4.6 Discussion

Students' experiences and interpretations were around views and how they related with the rural context, the rural classroom, the mentors, and their peers. On commencing TP, most students displayed blurred and pessimistic beliefs, comprehensions and expectations of teaching, working and living in rural settings. These anxieties were however dispelled after experiencing rurality. Eight students had anticipated learner language problems but these anxieties were dissipated as learners spoke and understood English. Sherwood (2000) laments the many stereotypes that exist about rurality and rural education, with descriptions related to unsophisticated, low-level intellectual capability and conservative nature of rural learners. Such stereotypes view rurality and rural learners as synonymous with educational and social deficiencies, and needs (Moletsane, 2012; Pennefather, 2011).

The well-maintained school environment, teaching/learning culture and the welcome students received amazed them. This contradicted their previous misconceptions around lost moral values, indiscipline and demotivation to teaching/learning in rural schools. The mythologies and misconceptions were disrupted after interacting with learners, teachers, the environment and participating in both in- and out-of-class activities. Adie and Barton (2012) advise that ITE and the novice years are critical for unsettling engrained myths and misconceptions of rurality.

All participants confirmed valuable experiences from, and enjoyed classroom practice. Such hands-on learning is what Mukeredzi and Mandrona (2013) defined as teaching/learning for understanding, which is an effective way of learning how to teach specific learners, in specific contexts. The all-encompassing context at MziwaXolo school with an enabling RTEP team on-spot support seemingly fostered students' confidence in classroom practice and rurality. Many students commended learners and teachers for their enthusiasm and commitment to work notwithstanding severe under-resourcing, erasing fallacies about demotivation in rural teachers and learners (Kiggundu & Nayimuli, 2009). Participants developed better understanding of under-resourcing challenges in rural schools but argued that this should not be an alibi for poor teaching.

Mentoring makes an effective vehicle for professional learning through reflection as students learn about the "self" in context. Many students commended their mentors for modelling lessons, guiding and giving them developmental critique and feedback on their teaching, and for promoting reflection, contrary to their previous misconceptions about demanding, unsupportive mentors who overworked students. Students who experienced ineffective mentoring had expected to benefit from mentoring through guidance, constructive feedback and specifically what needed doing to promote professional learning. While these students appreciated emotional support, that alone often brings frustration because students need developmental critique to build their own teacher identities (Hyland & Lo, 2006). Mentors are expected to appreciate students as individuals who require own teacher identity and teaching style. Two students apparently could not "find themselves" as teachers because mentors flooded them with their teaching styles and ideas. Such mentoring strategies often confuse students making them wonder whether to enact mentor suggestions or proceed with own ideas.

Some mentors are ineffective due to ignorance, lack of understanding/clarity on mentoring roles and responsibilities, and absence of active school-university liaison/coherence/partnerships (Nyaumwe & Mtetwa, 2011). Such issues often affect mentors' approaches to developing students' professional learning as generally, mentors do not experience effective training or receive clear guidance on the content of mentoring (Gershenfeld, 2014). Other mentors may just be experienced class-room practitioners who lack capacity for collegial training. Mentoring is not an instinctive process, but needs making teaching elements visible, and breaking the strategies into step-by-step components for the student (Mukeredzi & Mandrona, 2013). Again, rural school teachers often lack active participation or access to staff development courses and activities unlike their urban counterparts (Islam, 2012). Other mentors may not have experienced good mentoring themselves, given that what teachers do or do not do is often in response to their prior experiences. These mentors attended a once-off university mentor training workshop. Seemingly, the workshop was inadequate for effective learning of mentoring knowledge and skills.

Practicum is acknowledged as generally stressful, particularly in rural schools where many complexities come into play. Structured collaborative conversations were intended to offer students an additional supportive layer to their discussions and individual reflections on their rural TP experiences. Prince et al. (2010) contend that other vital characteristics of teacher professional learning include collaboration and entrenchment in classroom practice. Students also saw these collective engagements as fundamental for learning, confidence development and celebrating their achievements (Prince et al., 2010). Given the often numerous TP challenges, it becomes vital to acknowledge when processes work out smoothly. Confidence is generally related to an individual's level of self-esteem, and to optimism, which promotes one's self-awareness and self-belief in their positive achievements. It therefore makes a fundamental teacher attribute which affects their classroom communication and instructions.

4.7   Conclusion and Implications

This chapter explored students' TP experiences and interpretations of those experiences within the context of a rural school-university partnership model addressing rural school teacher development. It may appear unconvincing that a deep understanding of rurality developed during a four-week practicum, but data suggests that students developed a sense of rurality which dissipated some of their fallacies, seemingly increasing their employment possibilities in rural settings. This may ultimately stimulate their interest for teaching in rural schools. When rural school TP is organized for students to encounter and create their own understandings, this creates prospects for re-examining and disrupting existing illusions about rurality. Adie and Barton (2012) suggest that such encounters stimulate "ruralisation" of the mind which can clear individualistic young teacher beliefs that rural village schools turn individuals into "village men" (Monk, 2007). Students need immersion in rural settings, with hands-on experiences, and reflection to stimulate their dreams about job opportunities in these contexts.

Islam (2012) argues for teacher preparation oriented to students' understanding of rurality and how quality education could be delivered to rural areas. While teacher preparation for rurality during ITE could be a development avenue which invests in youth who choose a teaching pathway, this may be a starting point for supporting rural teachers, learners, and communities (Islam, 2012). Given the diversity in the South African education sector, teacher education should focus on quality education for varied contexts, with particular attention being paid to rural contexts. While the responsibility may be upon university education faculties to prepare enthusiastic and able teachers for rurality, this is a complex issue which demands more than short-term approaches and quick-fixes, but collaborative and holistic efforts of the tripartite: teacher education institutions, education departments, and interested parties to seriously rethink and invest in teacher preparation for rural education development.

This model of student teacher professional development on TP which uniquely involved a relatively large team of students from diverse backgrounds, ages and experiences to live in community specifically to learn from the context and from each other promoted collaborative reflective engagements. Students teachers experienced learning with and from one another as a community for professional learning through collaborative reflection. The on-going support and discussion with peers and supervisors, promotes collaborative capability as students sit beside, share and feed off each other thus, professionally learning with and from one another (Mukeredzi, 2015). In addition, the in-built opportunities for systematic reflection following reflective questions in this unique model would foster students' reflection on their experiences, interpretations and perceptions of the rural context practicum.

Regrettably, this is a small research project based on a structured model with hypothetical underpinnings for planning rural teacher preparation. However, given the resources involved, a TP model of this nature may be pragmatically unsustainable for replication to scale. Consideration of TP models that attach student cohorts to rural schools, with structures for collaboration and reflection could offer possible starting point.

Acknowledgements I am grateful to the RTEP leaders for giving me this invaluable opportunity. I am particularly thankful to Professor Relebohile Moletsane, the JL Dube Chair for Rural Education and my Post Doc mentor, for her unfailing support and encouragement throughout my research activities.

References

Adie, L., & Barton, G. (2012). Urban pre-service teachers' conceptions of teaching in rural communities. *Australian Journal of Teacher Education, 37*(6), 111–123. Retrieved from http://dx.doi.org/10.14221/ajte.2012v37n6.7.

Arnold, M. L., Newman, J. H., Gaddy, B. B., & Dean, C. B. (2005). A look at the condition of rural education research: Setting a difference for future research. *Journal of Research in Rural Education, 20*(6). Retrieved from http://jrre.psu.edu/articles/20-6.pdf.

Balfour, R. (2012). Rurality research and rural education: Exploratory and explanatory power. *Perspectives in Education, 30*(10), 9–18.

Brady, L. (2002). School university partnerships: What do the schools want? *Australian Journal of Teacher Education, 27*(1). http://dx.doi.org/10.14221/ajte.2002v27n1.1.

Cohen, L., Manion, L., & Morrison, K. (2012). Research methods in education. *Professional Development in Education, 38*(3), 507–509.

Cole, P. (2012). *Linking effective professional learning with effective teaching practice, PTR Consulting from.* http://www.aitsl.edu.au/verve/_resources/Linking_effective_professional_learning_with_effective_teaching_practice_ _Cole.pdf.

Corbett, M., & White, S. (2014). Why put the rural in research? In S. White & M. Corbett (Eds.), Doing educational research in rural settings: Methodological issues, international perspectives and practical solutions (pp. 1–5). New York, NY: Routledge.

du Plessis, P. (2017). Challenges for rural school leaders in a developing context: A case study on leadership practices of effective rural principals. *Bulletin for Christian Scholarship, 82*(3). Available at: https://doi.org/10.19108/koers.82.3.2337.

Erlingsson, C., & Brysiewicz, P. (2017). Hands-on guide to doing content analysis. *African Journal of Emergency Medicine, 7,* 93–99.

Gardiner, M. (2008). *Issues in Education Policy: A report on education in rural areas.* Centre for Education Policy Development: Pretoria.

Gershenfeld, S. (2014). A review of undergraduate mentoring programs. *Review of Educational Research September, 84*(3), 365–391. https://doi.org/10.3102/0034654313520512.

Green, B. (2008). *NSW rural teacher education project.* Wagga Wagga: Australia, Centre for Information Studies, Charles Sturt University.

Greenough, R., & Nelson, S. R. (2015). Recognizing the variety of rural schools. *Peabody Journal of Education, 90*(2), 322–332. https://doi.org/10.1080/0161956X.2015.1022393.

Gustafsson, M. (2016). *Teacher supply and the quality of schooling in South Africa: Patterns over space and time* (Working Paper No. 3). Stellenbosch: Stellenbosch University, Department of Economics.

Hamm, Z. (2014). Rural community research process as outcome: Approaching the community. In M. Corbett & S. White (Eds.), *Doing educational research in rural settings: Methodological issues, international perspectives and practical solutions* (pp. 88–103). New York, NY: Routledge.

Haugalokken, O. K., & Ramberg, P. (2007). Autonomy or control: Discussion of a central dilemma in developing a realistic teacher education. *Norway Journal of Education in Teaching, 33*(1), 55–69.

Hlalele, D. (2014). Rural education in South Africa: Concepts and practices. *Mediterranean Journal of Social Sciences, 5*(4), 462–469.

Hugo, W., Jack, M., Wedekind, V., & Wilson, D. (2010). *The state of education in Kwazulu-Natal: A report to the Provincial Treasury.* Pietermaritzburg: KZN Provincial Treasury.

Hughes, J. (2013). Cameos, supporting roles and stars: Citation and reflection in the context of initial teacher education. *Educational Research, 55*(1), 16–30.

Hyland, F., & Lo, M. M. (2006). Examining interaction in the teaching practicum: Issues of language, power and control. *Mentoring & Tutoring: Partnership in Learning, 14*(2), 163–186.

Islam, F. (2011). School-University partnerships in preparing new teachers: Possibilities and limitations. In F. Islam, C. Mitchell, N. de Lange, R. Balfour, & M. Combrinck (Eds.), *School–university partnerships for educational change in rural South Africa* (pp. 41–58). New York, NY: Edwin & Mellen.

Islam, F. (2012). Understanding pre-service teacher education discourses in Communities of Practice: A reflection from an intervention in rural South Africa. *Perspectives in Education, 30*(1), 19–29.

Johnson, J., & Strange, M. (2009). *Why rural matters 2009: State and regional challenges and opportunities.* Retrieved from http://files.eric.ed.gov/fulltext/ED516650.pdf.

Kiggundu, E., & Nayimuli, S. (2009). Teaching practice: A make or break phase for student teachers. *South African Journal of Education, 29,* 345–358.

Kline, J., White, S., & Lock, G. (2013). The rural practicum: Preparing a quality teacher workforce for rural and regional Australia. *Journal of Research in Rural Education, 28*(3), 1–13. Retrieved from http://jrre.psu.edu/articles/28-3.pdf.

Lietz, C. A., & Zayas, L. E. (2010). Evaluating qualitative research for social work practitioners. *Advances in Social Work, 11*(2), 188–202.

Lingam, G. I. (2012). Preparing teachers for rural schools: An empirical evidence from a Fiji case. *Greener Journal of Educational Research, 2*(2), 001–012. www.gjournals.org.

Mahlangu, V. P., & Pitsoe, V. J. (2013). The changing landscape in the conditions of service for teachers in South Africa. *Journal of Social Science, 36*(1), 69–75.

Mauthner, N. S., & Doucet, A. (2003). Reflexive accounts and accounts of reflexivity in qualitative data analysis. *Sociology, 37,* 413–431. Retrieved from http://dx.doi.org/10.1177/003803850303 73002.

Masinire, A. (2015). Recruiting and retaining teachers in rural schools in South Africa: Insights from a rural teaching experience programme. *Australian & International Journal of Rural Education, 25*(1), 2–14.

Miller, L. C. (2012). *Understanding rural teacher recruitment and the role of community amenities* (CEPWC Working Paper No. 1). Retrieved from http://curry.virginia.edu/resource-library/Miller RuralTeacherRetention.

Mitchell, C., de Lange, N., Balfour, R., & Islam, F. (2011). Transforming teacher education? A rural teacher education project experience. In F. Islam, C. Mitchell, N. de Lange, R. Balfour, & M. Combrinck (Eds.), *School–university partnerships for educational change in rural South Africa* (pp. 59–82). New York, NY: Edwin & Mellen.

Moletsane, R. (2012). Repositioning educational research on rurality and rural education in South Africa: Beyond deficit paradigms. *Perspectives in Education, 30*(1), 1–8.

Monk, D. H. (2007). Recruiting and retaining high-quality teachers in rural areas. *The Future of Children, 17*(1), 155–174. https://doi.org/10.1353/foc.2007.0009. Retrieved from http://muse. jhu.edu/journals/foc/summary/v017/17.1monk.html.

Mukeredzi, T. G. (2013). Professional development through teacher roles: Conceptions of professionally unqualified teachers in rural South Africa and Zimbabwe. *Journal of Research in Rural Education, 28*(11), 1–16. Retrieved from http://jrre.psu.edu/articles/28-11.pdf.

Mukeredzi, T. G. (2015). Creating space for Pre-service teacher professional learning during practicum: A teacher educator's self-study. *Australian Journal of Teacher Education, 40*(2), 126–145.

Mukeredzi, T. G. (2016). The "Journey to Becoming": Pre-service teachers' experiences and understandings of rural school practicum in a South African context. *Global Education Review, 3*(1), 88–107.

Mukeredzi, T. G., & Mandrona, A. R. (2013). The journey to becoming professionals: Student teachers' experiences of teaching practice in a rural South African context. *International Journal of Educational Research, 62,* 141–151.

Murphy, P. J., & Angelski, K. (1997). Rural teacher mobility: A report from British Columbia. *Rural Educator, 18*(2), 5–11.

Myende, P., & Chikoko, V. (2014). School-university partnership in a South African rural context: Possibilities for an asset-based approach. *Journal of Human Ecology, 46*(3), 249–259.

Nyaumwe, L. J., & Mtetwa, D. K. (2011). Developing a cognitive theory from student teachers' post-lesson reflective dialogues on secondary school mathematics. *South African Journal of Education, 31,* 145–159.

Pasensie, K. 2015. *Bringing rural education into the fold* (Catholic Institution of Education Briefing paper No. 401). Cape Town: SACBC Parliamentary Liaison Office. Available online: http://www.cplo.org.za/wp-content/uploads/2015/12/BP-401-Bringing-Rural-Education-intothe-Fold-Dec-2015.pdf.

Pennefather, J. (2011). Landscape shapes mindscape: Partnerships as agency in a community of learning. In F. Islam, C. Mitchell, N. de Lange, R. Balfour, & M. Combrinck (Eds.), *School–university partnerships for educational change in rural South Africa* (pp. 211–230). New York, England: Edwin & Mellen.

Plunkett, M., & Dyson, M. (2011). Becoming a teacher and staying one: Examining the complex ecologies associated with educating and retaining new teachers in rural Australia. *Australian Journal of Teacher Education, 36,* 32–47.

Putnam, R., & Borko, H. (2000). What do new views of knowledge and thinking have to say about research on teacher learning? *Educational Researcher, 29*(1), 4–15.

Prince, T., Snowden, E., & Mathews, B. (2010). Utilising peer coaching as a tool to improve student teacher confidence and support the development of classroom practice. *Literacy Information in Computer Education Journal, 1,* 45–51.

Roberts, P., & Green, B. (2013). Researching rural places: On Social Justice and Rural Education. *Qualitative Inquiry, 19,* 765–774.

Rural Education Policy. (2018). *South Africa Rural Education Policy*. Pretoria: Department of Basic Education.

Rural Teacher Education Project. (2012). *Recruitment Brochure*. Durban: University of KwaZulu-Natal.

Savides, M. (2017). *SA teachers not qualified or teaching the wrong subjects*. https://www.businesslive.co.za/bd/national/education/2017-06-06-sa-teachers-not-qualified-or-teaching-the-wrong-subjects/.

Shank, M. (2005). Mentoring among high school teachers: A dynamic and reciprocal group process. *Mentoring and Tutoring, 13*(1), 73–82.

Sharplin, E. D. (2009). *Getting them out there: A rural education field trip*. International Symposium for Innovation in Rural Education, Improving Equity in Rural Education, Armidale, NSW.

Sherwood, T. (2000). Where has all the "rural" gone? Rural education research and current federal reform. *Journal of Research in Rural Education, 16,* 159–167.

Statistic South Africa. (2017). *General Householld Survey*. Pretoria, South Africa.

Sullivan, K., McConney, A., Perry, L. B. (2018). A comparison of rural educational disadvantage in Australia, Canada, and New Zealand. *SAGE Open, 8*(4), 1–12. DOI:http://doi.org/10.1177/2158244018805791.

Wedekind, V. (2005). *Report for UNESCO on conditions affecting rural teachers in South Africa*. Pietermaritzburg: University of KwaZulu-Natal.

White, S., & Kline, J. (2012). *Renewing rural and regional teacher education curriculum: Final Report*. Australian Teaching and Learning Council. Retrieved from www.rrrtec.net.au.

World Bank. (2013). Urban population (% of total). Retrieved from http://data.worldbank.org/indicator/SP.URB.TOTL.IN.ZS.

Tabitha Grace Mukeredzi originally from Zimbabwe, but now a resident of South Africa, is an Associate Professor at the Durban University of Technology Faculty of Arts and Design, in the Adult Education Unit of the School of Education, based at the Education Campus in Pietermaritzburg 80 km west of Durban. Her research and publication interests are around teacher education, teacher learning, teacher professional development, teacher knowledge, rural education, mentoring and adult and community education including prison education.

Part III
Programmes and Services Attuned to Rural Schools and Communities

Chapter 5
Innovations in Providing Quality Gifted Programming in Rural Schools Using Place-Conscious Practices

Amy Price Azano and Carolyn M. Callahan

Abstract This chapter examines barriers to providing programming for gifted rural students and offers innovative solutions to addressing common challenges in rural schools drawing from a case study from the United States context. Gifted rural students often experience opportunity gaps compared to their non-rural peers related to limited funding, geographic location, and misunderstandings about gifted learners. These barriers lead to challenges in identifying and providing appropriate instruction and programming for gifted learners in rural schools. Using place as a theoretical, methodological, and pedagogical foundation, we position giftedness and rurality as social constructs and provide possibilities for mitigating challenges to include alternative identification strategies and place-conscious curriculum. The chapter concludes with practical takeaways for the field.

Keywords Gifted education · Place-conscious curriculum · Social construct · High poverty schools

5.1 Introduction

How can rural schools and communities foster their students' achievement and talent development? In this chapter, we explore the provision of programming for gifted (i.e., high potential) rural students, examining both the barriers to enrichment and acceleration in academic domains such as mathematics, science, social studies, and English language arts (e.g., reading, and writing, and speaking), as well as innovative solutions to address these common challenges. We do so drawing from a case study from the United States standpoint.

A. P. Azano (✉)
School of Education, Virginia Tech, Blacksburg, VA, USA
e-mail: azano@vt.edu

C. M. Callahan
School of Education and Human Development, University of Virginia, Charlottesville, VA, USA

© Springer Nature Singapore Pte Ltd. 2021
S. White and J. Downey (eds.), *Rural Education Across the World*,
https://doi.org/10.1007/978-981-33-6116-4_5

We have written elsewhere (e.g., Azano, Callahan, Brodersen, & Caughey, 2017; Callahan & Azano, 2019) about the circumstances relating to achievement and opportunity gaps between rural and non-rural students, and also between students from families with lower incomes and their more economically advantaged peers. The challenges to reducing achievement and opportunity gaps are persistent both in gifted education and rural schooling (Thomson, De Bortoli, & Buckley, 2013). These interactions between issues in gifted education and rural education should be addressed across the various facets of gifted programming, including the identification of gifted students, grouping arrangements, and curricular and instructional modifications. Structural challenges in providing adequate education to gifted students in rural environments include state, regional, and local gifted education policies and differing levels of funding for gifted programs.

These circumstances create major obstacles for small rural schools that are often already stretched financially or are located in geographic areas where delivering certain types of gifted programming (e.g., special schools or competitive academic teams) proves difficult. In addition to structural barriers, pervasive misunderstandings and myths about rural students and gifted learners make advocating for their needs additionally challenging. For example, expectations that all gifted students have high IQ scores or must appear to be like Albert Einstein, or that gifted students must be advanced readers, or that gifted students are always the highest achievers in the classroom thwart the process of finding talents and modifying services and creating appropriate curriculum and instructional modifications.

To address the complex field of rural gifted education, we provide both an overview of the complicated issues in identifying and providing appropriate curriculum and instruction to rural gifted students and innovative strategies to further efforts for their effective education. We also provide a discussion of how *place* was used as a theoretical, methodological, and pedagogical foundation in a five-year research project designed to mitigate the challenges by honoring local communities and supporting students with high academic potential.

The initial focus of the chapter explicates major issues in rural gifted education internationally, using place as a theoretical lens for interpreting and making sense of both affordances and barriers. For example, we provide a description of barriers including fewer specialists in gifted education, limited resources, fewer program options, and fewer research opportunities and field trips (Alston & Kent, 2003; Burney & Cross, 2006; Jarzabkowski, 2003; Hébert & Beardsley, 2001; Riley & Bicknell, 2013), and then we provide a discussion that acknowledges these challenges while also advocating for context rich resources that support gifted education. In so doing, we examine the ways "giftedness" and "rurality" are socially constructed and how these understandings affect programming.

This foundational overview is followed by a review of strategies to minimize these challenges, including specific examples from rural schools that have overcome barriers to provide quality services for their students. We provide an overview of the place-conscious methods used in our work to develop and implement an alternative process for identifying gifted students in rural schools. The alternative identification process yielded an increase in identified gifted students in all of our participating districts through implementation of place-conscious professional development and using local norms as a reference for including high-potential learners in gifted education programming. The discussion of alternative identification strategies is followed by presentation of an empirically validated curriculum model and illustrations of strategies for integrating place-based pedagogy drawn from geographically and culturally relevant examples. The modifications presented provide exemplars for engaging and challenging rural students in gifted programs regardless of geographic locale. We conclude with practical takeaways for the field.

5.2 Theoretical Grounding

A discussion of rural gifted education must begin with the acknowledgment that giftedness and rurality are both social constructs and that they are both framed in terms of relative presence or absence of a set of traits believed to differ across people or geography. These constructs are also based on values relative to those traits and also how the value of gifts (how they are honored and nurtured) can be deeply contextualized. Here we provide a theoretical grounding for this work to discuss the ways in which giftedness and rurality are socially constructed and how place can serve to make meaning in theory, research and practice.

5.2.1 Giftedness as a Social Construct

If we agree that the concept of giftedness exists because of a need by humans to describe what they believe are important differences in the way humans learn and perform and that they assign values to those traits, then we see giftedness as a social construct. In the framework where giftedness exists as a social construct, different cultures are likely to define giftedness in terms of the norms, beliefs, values, and priorities of a people, as well as from the socio-historical and socio-political realities of a country or region (Davis, Rimm, & Siegle, 2010). This is the case when one examines the definitions of giftedness adopted across nations and even within regions of nations (the deep South or the Midwest in the United States, for example). Heuser, Wang, and Shahid (2017) have analysed the myriad conceptions of giftedness around the world and identified four dimensions along which the definitions of giftedness fall:

1. defining giftedness as cognitive achievement and/or aptitude versus defining it as excellence in both academic and non-academic areas, such as sports, music, arts, and soft skills;
2. giftedness as aptitude versus achievement;
3. giftedness as nature or as nurture; and

4. giftedness as associated with individualism versus giftedness as associated with collectivism.

Heuser, Wang, and Shahid (2017) further identify countries which exemplify points along each dimension. For example, in their discussion of dimension (1), they name Austria, Germany, Ireland, Hong Kong, Hungary, Korea, the Netherlands, Poland, Switzerland, Taiwan, and the United Kingdom as conceptualizing giftedness as exceptional acumen in multiple areas that include both academic and non-academic domains. To illustrate one extreme on dimension (2), they identify Beijing, Hong Kong, and Taiwan as nations where high scores on IQ tests serve as the measure to identify students with cognitive excellence. To contrast the different poles of the third dimension, Heuser, Wang, and Shahid note that the Shona and Ndebele cultures of Zimbabwe perceive giftedness to be a result of an individual's predispositions as well as environmental factors that are supportive of the enhancement of innate ability, while the cultures of Austria, Germany, and the Netherlands stress the importance of nurture. Finally, they note the Maori (New Zealand), for instance, look to the collective, or belonging to the group, as integral to intelligence and note that an extraordinary individual performance may not be consonant with their understandings of giftedness.

Recent discussions of giftedness in the United States present a conception which has been identified as transactional (e.g., Barab & Plucker, 2002; Hymer, 2009; McWilliams & Plucker, 2014; Plucker et al., 2017). In this construction of the definition of giftedness the authors move from a static conception of giftedness in which a stable set of traits "exists" in the individual to one in which giftedness is considered to be an emergence of gifts and talents as an individual with potential interacts with the conditions in the physical, social, and intellectual environment. Accordingly, individuals may or may not manifest giftedness depending on the circumstances in which they are born and educated, and they may manifest the traits in unique ways depending on factors in their environment.

5.2.2 Rural as a Social Construct

We argue that not only is giftedness a social construct but so, too, is rural. While there are demographic variables that nations and regions use to assign the label of rural (most often based on geography and population density), those criteria differ internationally across geographic areas. Importantly, the social construct of rurality reflects the underlying recognition that areas designated as rural are not homogeneous, and like giftedness, the social construction of rurality reflects the notion that rural can have many meanings. Chigbu (2013) offered a definition of rurality that exemplifies this social construction, characterizing rurality as "a condition of place-based homeliness shared by people with common ancestry or heritage and who inhabit traditional, culturally defined areas or places statutorily recognized to be rural" (p. 815). As Rousseau (1995) noted in a description of the construct of rurality in Britain, rurality is often seen as the opposite of urbanicity or an idyllic place where one can escape from urban life to "rolling landscapes or bleak moors…with smiling farmers leaning on farm gates" (p. 1). In contrast, other conceptions of rurality may be just the opposite—one of relative poverty, lack of sophistication, and lower motivation associated with those lacking ambition to leave rural areas. These social constructs are often translated into stereotypes that inhibit positive thinking about the potential of gifted students in rural communities.

Others have written specifically about the challenges in defining rural (e.g., Azano, Downey, & Brenner, 2019; Corbett, 2016; Rasheed, 2019) and the boundary of rural for the purposes of rural education research (see Biddle, Sutherland, & McHenry-Sorber, 2019; Coladarci, 2007). Rasheed (2019) notes that organizations attempting to define and categorize rural fall short because they "do not provide understandings of the diverse populations and cultures in rural areas" (p. 4). We see evidence of that in the part of Chigbu's (2013) definition that references "people with a common ancestry or heritage" (p. 815). As populations in rural areas have shifted in recent years, in the United States and in other countries affected by the migrant crisis of the past decade, it is essential to continually and critically examine such definitions to ensure that as rural educators and researchers, we avoid falling back on outdated, narrow perceptions of the students we endeavor to serve.

For purposes of this chapter, and based on our five years of providing an alternative for gifted programming in rural schools, we have adopted a definition of giftedness that first reflects "potential or demonstrated capacity in the specific aptitude of processing language and producing products that reflect a high level of competence in expression using language" (Callahan & Azano, 2021). The second part of our definition ties recognition of capacity to the specific environment of the students. In other words, we ask educators to recognize the characteristics that reflect talent in the language arts domain as they manifest in students living in the specific rural communities. For example, some of the districts who participated in our project were situated in coastal communities where many families work in the fishing industry. Accordingly, teachers might view students who are able to provide an elaborate and detailed oral account of the steps involved in pulling in shrimp (prawns) from fishing nets as exhibiting signs of giftedness. Other specific academic areas could be adopted in expanding the definition to highlight other domains of academic focus.

5.2.3 Place as Meaning Making

We use "place" throughout this work to call attention to the ways we intentionally consider local contexts in our work. Theoretically, we position the very concepts of giftedness and rurality to be place dependent, informed by communities, local norms, and cultures. A critical pedagogy of place (Gruenewald, 2003) couples place-based pedagogy with critical theory—or the idea of leveraging place, the "social and ecological places people actually inhibit" (p. 3)—and the idea that we should critically "challenge the assumptions, practices, and outcomes taken for granted in dominant culture and in conventional education" (p. 3). Gruenewald presented a critical pedagogy of place as the "best of both worlds" and suggested it "offers a much needed framework for educational theory, research, policy, and practice" (p. 3). We find this a helpful frame in thinking about how local contexts influence conceptions of both giftedness and rurality and how dominant narratives about gifted people and rural places may present a discord in terms of practice and policy. We embrace *critical* stances on place by addressing an opportunity gap for rural students and advocating for increased identification of, and services for, gifted students in rural communities. Place is also used to consider the diversity of rural places and the affordances for meaning making when students are given the opportunity to connect curricula with places they care about. In this way, we aim to use place as curricular intervention as a means of dialogue about the interactions between environments and education (Gruenewald, 2003). More broadly, the focus of our research and examples provided in the chapter point to a critical pedagogy of place that "evaluates the efficacy of critical, place-based approaches to education" (p. 10).

5.3   Challenges in Recognizing and Serving Gifted Students in Rural Environments

The view of giftedness as a social construct accounts for policies around the identification of and programmatic activities for children and adults who are gifted, as well as the attitudes toward those individuals. The review of global orientations to giftedness by Heuser, Wang, and Shahid (2017) also presents strong arguments that perceptions of giftedness influence policy and program formation. As they note, the norms of the community, commonly held beliefs and attitudes, underlie the social construct of giftedness when translated into definitions, identification practices, and programs that have significant impacts on who is served and how. That is, the dominant social construct can either serve to provide a broad and inclusive orientation to giftedness or a very narrow orientation to giftedness. For example, when the definition of giftedness is narrowly conceived as exceptionally high intelligence, then identification is framed only in terms of scoring high on intelligence tests using national norms, and the population of individuals who are identified are primarily those who have been privileged to have greater opportunities to learn both in school and outside of school. As students in rural schools may have fewer opportunities to learn than other students (e.g., suburban students with higher family incomes; Lohman, 2013), there is diminished likelihood that all students with potential will be recognized and served. These opportunity gaps and subsequent achievement/excellence gaps between rural and non-rural students have been documented in the United States and other countries. For example, Hernández-Torrano (2018) documented the existence of excellence gaps between urban and rural students in Spain, with urban students scoring higher than rural students on measures of verbal and numerical reasoning, as well as in measures of fluency, flexibility, originality, and elaboration, which he attributed to limited opportunities to develop talent in rural environments.

When such narrow conceptions prevail, students from rural schools characterized by high poverty, students from historically marginalized racial and ethnic groups, students who are second-language learners, and students with disabilities are less likely to be identified as gifted. In rural school districts, particularly high poverty rural school districts where teachers have limited opportunity for exposure to newer conceptions of giftedness due to lack of funding for professional development, notions of giftedness as limited to high scores on intelligence tests likely prevail.

The demographics of rural and the conceptions of rurality also present challenges to providing quality services to gifted students in those areas. In the realm of demographics, low population density combined with the distance from resources and enrichment opportunities are, of course, a major challenge. Low enrollment of students in a school is correlated with low numbers of identified students, which limits the feasibility of offering options such as part-time or full-time classes for gifted students. A remote location means gifted students likely do not have equal access to special "magnet" schools that bring together gifted students from neighboring communities, and opportunities to participate in special events structured for gifted students, such as mathematics competitions, are likely limited as well. As we see increasing levels of poverty[1] and decreasing levels of education attainment in rural areas, the obstacles to quality education increase. High poverty across a community results in fewer resources for schools. The lack of resources manifests in fewer staff with backgrounds in gifted education; fewer opportunities for professional development; less access to specialized, quality curriculum for gifted students; and less access to enrichment opportunities that are available in more affluent suburbs and urban areas (Callahan & Azano, 2019). In fact, challenges to accessing basic internet services can adversely influence opportunities to learn for rural students who often do not have the internet connectivity at home needed to complete assignments (Fazlullah & Ong, 2019). Lack of internet connectivity also impedes replication of successful online programs such as the one offered to rural mathematically gifted students by Watson and Graham (2009) in Great Britain.

While definitions of giftedness, opportunities to learn (Callahan, 2018; Lohman, 2013), and rural demographics can influence gifted education resources and programming, so can possible bias in instruments used in the identification of gifted students. The use of some assessment tools and the ways scores are interpreted can result in under-identification of rural students, particularly those from families with relatively low incomes (Brodersen, Bruner, & Missett, 2018; Matthews & Peters, 2018; Worrell, 2018). Moreover, as evidenced in our research, financial resources might influence the process by which rural students are referred for gifted programming.

---

[1]Poverty rates in the United States, for example reached 24.2% in 2009 and continued to rise, reaching 25.2% in 2014. When considering "deep poverty" (families earning less than half of the poverty threshold) the numbers increased by almost 4.5% between 2007 and 2014. Further, the number of people attaining four-year college degrees in urban areas overtook the rural ones by 13%, in 2014 a gap that has continued to widen over more than a decade (https://modernfarmer.com/2015/12/the-state-of-rural-america-2015/).

For example, a referral process dependent on parent and teacher nominations may unintentionally privilege some students over others. For example, there is a reliance on parental nomination in India (Kurup & Maithreyi, 2012), which, because of lower literacy rates in rural community castes, leads to inequitable identification; that is, parents more familiar with the educational system and aware of the option for nomination/referral are more likely to access the process. Additionally, in rural schools if the process relies solely on teacher nominations, students who do not fit traditional archetypes of giftedness may be overlooked (Siegle & Powell, 2004). We argue that universal screening devices (assessment tools given to *all* children) can help minimize bias and increase representation among students with fewer opportunities to learn, students from low-income families, and minority student populations (Card & Giuliano, 2015).

5.4 Innovative Strategies to Minimize Challenges in Identifying and Providing Appropriate Curriculum and Instruction to Gifted Learners in Rural Schools

In our work, we have used specific strategies to mitigate challenges to providing gifted education services in rural schools, beginning with the identification process. Universal screeners are highly recommended (Card & Giuliano, 2015) as a critical step in creating an appropriate pool of students for consideration for gifted services. However, in schools where financial resources are not available to purchase and score additional cognitive ability tests, scores on government-mandated standardized tests can be used as a second-choice as long as students' scores are interpreted using local norms and ceiling effects do not minimize assessment of full potential. However, it is critical to use data that are related to the area of talent being considered (i.e., using scores on assessments of mathematics for screening students for with advanced mathematical performance.) Further, it is important to recognize the limitation of using achievement test scores for assessing potential. Importantly, *all* students should be evaluated using multiple data points, including test and non-test sources (Australian Association for the Education of the Gifted and Talented, n.d.; National Association for Gifted Children, 2010; Northern Territory Government Department of Education, 2016). A combination of measures can be used with tests scores including portfolio and performance assessments and teacher ratings (with appropriate teacher training, Peters & Gentry, 2010) to evaluate which students might benefit from advanced instruction. It is important to note that a range of valid assessments should be used to ensure that a variety of gifts and talents (e.g., mathematical, writing) are assessed uniquely. That way, giftedness in one domain can be recognized, and accommodations made to ensure appropriate instruction in that area, even if giftedness is not recognized in other subjects or domains.

However, these strategies alone will not ensure equitable identification of gifted students from rural areas, especially those from high poverty and/or remote communities who may have experiential gaps that restrict assessment of potential when only nationally normed scores from standardized measures are considered. Using local norms, calculated by comparing a student's scores to those of other students in the same school district or school building, ensures that students are being evaluated within a particular context as opposed to dissimilar contexts where opportunities to learn (Lohman 2013) might be different.

5.4.1 A Case Study of Alternative Identification in Rural School Districts

In Promoting PLACE in Rural Schools, a federally funded grant project in the United States, we applied the aforementioned strategies to increase the number of gifted students in 14 participating rural districts in the southeastern United States. Districts were considered for participation if 50% or more students were eligible to receive free or reduced-price lunches through a federal program based on families' relatively low incomes (this is a common way for U.S. researchers to describe the socioeconomic status of schools). In the project, we found that only five of the 14 districts screened students by administering a common assessment tool (universal screening) in their identification processes while the other districts relied on a referral process. Moreover, when students were assessed (even through the referral process), districts often applied arbitrary "cut-off" scores based on national norms on standardized tests for selection of students. For example, one participating district required students to score in the 96th percentile based on national norms on an IQ test; that is, students had to score higher than 96% of other same-aged children *nationally* to be included in the gifted education program. As a result of adhering to strict criteria, we found that many districts had very few students in their gifted programs.

As part of our work, we implemented two place-conscious efforts to address identification of students in the area of language arts (reading, writing, and speaking). First, we administered the *Cognitive Abilities Test*-Verbal Battery Level 9 (CogAT-V; Lohman, 2011) as a universal screener to all second graders in participating districts and computed students' percentile scores based on local norms (Lohman, 2012). We then provided place-conscious and rural-focused professional development to all second grade teachers in participating districts before they completed three subscales (motivation, creativity, and reading) of the *Scales for Rating the Behavioral Characteristics of Superior Students* (SRBCSS; Renzulli, et al., 2010) for each one of their students. The professional development provided an overview of characteristics common to students gifted in the language arts as well as a description of the ways such gifts and talents may manifest in rural students. A group discussion allowed teachers to articulate the ways they saw evidence of giftedness in their own students, ensuring a common understanding of how students' behaviors may indicate talent. Teachers completed ratings of all students in their second grade classrooms following the training, Norms for the ratings were calculated based on the overall school ratings and the individual teacher's classroom ratings (to account for rater leniency or strictness bias).

Results from the CogAT-V and SRBCSS were then presented to district administrators in a spreadsheet that displayed scores of high-potential students, indicating their nationally normed and locally normed scores. We advised administrators to use the locally normed scores for identification of students to be included in gifted and talented programming with an intentional effort to "find" students who might have been missed or previously overlooked by other identification means. As a result of these meetings, each district increased the number of students served in its programs.

5.4.2 Quality Curriculum for Gifted Learners that Reflects Place-Based Curriculum

During the identification process, districts were randomly assigned to treatment and control groups. Control districts included the additionally identified students (along with already identified gifted students) into their "business as usual" gifted education programs. By comparison, treatment districts were provided a place-based curriculum consisting of four language arts units for grade three (poetry and folklore) and grade four (research and fiction) to be offered to both the school-district identified students and those subsequently identified through the processes described above. Schools in both groups continued to use the service delivery and grouping model in place in their respective districts; in some cases, the classroom teacher used the curriculum to differentiate instruction for identified students in her class, while in other cases, the gifted specialist taught the curriculum to small groups of identified gifted students using a pull-out model.

We developed four modified language arts units based on the CLEAR curriculum model (Azano, Missett, Tackett, & Callahan, 2018). *CLEAR* (Challenge Leading to Engagement, Achievement, and Results) is a curriculum developed from three well-regarded models in gifted education: differentiation (Tomlinson, 1995, 1999a, 1999b, 2018), the Schoolwide Enrichment Model (SEM; Renzulli & Reis, 1985, 2000), and the depth and complexity model (Kaplan, 2005, 2018). Added to the elements derived from these three approaches to curriculum development for gifted students are the fundamental foundations of quality curriculum: formative assessment, clearly specified learning goals, data driven learning experiences, authentic products, and rich curriculum.

Further, for Promoting PLACE, we modified the curricula to incorporate aspects of rurality (e.g., substituting passages set in cities with those depicting farm life). We then further individualized the curricula for each treatment district based on survey responses from elementary teachers who shared details about the geography, industry, and other characteristics of the particular rural communities in which they taught. For example, for students learning in mountainous regions heavily dependent on agriculture, we incorporated poems and related activities drawing on those environmental features; for rural areas near the ocean, poems with coastal imagery were incorporated. Common task requirements throughout the units drew on place-specific references or provided opportunity for place reflections. For example, after students read William Carlos Williams' *The Red Wheelbarrow*, they learned about the poet's upbringing in rural New York. When they were tasked with writing a similar type of poem, they were encouraged to include artefacts from rural places important to them (see Fig. 5.1).

Similarly, after reading "Mississippi Origins" by Anna Journey, students were invited to reflect on daily events in their rural communities (see Fig. 5.2).

Finally, in the folklore unit, students were asked to make connections between content and context (see Fig. 5.3).

Encourage students to go somewhere different every day and write about their surroundings, especially rural places that are special to them. Emphasize that they should look for things either common to where they are or unique to their surroundings, community, or place. Encourage students to write their names on the outside cover and to keep it in their backpacks or coat pockets—wherever they are most likely to use it on a moment's notice.

Fig. 5.1 Using artefacts to stimulate consideration of place in writing

Afterwards, allow students to share out one family or everyday ritual that they have that is tied to place (i.e., feeding the chickens in the mornings, helping cook cornbread, going to church on Sunday, attending family reunions, etc.).

Fig. 5.2 Using events or rituals to stimulate consideration of place in writing

Fig. 5.3 Stimulating
connections between student
sense of place and literature

PLACE

Ask students if
they have a
wooded area or
forest near their
homes, or perhaps
a place they have visited. Did
that wooded place have any
fairytale-like qualities? Or, if
students have ever visited the
city, ask how the tall buildings
could be like the forest or
woods.

5.5   Teacher Support

Teachers in rural schools who deliver gifted services often have little time or support for developing curricula for advanced students, and they may not have had training in how to make appropriate curricular and instructional modifications for gifted students. This can be especially challenging because itinerant teachers often work at multiple sites and with multiple grade levels necessitating multiple preparations. Understanding these challenges, we provided professional development sessions each summer for the gifted and general education teachers who would be implementing the units. However, in order for the project intervention to be sustainable, we knew the trainings needed to be brief and replicable by district staff. And we incorporated specific directions, supplemental information, and icons representing quality differentiation in each lesson to illustrate important principles of differentiation to support on-going professional learning.

Rural gifted education teachers can experience professional isolation (Azano et al., 2014), making it more difficult to implement gifted curricula and related interventions. Additionally, we have found that some rural gifted teachers may encounter resistance from administrators or other teachers in their schools who may believe gifted education detracts from other, more needed educational pursuits they deem to be of higher priority for the school or the student. Therefore, we sought to support teachers by orienting them thoroughly to underlying principles of quality curriculum for gifted students prior to introducing them to the curriculum, which was documented as effective by a randomized controlled trial (RCT) experiment (Callahan et al., 2015). We offered continued support within the curriculum itself by building in multiple lessons that had specific place references, incorporating specific assessment tools with explicit directions for modifying curriculum based on students' readiness and interest, and as noted above by using icons to highlight the introduction of increased depth and complexity of curriculum. By building in specific tasks that required authentic production, we could provide repeated models of ways in which curriculum is appropriately modified for gifted students. Teachers did not have to search for a program or resources that would be relevant to students in Appalachia or the fishing communities of the coast—those resources were built into the curriculum the teachers used. Teachers could then attend to the foundational aspects in the unit (i.e., differentiation, depth, complexity, and authentic investigation and product creation).

We also worked to foster a sense of community with the gifted resource teachers by establishing a professional partnership and serving as colleagues for teachers who may have felt isolated by their position. In application of the model, rural schools should consider how to foster community and provide support, either with neighboring school districts, via the internet, or with local/regional universities.

5.6 Conclusion

We have outlined the challenges of identifying and serving gifted students in high poverty rural schools and then described a strategy for addressing those challenges. Our research has verified that the use of multiple, distinctly different types of instruments (teacher rating scales and standardized cognitive assessments), local norms, and judgments of students' profiles as described above yields an expanded pool of students who should be provided gifted education services. Further, we were able to verify that teacher ratings and standardized cognitive assessments are moderately correlated, but sufficiently independent to warrant the time (teachers') and expense (tests and test scoring) of using multiple measures. Interestingly, our research revealed that many students who were not identified by their school districts—but who *were* identified using our alternative criteria—scored at the same level of performance on the CogAT as students identified traditionally (Callahan et al., submitted for publication). Even more crucially, our study showed that offering a curriculum designed for advanced learners in rural schools resulted in significantly higher average scores for Promoting Place students compared to traditionally identified students on the Iowa Assessments in the areas of Reading, Written Expression, and on the Total scores; higher, but not significantly higher, scores on the Iowa Vocabulary subtest; and Promoting Place students scored equally well on writing tasks and unit tests (Callahan et al., submitted for publication). These findings invalidate claims that alternative assessment leads to the inclusion of students less capable of high levels of achievement. Finally, there were significantly greater gains for the treatment group (compared to the control group on the Iowa Assessments of Reading, Vocabulary, and Written Expression), treatment groups significantly outperformed control group students on unit tests in poetry and research, and the average difference in scores for the folklore and fiction units was positive (favoring the treatment group) though not statistically significant.

Acknowledgements The research reported here was supported by the U.S. Department of Education, under the Jacob K. Javits Gifted and Talented Students Education program, through Grant S206A140034-17.

References

Australian Association for the Education of the Gifted and Talented. (n.d.). *The identification of gifted and talented students.* Author. http://www.aaegt.net.au/?page_id=753.

Azano, A. P., Callahan, C. M., Brodersen, A., & Caughey, M. (2017). Responding to the challenges of gifted education in rural communities. *Global Education Review, 4*(1), 1–16.

Azano, A. P., Downey, J., & Brenner, D. (2019). Preparing pre-service teachers for rural schools. In J. Lampert (Ed.), *Oxford research encyclopedia of education.* New York, NY: Oxford University Press. (Published first online).

Azano, A. P., Missett, T. C., Tackett, M.E., & Callahan, C. M. (2018). The CLEAR curriculum model. In C. M. Callahan & H. Hertberg-Davis (Eds.), *Fundamentals of gifted education: Considering multiple perspectives* (2nd ed., pp. 293–309). New York, NY: Routledge.

Barab, S. A., & Plucker, J. A. (2002). Smart people or smart contexts? Cognition, ability, and talent development in an age of situated approaches to knowing and learning. *Educational Psychologist, 37,* 165–182. https://doi.org/10.1207/S15326985EP3703_3.

Biddle, C., Sutherland, D. H., & McHenry-Sorber, E. (2019). On resisting "awayness" and being a good insider: Early career scholars revisit Coladarci's swan song a decade later. *Journal of Research in Rural Education, 35*(7), 1–16. Retrieved from: https://doi.org/10.26209/jrre3507.

Brodersen, A. V., Brunner, M. M., & Missett, T. C. (2018). Traditional Identification Instruments. In C. M. Callahan & H. Hertberg-Davis (Eds.), *Fundamentals of gifted education: Considering multiple perspectives* (2nd ed., pp. 103–115). New York, NY: Routledge.

Callahan, C. M. (2018). Identification. In C. M. Callahan & H. L. Hertberg-Davis (Eds.), *Fundamentals of gifted education: Considering multiple perspectives* (pp. 94–102). New York, NY: Routledge.

Callahan, C. M., & Azano, A. P. (2019). Place-based gifted education in rural schools. In S. Smith (Ed.), *International handbook of giftedness and talent development in the Asia-Pacific.* New York, NY: Springer. First Online: 26 July 2019. https://link.springer.com/referenceworkentry/10.1007%2F978-981-13-3021-6_25-1.

Callahan, C. M., & Azano, A. P. (2021). Overcoming structural challenges related to identification and curricula for gifted students in high poverty rural schools. In R. J. Sternberg & D. Ambrose (Eds.), *Conceptions of giftedness and talent worldwide perspectives.* Cham: Palgrave Macmillan.

Callahan, C. M., Azano, A. P., Park, S., Brodersen, A., Caughey, M., & Bass, E. (Submitted for publication). Consequences of implementing alternative strategies for identifying gifted students. *Gifted Child Quarterly.*

Card, D., & Giuliano, L. (2015). *Can universal screening increase the representation of low income and minority students in gifted education?* (NBER Working Paper No. 21519). Retrieved from: http://www.nber.org/papers/w21519.

Chigbu, Uchendu Eugene. (2013). Rurality as a choice: Towards ruralising rural areas in sub-Saharan African countries. *Development Southern Africa, 30,* 812–825. https://doi.org/10.1080/0376835X.2013.859067.

Coladarci, T. (2007). Improving the yield of rural education research: An editor's swan song. *Journal of Research in Rural Education, 22*(3), 1–9.

Corbett, M. (2016). Rural futures: Development, aspirations, mobilities, place and education. *Peabody Journal of Education, 91*(2), 270–282.

Davis, G. A., Rimm, S. B., & Siegle, D. (2010). *Education of the gifted and talented* (6th ed.). Upper Saddle River, NJ: Prentice Hall.

Fazlullah, A., & Ong, S. (2019). *The homework gap: Teacher perspectives on closing the digital divide.* San Francisco, CA: Common Sense Media.

Gruenewald, D. A. (2003). The best of both worlds: A critical pedagogy of place. *Educational Researcher, 32*(4), 3–12.

Hernández-Torrano, D. (2018). Urban–rural excellence gaps: Features, factors, and implications. *Roeper Review, 40*(1), 36–45.

Heuser, B. L., Wang, K., & Shahid, S. (2017). Global dimensions of gifted and talented education: The influence of national perceptions on policies and practices. *Global Education Review, 4*(1), 4–21.

Hymer, B. J. (2009). Beyond compare? Thoughts towards an inclusional, fluid, and nonnormative understanding of giftedness. In T. Balchin, B. Hymer, & D. J. Matthews (Eds.), *The Routledge international companion to gifted education* (pp. 299–307). London, England: Routledge.

Kaplan, S. (2005). Layering differential curricula for gifted and talented. In F. A. Karnes & S. Bean (Eds.), *Methods and materials for teaching gifted students* (pp. 107–132). Waco, TX: Prufrock Press.

Kaplan, S. N. (2018). Differentiating with depth and complexity. In C. M. Callahan & H. L. Hertberg-Davis (Eds.), *Fundamentals of gifted education: Considering multiple perspectives* (2nd ed., pp. 270–278). New York, NY: Routledge.

Jarzabkowski, L. (2003). Teacher collegiality in a remote Australian School. *Journal of Research in Rural Education, 18,* 139–144.

Kurup, A., & Maithreyi, R. (2012). A review of challenges in developing a national program for gifted children in India's diverse Context. *Roeper Review, 34,* 215–223. https://doi.org/10.1080/02783193.2012.715332.

Lohman, D. F. (2011). *Cognitive abilities test (Form 7).* Rolling Meadows, IL: Riverside.

Lohman, D. F. (2013). Identifying gifted students: Nontraditional uses of traditional measures. In C. M. Callahan & H. L. Hertberg-Davis (Eds.), *Fundamentals of gifted education: Considering multiple perspectives* (pp. 112–127). New York, NY: Routledge.

Matthews, M. S., & Peters, S. J. (2018). Methods to increase the identification rate of students from traditionally underrepresented populations for gifted services. In S. Pfeiffer, E. Shaunessy-Dedrick, & M. Foley-Nicpon (Eds.), *APA handbook of giftedness and talent* (pp. 317–331). Washington, DC: American Psychological Association.

McWilliams, J., & Plucker, J. (2014). Brain cancer, meat glue, and shifting models of outstanding human behavior: Smart contexts for the 21st century. *Talent Development and Excellence, 6*(1), 47–55.

National Association for Gifted Children. (2010). *Pre-k–Grade 12 gifted programming standards.* Washington, DC: Author.

Northern Territory Government Department of Education. (2016). *Guidelines and procedures: Gifted education.* Author. https://education.nt.gov.au/__data/assets/pdf_file/0011/439148/Gifted-and-Talented-Education-Guidelines.pdf.

Peters, S. J., & Gentry, M. (2010). Multigroup construct validity evidence of the HOPE Scale: Instrumentation to identify low-income elementary students for gifted programs. *Gifted Child Quarterly, 54,* 298–313. https://doi.org/10.1177/0016986210378332.

Plucker, J. A., Makel, M., Matthews, M. S., Peters, S. J., & Rambo-Hernandez, K. E. (2017). Blazing new trails: Strengthening policy research in gifted education. *Gifted Child Quarterly, 61,* 210–218. https://doi.org/0016986217701838.

Rasheed, M. (2019). Context and content in rural gifted education: A literature review. *Journal of Advanced Academics, 26,* 1–24. First Published online October 4, 2019. https://doi.org/10.1177/1932202X19879174.

Renzulli, J. S., & Reis, S. (1985). *The schoolwide enrichment model: A comprehensive plan for education excellence.* Mansfield Center, CT: Creative Learning Press.

Renzulli, J. S., & Reis, S. (2000). The Schoolwide Enrichment Model. In K. Heller, F. Monchs, R. Sternberg, & R. Subotnik (Eds.), *The international handbook of giftedness and talent* (2nd ed., pp. 367–382). Oxford, UK: Elsevier.

Renzulli, J. S., Smith, L. S., White, A. J., Callahan, C. M., Harman, R. K., Westberg, K. L., …, Systema Reed, R. E. (2010). *Scales for rating the behavioral characteristics of superior students*. Waco, TX: Prufrock Press.

Riley, T., & Bicknell, B. (2013). Gifted and talented education in New Zealand schools: A decade later. *APEX: The New Zealand Journal of Gifted Education, 18*(1). Retrieved from www.gifted children.org.nz/apex.

Rousseau, N. (1995). What is rurality? *Occasional Paper of the Royal College of General Practitioners, 7*, 1–4.

Thomson, S., De Bortoli, L., & Buckley, S. (2013). *PISA 2012: How Australia measures up: The PISA 2012 assessment of students' mathematical, scientific and reading literacy*. ACER: Camberwell, Victoria. Retrieved from http://www.acer.edu.au/ozpisa/reports.

Tomlinson, C. A. (1995). *How to differentiate instruction in mixed-ability classrooms*. Alexandria, VA: ASCD.

Tomlinson, C. A. (1999a). *The differentiated classroom: Responding to the needs of all learners*. Alexandria, VA: ASCD.

Tomlinson, C. A. (1999b). *How to differentiate instruction in mixed-ability classrooms* (2nd ed.). Alexandria, VA: ASCD.

Tomlinson, C. A. (2018). Differentiated instruction. In C. M. Callahan & H. L. Hertberg-Davis (Eds.), *Fundamentals of gifted education: Considering multiple perspectives* (2nd ed., pp. 279–292). New York, NY: Routledge.

Siegle, D., & Powell, T. (2004). Exploring teacher biases when nominating students for gifted programs. *Gifted Child Quarterly, 48,* 21–29.

Watson, B., & Graham, T. (2009). Rural schools mathematics projects. *Mathematics in School, 38*(3), 17–19.

Worrell, F. C. (2018). Identifying gifted learners: Utilizing nonverbal assessment. In C. M. Callahan & H. Hertberg-Davis (Eds.), *Fundamentals of gifted education: Considering multiple perspectives* (2nd ed., pp. 125–134). NY: Routledge.

Amy Price Azano an Associate Professor at Virginia Tech, is a teacher educator in the School of Education. Her scholarship focuses on issues of equity for rural learners. She was the co-principal investigator on Project PLACE, and is the principal investigator on two funded projects promoting educational equity and sustainable programming for gifted learners in high-poverty rural Appalachian schools. She has published numerous journal articles and book chapters, co-authored a curriculum series with Prufrock Press, and has been an invited speaker on issues related to rural education in the U.S. and abroad. She is a coauthor of *Teaching in Rural Places: Thriving in Classrooms, Schools, and Communities*, and currently serves as Chair of AERA's Rural Education Special Interest Group.

Carolyn Callahan is the Commonwealth Professor of Education Emeritus at the University of Virginia and has been principal investigator on projects of the National Center for Research on Gifted Education (formerly NRC/GT), and principal investigator on five Javits grants including Project PLACE, focusing on the identification and provision of services to rural gifted students. Her work has focused on curriculum development and implementation. She has been recognized as Outstanding Professor of the Commonwealth of Virginia and Distinguished Scholar of the National Association for Gifted Children and has served as President of the National Association for Gifted Children and the Association for the Gifted, and as Editor of Gifted Child Quarterly. She is the co-editor of the recently published book, Fundamentals of Gifted Education: Considering Multiple Perspectives (2nd ed.) and Critical Issues in Gifted Education (3rd ed.).

Chapter 6
Building School-Migrant Family Connections in Culturally- and Linguistically-Diversifying Rural Communities: A Participatory Study From Australia

Margaret Kettle

Abstract Migration is presenting challenges and opportunities for rural education. In Australia, migration policy has long involved schemes directing migrants into regional areas to supplement workforces. This chapter reports on a study of skilled migration in a rural area of Queensland, a large decentralised state in the north-east of Australia. The study was an exploratory case study of the connections, or lack of them initially, between migrant families and the local secondary school. The study utilised the concept of connections, both as a response to policy initiatives and because of the literature on the benefits of school-family connections for students' academic adjustment and achievement. The research prioritised participation through use of interviews, focus groups, student photo-ethnographies and a social event led by the researcher, during which all participants heard—often for the first time— the views of other stakeholders. The school principal and teachers learned about the language brokering responsibilities of the students; the parents—the Australian curriculum; and the students—the commitment of teachers and parents to their school success. The chapter concludes with a discussion about the development of connections—their enabling conditions and the benefits for educational stakeholders in rural communities undergoing cultural and linguistic change as a result of migration.

Keywords Migration · Case study · English as an additional language · Community

6.1 Introduction

Migration is presenting challenges and opportunities for rural education. In Australia, migration policy has long involved schemes directing migrants into regional areas to supplement workforces and sustain communities (Hugo, Khoo, & McDonald, 2006). Indeed, barely a month goes by in Australian politics without a media report citing

M. Kettle (✉)
Faculty of Education, Queensland University of Technology, Brisbane, QLD, Australia
e-mail: m.kettle@qut.edu.au

© Springer Nature Singapore Pte Ltd. 2021
S. White and J. Downey (eds.), *Rural Education Across the World*,
https://doi.org/10.1007/978-981-33-6116-4_6

government calls for migrants and refugees to be settled in regional and rural areas (e.g. Kainth, 2018; Koziol, 2019; van Kooy & Wickes, 2019). The impetus for the calls is the bolstering of depleted workforces and low-population communities that struggle to attract and retain labour for local industries (Regional Australia Institute, 2018; Wright, Clibborn, Piper, & Cini, 2016).

While governments and regionally focused organisations advocate for migrants to strengthen workforces in agriculture, food processing and health care, little consideration is given to schools and the enrolment of children with minimal experience of the Australian school system and at times, low levels of academic English proficiency. Academic language proficiency refers to competence in the language required for schooling, namely the grammars, vocabulary and text types associated with different academic disciplines. The concepts are often scientific and abstracted, and the texts lexically dense and prescriptive in terms of genre structure (e.g. Halliday, 1985; Kettle & Ryan, 2018). For rural schools that are geographically isolated, access to specialist English language support is often limited, and the relatively new phenomenon of migration to the area may mean that teachers are inexperienced in addressing the needs of students with English as an additional language or dialect (EAL/D). Furthermore, for schools hoping to encourage a whole-of-family approach, migrant parents frequently feel ill-equipped to assist their children because of fears about their own English capabilities and unfamiliarity with the Australian curriculum.

This chapter reports on a study of one Australian secondary school's innovative responses to increased skilled migration and its efforts to bring together the principal, teachers, students and parents. The focus of the study was school-migrant family connections and the ways that the stakeholders could begin the process of initial introductions followed by growing contact and communication. The study adopted a participatory design and at the instigation of the school principal, was both the catalyst and chronicler of increasing school-migrant family interactions and a willingness to connect around student welfare and outcomes.

6.2 The Context

The secondary school in the case study (to be known here as The School) lies approximately 150 kilometres from Brisbane, the capital city of Queensland. The school has an Index of Community Socio-Education Advantage (ICSEA)[1] in the 900s which means that the students attending the school have lower education advantage than the average Australian student (Australian Curriculum, Assessment and Reporting Authority [ACARA], 2015); indeed, the school's ICSEA placed it among the 15 least advantaged schools in the state. According to the Australian Bureau of Statistics (ABS) data census data, the local town's population is around 4700 with most

[1]ICSEA is calculated on geographical location, parents' education levels and occupations, and the proportion of Indigenous students at the school. The average value for ICSEA is set at 1000 ACARA (2015).

people born in Australia (82%) followed by Brazil (3%), Philippines (2%), England (2%), New Zealand (1.5%) and Cook Islands (0.3%) (ABS, 2018). English is the dominant home language (88%) with the other languages spoken at home being Portuguese (3%), Filipino languages, e.g. Tagalog (2%), and Tongan (0.2%). Major industries in the area are meat processing and aged-care residential services (ABS, 2018).

Reflecting the economic migration conditions particularly in relation to employment in the beef-processing plants, The School has experienced increasing enrolments of English as an additional language (EAL) students over the past seven years. From 1% of the school population in 2013 to 9% in 2014, the EAL population peaked at 11% in 2015. At the time of the study, from 2017–2018, the EAL population was respectively, 9% (2017) and 7% (2018) (ACARA, 2019). Most of the EAL students were Brazilian and the children of workers employed in the abattoirs. Others were from the Cook Island with parents also working in the meatworks while some were from Filipino-background with parents employed in aged-care and automotive services.

At The School, the changing student demographics generated important pedagogical and social questions. From a pedagogical point of view, the school principal and teachers were committed but unsure about how best to teach the EAL students. From a social point of view, the Department of Education and Training (DET)[2] was prioritising parent and community connections as a means of building familiarity into the learning contexts of the students. In its *Advancing Education* plan for Queensland, the Department (2018) defined partnering for success as including engaging and collaborative relationships with parents. Furthermore, in its *Parent and Community Engagement Framework* (2019) policy, the department explicitly acknowledged the importance of quality partnerships between teachers and parents as a means of improving student learning and wellbeing. The understanding articulated in the policy is that learning is not confined to the classroom and creating a holistic environment of school, family and community can contribute to student outcomes (The State of Queensland [Department of Education], 2019). Of particular focus in the policy is devising practices that support inclusion and communication between schools and parents from diverse cultural and linguistic backgrounds. These practices include teachers learning about the home cultures of their students.

For The School, the benefits to student learning of connecting with families were obvious. The school principal and teachers regularly emailed parents[3] and sent home newsletters with the students; they also reported calling parents to talk about their child. The problem from The School's point of view was that despite efforts to communicate with parents, there was little or no response from the latter. The teachers talked of sending home invitations for parents to attend teacher-parent conferences as well as phone-calls with concerns about their child's attendance and classroom

---

[2]The Queensland Department of Education and Training (DET) has since been named the Department of Education (DoE).

[3]Following the Department of Education policy, 'parent' refers to parents, step-parents, carers and families.

behaviour. The lack of interaction fed a level of frustration among the principal and teachers and fired an interest in rethinking communication with migrant families.

For the school principal, connection with families was a priority; he recognised that it was linked to improved student learning and positive school-community engagement. His decision to involve the school in the research project aligned with the Departmental policy of seeking ways to better understand the home context of migrant students, and to devise practices that promoted inclusion and partnerships with families. The rationale in the research was that the process would be responsive and reciprocal, that is, considerate of all participants' circumstances and concerns, and committed to reciprocity of learning for everyone.

As a result, the research project had three objectives for developing school-migrant family connections: (i) to identify the conditions and concerns of the key stakeholders, namely, the school principal, teachers and migrant students and parents; (ii) to initiate contact and information-sharing between the stakeholder groups; and (iii) to institute more formalised mechanisms for ongoing communication and connection between the groups. Three expected benefits of the study accorded with Departmental policy and the values of The School: (i) greater knowledge and understanding among school personnel of migrant family lives and the contributions of parents to the schooling of their children; (ii) increased knowledge and confidence on the part of families to interact with teachers and school personnel; and (iii) improved trust in the school as a place of welcome and respect for migrant families. A side benefit of the study was the possibility of the researcher sharing second language pedagogies and strategies with teachers for use in their classes with EAL/D students.

6.3   The Literature

Migration literature in Australia is extensive and covers the topic from economic, social, political and increasingly ethnolinguistic perspectives. Migration holds particular significance for Australia: aside from Indigenous Australians, everyone else is the product of a migration story with Australia continuing to be one of the world's major 'immigration' nations, along with Canada, New Zealand and the United States (Organisation for Economic Co-operation and Development [OECD], 2014; Phillips & Simon-Davies, 2014). In terms of economic migration, that is, the recruitment of migrants to address labour market needs, the impact in Australia in terms of population, workplaces and the economy is unmatched in other advanced economies (Wright et al., 2016). Australia is seen as having managed its economic migration quite well, with high intakes of skilled and work-oriented migrants and the avoidance of large-scale social and political upheavals witnessed in other countries. Indeed, Australia has moved largely from its legacy as a settler country to one that issues more temporary than permanent visas (Collins, 2019; Wright et al., 2016). This shift away from permanent settlers to a three-times larger intake of temporary migrants, mainly international students, working holiday makers and skilled workers, is considered a major change in focus for Australian immigration policy. Consequently, there are calls for the social and economic effects of large-scale, long-term temporary migration to be researched more comprehensively (Collins, 2019; Phillips, 2013).

The study reported in this chapter links to economic migration because the skilled migrants moving to regional and rural areas in Australia are largely motivated by work opportunities and labour shortages. The literature below canvasses Australia's migration policy and visa categories in order to highlight the conditions, often precarious, surrounding families' experiences of living and working as temporary skilled workers in Australia. I also present literature on school-family connections and the experiences of migrant families in their interactions with schools in other settler countries, particularly the USA and Canada. Finally, theoretical concepts linking culture and connections are introduced, drawing on Anne Freadman's (2001) work on outsiderness and insiderness, and Iris Marion Young's (2006) concept of reciprocal responsibility in the formation of socially just connections. These principles provide the explanatory tools for understanding the complex nature of school-migrant connections in rural contexts undergoing cultural and social change. While the research presented here pertains to a rural community in Australia, the situation is mirrored throughout Australia and in other countries where communities are recruiting economic migrants to sustain workforces and deliver occupational expertise.

6.3.1 Migration Patterns in Australia

According to OECD (2019) data, the management of migration programmes is not restricted to Australia; indeed, many member countries are actively managing their temporary migration programmes to align with labour needs. In 2017 labour migration (also referred to as economic migration) increased significantly to 4.9 million people in OECD countries, a rise from 4.4 million in 2016 (OECD, 2019). Poland was the top recruiter, overtaking the USA. Australia's economic migrant intake increased by 1% in 2017. The clear orientation in OECD member countries' migration policies is resourcing labour demands and making adjustments that improve the selection of people with much needed skills (OECD, 2019).

In Australian migration policy, there are different visa categories—permanent and temporary—as introduced above. The permanent visa category comprises two programmes: (i) skilled migrants and families; and (ii) the Humanitarian programme for refugees and those in refugee-like situations (Phillips & Simon-Davies, 2014). The temporary visa category affects international students on study visas for the duration of their courses and long-term temporary skilled business visas, known previously as Sub-class 457 visa which was introduced in 1996 but renamed the Temporary Skill Shortage (TSS) visa (Sub-class 482) in 2017 (Department of Immigration and Border Protection [DIBP], 2017; Kettle, 2018). Visa adjustments are ongoing with the Australian government introducing two new temporary visas for regional workers as recently as December 2019—Sub-classes 489 and 491 (International English Language Testing System [IELTS], 2020). While numbers of permanent visas are capped by the Australian Government, temporary visas are uncapped and are issued in response to demand. Temporary visa holders can apply for permanent residency, although this transition is subject to certain conditions such as age, skill assessments, health checks and English language proficiency levels. Recent shifts in government policy have mandated English language proficiency in speaking, listening, reading and writing at IELTS level 6—Competent English user—in order to be eligible for permanent residency (IELTS, 2020).

Another consideration in Australia is the management of migration of supply workers to regional and rural areas; indeed, managed migration in state- and regional-based schemes has long been a feature of Australian policy (Hugo et al., 2006). In 2015–2016, three in ten skilled migrants in the state of Queensland where the study was conducted were sponsored under the Regional Sponsored Migration Scheme (RSMS) which "enables employers in regional and low population growth areas to sponsor a highly skilled worker from overseas … to live and work in regional Australia" (The State of Queensland [Queensland Treasury] 2019, p. 7). An example of regional migration is the town of Biloela in central Queensland which hosts a total population of approximately 5750. Biloela has been named by the Regional Australia Institute (2017) as an exemplar town for welcoming migrants and increasing the workforce in the local abattoir and on farms, as well as in medical and aged care facilities and schools.

For the skilled migrants in the study, their town was closer than Biloela to a large regional centre and the state capital of Brisbane. They were on 457 visas under the nominated category of "skilled meat worker". Many of the women identified their jobs as slicers while their husbands or partners were often involved with the heavier work of boning. The meat industry labour agreement defines their duties as including "cutting meat to separate meat, fat and tissue from around bones" (Department of Immigration and Border Protection [DIBP], n.d.). The agreement requires that they have a level of English (IELTS Level 5—Modest User of English) and that their workplace—the abattoirs—provide language support such as the use of interpreters and multilingual signs. While concerns about the exploitation of temporary migrants, especially those from non-English-speaking backgrounds, have been raised (e.g. Collins, 2019; Phillips, 2013), the concerns among many of the Brazilian migrants in the study were the precariousness of their employment. The instability included shift reductions due to a lack of cattle during droughts and bushfires, as well as the high IELTS English language score required at the end of their 3.5–4 year visa period to avoid being sent back to Brazil with their children.

6.3.2 School-Family Connections

As noted above, the current policy settings in Queensland favour successful part-nering relationships between schools and parents as a means of improving student learning and wellbeing (The State of Queensland [Department of Education], 2019). Operating in conjunction with this policy is the priority for inclusive practices that support communication between schools and families from diverse backgrounds. In the school-family connections literature, a definitive report is that by Henderson and Mapp (2002) which reviewed and synthesised studies on the nature of these connections and their impact on student achievement in the USA. The selection of 51 studies in the report was guided by research on high-performing schools in the USA (e.g. Mayer, Mullens, & Moore, 2000) which found that high levels of parent and community involvement is one of the characteristics promoting student performance at school. The synthesis of studies by Henderson and Mapp (2002) focussed on family involvement in schools across all levels and regions of the USA as well as diverse populations in terms of income, ethnicity, educational level and occupation. The synthesis also included studies with different research methodologies and designs. The resulting report summarises key findings as follows (Henderson & Mapp, 2002, pp. 7–8):

- Students with involved parents in their school, irrespective of background and income, were more likely to: achieve higher grades and pass their classes; attend school regularly; have better social skills adjustment to school and classroom behaviour; graduate successfully and progress to postsecondary education.
- While some studies found that parents from all income, ethnic and education-level groups supported their children's learning at home, the most involved at school tended to be white, middle-class families.
- Teacher outreach to parents was found to make a difference to students' learning and was strongly associated with significant gains in students' performances in reading and maths.
- Schools successfully engaging with families from diverse backgrounds had three common characteristics: (i) a focus on building trusting relationships among teachers, families and community members; (ii) recognition and respect of families' needs as well as cultural and class differences; and (iii) embrace of a philosophy of partnership where "power and responsibility are shared" (p. 7).

While Henderson and Mapp (2002) highlight positives associated with successful school-family connections, Suárez-Orozco, Onaga, and de Lardemelle (2010) detail the particularities of migrant experiences which mitigate against successful partnerships. In their research with immigrant adolescents and their families in the USA, Suárez-Orozco et al. found that long hours of work and other parental obligations can reduce the amount of time that family members spend together. This reduces the capacity of parents to act as buffers for their children against the challenges of the migration experience. In addition, the faster acculturation and language development of their children means that some immigrant parents relinquish authority to their children, placing the children in sometimes stressful interpreter and language brokering roles. Other experiences relate to parental cultural expectations and/or a sense of dislocation in which parents entrust their children's education to the teachers, perpetuating a perception in the school that the parents are uninvolved in their children's education (Suárez-Orozco et al., 2010).

Misinterpretations on the part of teachers about a lack of migrant parent involvement have also been noted in Canadian research (Guo, 2011). Working with mainly

Chinese-background families, the research found that cultural and linguistic differences often prevented migrant parents from intervening in their children's education. Indeed, some families seldom attended school functions because their cultural expectations were that visits to the school occur only when their children are in trouble. Parents, however, cared passionately about their children's education and often used informal means such as the internet to inform themselves about the unfamiliar Canadian school system (Guo, 2011).

The specificity of education in rural settings with increasing multilingual migrant family settlement has been explored in some US research (e.g. Coady, 2019). As identified in other research, teachers in the US rural schools felt ill-equipped to address the linguistic and cultural differences of the students and their families, intensified by the geographical isolation and limited access to financial and social resources. Coady (2019) argues that the teachers deemed the differences were 'barriers' that impeded communication, connections and trust-building. For their part, the immigrant parents' concerns included fears about job stability, worries about their perceived lack of English and education, and challenges with how to support their children's education. The conclusion in the research was that school engagement with rural-based multilingual immigrant families needs to be contextualised and differentiated, with foundations in trust and care.

6.3.3 Theorising Cultural Practices and Socially just Connections

The literature above canvasses the factors that have been found to contribute to and mitigate against effective school-family connections. For the purpose of interpreting and understanding the data in the current study, theories of socially just connections and cross-cultural awareness were utilised. To begin, however, it is useful to consider theorisations by Piller and Lising (2014) about globalised food production and the place of workers, notably temporary skilled workers in large abattoirs such as those employing the migrants in this study. Piller and Lising (2014) argue that temporary meatworkers often live in small towns in rural Australia, or what they call Tiny Town, and work at large abattoirs that are key sources of income in Tiny Town—what the authors call Big Beef. The workers arrive in Australia without high levels of English and have few opportunities to improve their English language proficiency, either at work or in the community. The authors take a socially critical perspective arguing that the competitive nature of the global beef market means Big Beef uses English language proficiency (among other mechanisms) to manipulate flexibility into the labour supply; the migrant meatworkers are "little cogs in the global machine of neoliberal capitalism" (Piller & Lising, 2014, p. 56).

The precariousness of work conditions for temporary migrants is also the focus of Young's (2006) work on a social connection model of responsibility and global justice, although her example is sweatshops and the conditions in the global apparel industry. Young (2006, p. 130) argues that "global social and economic processes bring individuals and institutions into ongoing structural connection with one another" and that all stakeholders have a shared responsibility to ensure justice. The model recognises social cooperation and argues its value over blame as a means of ensuing justice not only for ourselves but for others as we are increasingly drawn into a system of social and economic interdependence. To define what socially just connection looks like, Young proposes a number of features: (i) promoting universal responsibility for all involved in the institutions and practices of interdependence; (ii) making visible the interactions within practices of interdependence with the view to effecting change, thus a forward-looking process of change that seeks "to enjoin those who participate by their actions in the process of collective action" (p. 122); and (iii) the sharing of responsibility for collective action by individuals, irrespective of privilege. Her point is that these conditions are necessary for the formation of socially just connections.

Young's notion of shared responsibility for justice evokes Freadman's (2001) work on cultural shift. Freadman (2001) argues the need for individuals in cross-cultural encounters to recognise how connections are made. By this she means the strategies that mediate cultural familiarity and unknownness. These concepts go to cultural "insiderness" and "outsiderness" and the ways that these social experiences can be mediated by action, for example, insiders enabling the passage of outsiders to the "inside" of accepted practices. The combined work presented above provides the explanatory tools for the actions and outcomes of the research study and the efforts of the school principal, teachers, parents, students and researcher to establish improved school-migrant family connections.

6.4 The Study

The study reported here built on an earlier Australian Research Council (ARC) project (ID:LP130100469) that focused on fostering digital participation in regional and rural communities. The project comprised a social living lab using technology to support and upskill volunteer home tutors teaching English language communication to migrant women employed in the abattoirs (see Kettle, 2018). The genesis of the current study was the recommendation of one of the home tutors to meet the high school principal; the tutor worked at the school and was aware of the principal's concern about the engagement and learning of the EAL students, particularly the Brazilians. The closeness of the community is such that some of the Brazilian women and their families in the ARC project also volunteered to participate in the current study.

The school principal was relatively new at the school, arriving from a large high school in a regional city with a significant Indigenous population and growing enrolments of refugee-background students. He was respectful of cultural and linguistic diversity, and alert to the need for greater connections with migrant families:

I don't think there is a good connection and it's got to be fostered. We have International Day and that's great and people come in and we dance and we have food and we sing and share those cultures. It's pretty amazing. … I would never change that, but it probably is tokenistic to some extent.

For him the importance of connections lay in their potential to promote student learning:

I want the parents to feel that they are part of this place and they can come here and talk to the kid's maths teacher or the head of the maths department or me – eventually so we are a partnership.

The subsequent study adopted a qualitative approach designed to collect a rich account of the experiences of the school personnel and migrant families in their inter-actions and expectations about schooling. The objective was to generate a descrip-tion of the participants' social reality of schooling and home life through verbal and graphic data that were trustworthy and transparent (Holliday, 2015). Moreover, it was intended that the research study would have elements of transferability, in other words, the descriptions would be rich enough to enable other researchers to evaluate the applicability of the study to their situations and practices (Lew, Yang, & Harklau, 2018).

The participants in the current study were the school principal, five English teachers (from a total teaching staff of 35), 13 students with parental permission and 10 families comprising either one or two parents. All were volunteers who had been invited by the school principal and teacher aide (the home tutor introduced above) to consider participating in the study. The researcher also met with the students to explain the objective and design of the study, with an invitation to discuss participa-tion with their parents. The teachers taught English as a compulsory subject and were therefore involved with all EAL students across multiple grade levels. The families were predominately Brazilian (9) and Filipino (1) with the students ranging from Grade 9–12 in the school (Table 6.1).

The data collection involved focus groups with the teachers, students and some families, and interviews with the school principal and other families as well as photo-graph collections from the students. (See Table 6.2 for a sample of the interview and focus group questions).

While the data collection with the school principal, teachers and students occurred at the school, the interviews and focus groups with parents took place away from the

Table 6.1 Profiles of the student participants

Grade	Nationality	Number and Sex
9	Brazilian	Female: 5 Male: 1
10	Brazilian	Male: 3
11	Brazilian	Male: 2
12	Filipino Brazilian	Female (Filipino): 1 Male (Brazilian): 1

Table 6.2 Participant groups with a sample of the interview questions

Participants	Interview and focus group questions
School principal	• Currently how do you see the connections between migrant families and the school? • Would you like to improve the connections? Why? • How do you propose improving connections?
English teachers	• Do you have many migrant-background students in your English classes? • What are the connections between you and the families of the migrant-background students? • Would you like to increase levels of interaction? Why/why not? How can you do this?
EAL/D students	• What is it like being a student at school with a (Brazilian/Filipino) background and home life? • What is it like operating across two communities? Do you enjoy it? Why? Why not? • How does your family interact with the school? Would you like more contact? Why? How?
Migrant parents	• Do you have much contact with your child's school? Why? Why not? • Do you feel comfortable going to the school? Why? Why not? • Would you like more contact with the school? Why? Why not? How can this occur?

school. Most interviews were conducted at the public town library but one was held in the participant's home between work shifts at the abattoir. The choice of the non-school public space was a response to feedback about parents' reluctance to come to the school and respect for their time and commitment to the study. All arrived at the library after a long day's work at the abattoirs while the Filipino mother worked in aged care and attended before her shift in the morning. As an acknowledgement of their participation, the parents received vouchers for the local supermarket.

While the study had a descriptive focus, it was also had an advocatory function that was directed at social change. The photographs by the students of their "school at home" space were designed to inform teachers of what the students' homes looked like and to dispel misconceptions about families' lack of engagement with their children's education. Further to the advocatory and transformative focus of the study, a culminating social event for all participants and interested school staff was held at the school. The event included afternoon tea and was intended as a gentle *entré* for parents into the school. At the social event, the researcher provided a rich picture of all participant groups' concerns, expectations and aspirations for school-family connection. For all the participants, it was the first time they had come together and provided a lively opportunity to discuss and negotiate possibilities for the future. As is often the case with qualitative research, the collection and analysis of data are often not separate (Holliday, 2015) and a description of the social event and its outcomes is presented at the end of this chapter.

The analysis proceeded incrementally with gradual focusing (Holliday, 2015) around codes such as key words and topics, and the assembling of themes. Following

the literature, key topics included student EAL/D proficiency, academic requirements, school-family contact and communication and migrant workplace conditions. The ensuing findings and arguments were finessed by the understandings of
socially responsible connections and collective action. The focus of the analysis was
to illuminate each stakeholder group's circumstances for the purpose of building
cross-cultural awareness and "insiderness"—the conditions for change and greater
connection.

6.5   Building Connections: Conditions and Processes

6.5.1   The School Principal and Teachers

The school principal reported that on arrival in the town, he had expected the small
community to be "a very white bread place" but found that both Indigenous and
migrant students, particularly from Brazilian and Filipino backgrounds, were significant parts of the school population. He was familiar with the research that shows
"the better the connection between families and the school, the better the results for
the kids" and considered this a key reason "for good parental contact with everyone".
But he identified that every high school "struggles to engage people because once you
leave primary school … it's a whole different dimension" with a notable difference
in secondary school being the involvement of multiple teachers and discrete subject
areas. The principal offered high praise to the teachers at the school but acknowledged their challenges teaching second language migrant students: "The teachers
here …really genuinely care about all the kids but they certainly feel inadequate in
their delivery to the kids who are EAL/D".

The principal was interested in the responses of the parents and students to the
research questions about ways to better promote communication with families. He
listed initiatives by the school: Facebook, "an amazing newsletter" with online and
paper copies; parent forums; an informal café for parent drop-ins; surveys; and an
electronic sign at the front of the school. He acknowledged that a significant number
of migrant parents worked at the meatworks and "are hard to contact". Out of concern,
the school had established an arrangement with the meatworks to pass on messages
to parents when the school's text messages to personal mobile phones elicited no
response. Despite the initiatives, the principal conceded he had no idea whether
migrant families were engaging with school information and was buoyed by the
possibilities in the study to hold a social event bringing stakeholders together at the
school:

> You (the researcher) have asked the kids as to how we can better communicate and you've
> asked the parents too. …How do we fix the communication problem? …I'd love to, if we
> could have a meeting with everyone who's from those (migrant) circumstances and they
> could tell me what they want. I'm up for anything.

The teachers, for their part, were mostly concerned about classroom level issues; these included students' English language capabilities, curriculum content and teaching methods, student length of residence in Australia, class behaviour, and reporting student progress to parents. The teachers' classes consisted of about one-fifth of EAL/D students; for example, two students in the combined Grade 11/12 class and five in the Grade 9 class of 23. The majority were Brazilian-background students who all spoke Portuguese at home. The small numbers meant the teachers were familiar with the students and their circumstances in class but the overall size of the school and its remoteness from the regional centre led the teachers to worry about the lack of community services; one commented that the town was "a dead zone"; another said that it was "like a nether region" with few services to support students and their families.

When referring to the English language proficiency, the teachers consistently referenced the length of time that the students had been in the school, and indeed, in Australia. They were cognisant that the language issue was not just English grammar but also school-based text knowledge: "it's not English; it's literacy". The teachers were mindful that cultural differences might exist among Brazilian families about education, for example, about attending meetings on time and bonding over food, but also recognised that "you can't lump all Brazilians in together …about their values and attitudes around education and learning". One teacher provided an account of a planning interview with a Brazilian student's father and noted that he was "very engaged and very interested in it and (the student) knew what she wanted to do". The teachers were in agreement that the parents' aspirations for their children post-school did not include employment in the abattoirs. One teacher's experience was that "the (parents) that come into meetings have said 'education's important; we want our kids to do well but we don't know what our kids are doing; we don't know what we're supposed to do'".

Like the parents, the teachers' accounts also highlighted concerns about not knowing what to do, except for them, the "not knowing" related to second language teaching pedagogies and how best to meet their EAL/D students' learning needs. One teacher expressed the universal view: "We've got no clue. …We're staggering around in the dark. We're finding out by accident what works with our kids". Despite self-doubts about their expertise and effectiveness, the teachers articulated numerous strategies that indeed, align with pedagogical recommendations for teaching second language students, including scaffolded tasks to promote cumulative learning; explicit teaching of text types such as paragraphs; multiple modes of providing instructions, e.g. visual, oral and graphics on posters; and conscious groupings of EAL/D students with more proficient English speakers (e.g. Gibbons, 2002; Hammond & Miller, 2015). Not so successful strategies for the teachers' included the use of Google Translate which they found time-consuming (three hours per night) and inaccurate. One teacher reported spending hours translating curriculum documents on the health effects of smoking, ending with students' "killing themselves laughing because of the way it came out in the translator". Most of the teachers described learning some words of Portuguese which they used in class, for example: "I've learned how to say *good morning* and *be quiet* and *hurry up*".

In terms of contact with families, the teachers were concerned about the lack of communication: "I've never spoken to any of (my EAL students') families, except one". Their attempts to communicate included leaving messages on answering machines and sending letters home. The teachers' rationale for communication was to provide support and report behaviour problems such as a lack of punctuality or poor attendance at school. For example, one teacher argued that she wanted to talk to parents more about, "what things they could be doing at home that would provide further support to what we're giving their kids in class, because we only have a small amount of time (with the students)—three times a week".

6.5.2   The EAL Students

All of the 13 students interviewed in the study were born overseas in either Brazil (12) or the Philippines (1). Of the 12 Brazilian students, all had school experiences that reflected economic migration and mobility in the meat processing industry, either to Australia after some schooling in Brazil or among Australian towns and cities with abattoirs. Three of the students in Grade 9 were from families that had migrated to Australia together, settling in another city before moving collectively to the current town. Two boys—in Grade 10 and 11—had been at the school for only two months, after their families had moved from a rural town in New South Wales and the Queensland capital, Brisbane, respectively. Only two of the students (in Grade 9) had undertaken all of their schooling in the town. The Filipino girl's parents were also economic migrants, with her mother initially leaving the family in the Philippines to work as a doctor's assistant in Saudi Arabia. On her return, the father left for Australia where he was employed as a motor mechanic in a remote town, and had relocated to the current town when his family joined him. The Filipino student started school in the current town in Grade 6 and at the time of the study had been voted one of the school's Grade 12 leaders o f he year.

The two Grade 9 Brazilian students noted that their parents were interested in becoming more involved at the school with one saying: "It is important for both families and schools to interact so the parents know what's happening and how they can help their children get better at school and get a better education". The interest of these families and the commitment to their children's education was evident in their attendance at the social event at the end of the study, despite never visiting the school before. In addition, most of the students talked of their parents' involvement in homework, particularly in relation to time management and social media use. For example, one student reported: "If I'm on my phone in the afternoon (mum's) like, do your stuff first, do your homework, get all that done, then go on your phone". In addition, the students described their "school at home" spaces, including office-type arrangements with a computer and printer, as well as the kitchen table (See Fig. 6.1 as an example).

The students' experiences also included extensive language brokering duties for their parents and other family members. Language brokering means that the students

Fig. 6.1 Home spaces for school-related work

were responsible for mediating the communication between their parents and key community members, due to their bilingual proficiency in the home language and English as the language of the community. The students referred to translating forms such as a driver's licence application, as well as interpreting in doctor's consultations and hospital appointments. One student reported that her mother always attended parent-teacher interviews at the school but wanted her daughter to accompany her, because "although she understands (English) but she doesn't speak; she's afraid of speaking". Another student talked of missing a week at school after his mother had two operations on her arm and he had to help her at home and also act as the language broker at the hospital. For him and his friends there was a great reluctance to share family information with the school, particularly about medical conditions: "it's a personal thing about your mum and stuff; something that the school wouldn't really have to know".

For some of the students, their continuous language brokering duties and their parents' low English proficiency meant that they saw little benefit in their parents meeting with teachers; at home, the students had to translate emails from the school for their parents and according to one student: "I don't like asking (my parents to go to the school) because they wouldn't understand it anyway since they don't really know how to speak English….So I just like do my own stuff with my teachers". For these students, it was understood that their parents, particularly their mothers, were in Australia primarily to see the children through school after which they would return to Brazil: "Work is too hard here compared to the life (my mother) can have over there".

6.5.3 The Migrant Parents

All the Brazilian parents attended the research interviews accompanied by their son or daughter who brokered communication between the parents and the researcher using English and Portuguese. The Filipino mother attended unaccompanied with the interview conducted in English.

The parents were universally interested in their children incorporating positive aspects of Australian culture into their lives but were also concerned about the maintenance of home culture and values, particularly language. For the Brazilians, this was in part because of their ongoing connection with family in Brazil and continuous mobility between the two countries. Families regularly returned home for holidays and at times were forced back to Brazil by family emergencies and visa issues. Some mothers contacted their families, notably their mothers regularly, sometimes daily, using communication apps such as Skype and Whatsapp. The cultural significance accorded to mothers and family ties aligned with one Brazilian student's comment: "I miss my grandma all the time because … every Sunday we talked to each other – and we just had this connection. Sometimes I do feel connected to Brazil". The preservation of Portuguese was a priority for the Brazilian parents especially reading and writing; one means of promoting Portuguese was through faith-based practices and the use of a Portuguese-language bible in church services.

All the families in the study, including the Filipino family, were in Australia on 457 visas. The decision for many of them was whether to progress from temporary visa status to permanent residency and then to citizenship. One student, interpreting for her mother, indicated her mother's goal was "permanent yeah and she's going to learn English to do the citizenship (test)". English proficiency was a worry for many of the parents although they conceded that they did not need much English on the production line at the meatworks. Portuguese signage was on display and most of the co-workers were either from Brazil or other countries, with only the occasional English-speaking Australian on the line.

The parents indicated overwhelming concern for their children's education, and indeed education was the motivation for many of them staying in Australia. Successful graduation from school in Australia meant a better future. One student reported her mother's comment: "My mum always tells me that if I'm not taking school seriously, they'll just put me in the abattoir. So like, it's her biggest nightmare for me to not take school seriously. She says that she never wants me to work there, in the abattoir". Echoing Guo's (2011) findings with Chinese-background parents in Canada, many of the migrant parents in the study felt little need to go to the school if their child was doing well and not getting into trouble. One student commented about her mother: "She says that, like only when asked to go (to the school), otherwise she just thinks like, I'm doing fine". One father stated that he was more attentive to his children's schooling when they were in primary school, a point that resonates with the school principal's observation. For the Brazilian parents, the nature of work at the abattoirs (slicing for many of the women and boning for the men) together with the length of shifts—from 5 a.m. to 3:30 p.m.—saw them tired in the afternoons after work and facing cooking dinner and other family duties. Nonetheless they were mindful of homework and checked on their children; one mother reported: "I make sure my kids do homework. Reading something".

A consistent theme in terms of assistance with schoolwork was the role of fathers. Many of the parents and students reported that it was the father who assisted them, often because he had greater English language proficiency. This student's account echoed that of many others: "We speak a lot, like always Portuguese, and then mum still barely speaks English so my dad is the one that basically helps us with our homework, if we need help". Several of the fathers indicated that they wanted to establish more contact with the school but were unable to because of the timing of school meetings:

> I think the ways for we to have more contact, that's my opinion, like, the school want to see the parent, they (should) make timings like we would be finishing, I suppose, 4:30. … But if you (say) – I want to see you two o'clock – we at work; we can't leave the work and come here.

Reflecting the participatory nature of the research, one father—with the assistance of his daughter—asked if the researcher could negotiate better meeting times with the school:

Father: Can you help us about that or not? … Please to organise this time for me to come.

Daughter: Like, would you be able to somehow talk to (the school) and make it easier for our parents to come in and talk to the them, like, about everything that's happening with everything?

6.6 Emerging Connections: Discussion

The participatory nature of the study meant that it had the dual function of generating rich experiential data about the participants as well as engaging them in interactions that were transformational in terms of their relationships with each other. The reflexive nature of the research meant that participation derived from a commitment to change that itself drove change, and an increased participation and connection between the stakeholders. The study functioned as a critical intervention that was enabled by a shared commitment to education and action, with people sacrificing valuable resources such as time to meet and engage in the study. Young (2006) notes it is with a sense of shared responsibility and a will to interdependence that collective action is possible. Generated through the study, a number of forward-focused actions were initiated between the school and families which lay the foundation for establishing and sustaining connections.

6.6.1 A Combined Social Event

The event was held at the school several months after the study was completed with participants invited by email as well as texts to the parents. All the teachers and professional staff at the school were invited to the event which was scheduled for 4 pm–5 pm in the school library and catered with afternoon tea. The event was a success, bringing together 16 people who had never interacted previously: the principal, teachers, a Head of Department, professional staff such as the attendance officer and chaplain, and Brazilian families who were at the school for the first time. The interactions were lively and comfortably bilingual, with fathers determined to use English and mothers speaking in Portuguese that was translated by the children. The event programme included a Powerpoint presentation by the researcher of the findings on each participant group's concerns about school-migrant family connections; an address from the principal with an invitation to families to engage in ongoing connection and communication; and questions from teachers and professional staff about ways to improve their teaching and communication with bilingual families. After the meeting, people continued to talk with each other, notably the principal and several fathers discussing the possibility of forming a migrant parent advisory group.

6.6.2 Changed Workplace Practices and the Parent Advisory Group

Several weeks after the social event the school principal wrote to Brazilian and Filipino-background families in Portuguese and Tagalog, inviting them to consider forming a parent advisory group. The Brazilian response was positive and led him to negotiate a change of shift-times with the abattoirs' management which enabled the parents to be paid while attending a meeting. The principal's subsequent email to the researcher was as follows:

> Thought you might like to see positive action from your input. Letter to all Braz homes-translated by (student name). I have got (company name) to agree to pay them for the hour of work while they attend the meeting- now that's something!

The first meeting of the principal and the Brazilian parents occurred at an abattoir three months later: "Had our first meeting with the Braz focus/reference group last week! Yeah. 5 parents. It was good to make a start".

6.6.3   Recruitment of a Community Liaison Officer and Further Research

Subsequent initiatives by the school have been the employment of a community liaison officer who is Brazilian and a former student at the school. In addition, the school and Brazilian families have committed to participation in further research, this time a Department of Education-funded study investigating the use of home languages—in this case, Portuguese—in the teaching and learning of Australian curriculum content.

These initiatives by the school principal and teachers with uptake by the parents and students are incremental but nonetheless, cumulative and forward-focused; each development creates momentum and possibilities for the next. Following Young (2006), the emerging connections between the school and migrant families appear built on tentative but growing trust forged from contact and communication. There is a shared responsibility by all stakeholders to participate in the forums aimed at improving students' academic outcomes and experiences at school. Central to bringing the stakeholders together was the research study, which itself built on previous connections with migrant families. The participatory nature of the study meant that it collected and made visible the practices of each group, which until then, had been invisible to the others. The school principal and teachers learned for the first time about the social and economic conditions of being a temporary migrant in Australia including the aspirations of migrant parents for their children.

The students heard about the care and concerns of their teachers, and the parents learned about the Australian curriculum and the benefits of family connections for learning as well as teachers' expectations for student behaviour and engagement. Together these new insights formed a new critical awareness that began the process of diminishing separateness and what Freadman (2001) calls the *outsiderness* of each group. Rather, a collective *insiderness* for all with each other was initiated. The collective action of the school personnel and families comprised not only committing to the study but also to the responsibility of being an agent of change, at a personal level and also in unison with others. This approach fostered an understanding of agency as a universal attribute including for migrant families and presented them as concerned and able partners in the development of connections with teachers and schools.

6.7   Conclusion

The study presented here was located in the dynamics of economic migration and the rise of long-term temporary migration in Australia. In particular, it focused on the settlement of temporary skilled migrants in rural towns for work in industries such as agriculture, food processing and social services, and the implications for their children in schools. Little research has been done on the teaching and learning of EAL/D students in Australian rural schools and in response, this study adopted a participatory approach to make visible the experiences of a rural high school community experiencing considerable social and cultural change as a result of growing migrant enrolments. The participants in the study comprised the school principal, English teachers, EAL/D students and their parents who worked mainly in abattoirs and aged care. The study garnered their respective accounts of teaching, learning, leadership and migration to provide a comprehensive picture of the experiences and expectations of schooling and to lay the foundation for growing connections that promote cross-cultural awareness and mutually responsible collective action.

Acknowledgements This research project was funded by a QUT Women in Research grant—Ethics ID:1700000836.

References

Australian Bureau of Statistics (ABS). (2018). *Australian demographic statistics, December 2017*. Retrieved from http://www.abs.gov.au/Ausstats/ABS@.nsf/7d12b0f6763c78caca257061001cc588/fa9c11f1913bdafcca25765100098359!OpenDocument.

Australian Curriculum, Assessment and Reporting Authority [ACARA]. (2015). *What does the ICSEA value mean?* Retrieved from https://docs.acara.edu.au/resources/About_icsea_2014.pdf.

Australian Curriculum, Assessment and Reporting Authority [ACARA]. (2019). *My school*. Retrieved from https://www.myschool.edu.au/.

Coady, M. R. (2019). *Connecting school and the multilingual home: Theory and practice for rural educators*. Bristol: Multilingual Matters. https://doi.org/10.21832/COADY3262.

Collins, J. (2019). Migration to Australia in times of crisis. In C. Menjívar, M. Ruiz, & I. Ness (Eds.), *The Oxford handbook of migration crises* (pp. 817–831). New York, NY: Oxford University Press.

Department of Immigration and Border Protection (DIBP). (n.d.). *Meat industry labour agreement*. Retrieved from http://www.border.gov.au/Trav/Work/Empl/Labour-agreements/meat-industry.

Department of Immigration and Border Protection (DIBP). (2017). *Abolition and replacement of the 457 visa: Government reforms to employer sponsored skilled migration visas*. Retrieved from http://www.border.gov.au/Trav/Work/457-abolition-replacement.

Freadman, A. (2001). The culture peddlers. *Postcolonial Studies: Culture, Politics, Economy, 4*(3), 275–295. https://doi-org.ezp01.library.qut.edu.au/10.1080/13688790120102651.

Gibbons, P. (2002). *Scaffolding language; scaffolding learning: Teaching second language learners in the mainstream classroom*. Portsmouth, NH: Heinemann.

Guo, Y. (2011). Beyond deficit paradigms: Exploring informal learning of immigrant parents. *The Canadian Journal for the Study of Adult Education, 24*(1), 41–59.

Halliday, M. A. K. (1985). *Spoken and written language*. Melbourne, VIC: Deakin University Press.

Hammond, J., & Miller, J. (Eds.). (2015). *Classrooms of possibility: Supporting at-risk EAL students*. Newtown: Primary English Teaching Association Australia (PETAA).

Henderson, A. T., & Mapp, K. L. (2002). *A new wave of evidence: The impact of school, family and community connections on students' achievement. Annual synthesis 2002*. Austin, TX: Southwest educational Development Lab.

Holliday, A. (2015). Qualitative research and analysis. In B. Paltridge & A. Phakiti (Eds.), *Research methods in applied linguistics: A practical resource* (pp. 49–62). London: Bloomsbury.

Hugo, G., Khoo S-E., & McDonald P. (2006). Attracting skilled migrants to regional areas: What does it take? *People and place, 14*(3), 26–36.

International English Language Testing System [IELTS]. (2020). *Five tips to claim superior English for your Points Test Visa.* Retrieved from https://ielts.com.au/articles/5-tips-to-claim-superior-english-for-your-points-test-visa/.

Kainth, S. (2018, October 15). New plan to settle migrants in regional areas. *Special Broadcasting Service (SBS).* Retrieved from https://www.sbs.com.au/language/english/new-plan-to-settle-migrants-in-regional-areas_1.

Kettle, M. (2018). Connecting digital participation and informal language education: Home tutors and migrants in a rural community. In M. Dezuanni, M. Foth, K. Mallan, & H. Hughes (Eds.), *Digital participation through social living labs—valuing local knowledge, enhancing engagement* (pp. 173–190). Cambridge, UK: Chandos Publishing.

Kettle, M., & Ryan, M. (2018). Using reflexivity to explain transitions in second language writing: Implications for international postgraduate students' academic success. In K. Spelman Miller & M. Stevenson (Eds.), *Transitions in writing* (pp. 169–198). Leiden, Netherlands: Brill.

Koziol, M. (2019, November 22). Government wants half of new refugees to be settled in 'regional' Australia by 2022. *The Sydney Morning Herald.* Retrieved from https://www.smh.com.au/politics/federal/government-wants-half-of-new-refugees-to-be-settled-in-regional-australia-by-2022-20191121-p53ct1.html.

Lew, S., Yang, A. H., & Harklau, L. (2018). Qualitative methodology. In A. Phakiti, P. De Costa, L. Plonsky, & S. Starfield (Eds.), *The Palgrave handbook of applied linguistics research methodology* (pp. 79–101). London: Palgrave Macmillan.

Mayer, D. P., Mullens, J. E., & Moore, M. T. (2000). *Monitoring school quality: An indicators report.* Washington, DC: Department of Education. National Center for Education Statistics. ED450473. http://nces.ed.gov/pubs2001/2001030.pdf.

Organisation for Economic and Cultural Development (OECD, September 18). (2019). *Humanitarian migration falls while labour and family migration rises.* Retrieved from https://www.oecd.org/migration/humanitarian-migration-falls-while-labour-and-family-migration-rises.htm.

Organisation for Economic and Cultural Development (OECD). (2014). *Migration policy debates: Who should be admitted as a labour migrant?* Retrieved from http://www.oecd.org/migration.

Phillips, J. (2013, March 13). *Temporary skilled migration and the 457 visa.* Parliament of Australia: Parliamentary library. Retrieved from http://www.file.com///C:/Users/Margaret%20Kettle/Documents/Articles%20and%20Publications%202017/Oakey_Social%20Living%20Lab/Temporary%20skilled%20migration%20and%20the%20457%20visa%20%e2%80%93%20Parliament%20of%20Australia.html.

Phillips, J., & Simon-Davies, J. (2014, May 14). *Migration to Australia: A quick guide to the statistics.* Parliament of Australia: Parliamentary library. Retrieved from https://apo.org.au/sites/default/files/resource-files/2014/05/apo-nid39659-1113921.pdf.

Piller, I., & Lising, L. (2014). Language, employment and settlement: Temporary meat workers in Australia. *Multilingua, 33*(1–2), 35–59. https://doi.org/10.1515/multi-2014-0003.

Regional Australia Institute. (2017). *Connecting migrants with new opportunities.* Retrieved from http://www.regionalaustralia.org.au/home/connecting-migrants-new-opportunities/.

Regional Australia Institute. (2018). *The missing workers: Locally-led migration strategies to better meet rural labour needs.* Retrieved from http://www.regionalaustralia.org.au/home/wp-content/uploads/2018/06/180510-The-Regional-Australia-Institute-2018-The-missing-workers_policy-paper_FINAL.pdf.

Suárez-Orozco, C., Onaga, M., & de Lardemelle, C. (2010). Promoting academic engagement among immigrant adolescents through school-family-community collaboration. *American School Counselor Association [ASCA], 14*(1), 15–26.

The State of Queensland (Department of Education). (2018). *Advancing education: An action plan for education in Queensland.* Retrieved from http://advancingeducation.qld.gov.au/Pages/default.aspx.

The State of Queensland (Department of Education). (2019). *Parent and community engagement.* Retrieved from https://education.qld.gov.au/parents-and-carers/community-engagement.

The State of Queensland (Queensland Treasury). (2019). *Overseas migration, Queensland, 2017–2018*. Retrieved from File:///E:/Articles%20and%20publications_2019/Qld_overseas-migration-qld-2017-18.pdf.

Young, I. M. (2006). Responsibility and global justice: A social connection model. *Social Philosophy & Policy, 23*(01), 102–130. https://doi.org/10.1017/S0265052506060043.

van Kooy, J., & Wickes, R. (2019, April 1). Settling migrants in reginal areas will need more than a visa to succeed. *The Mandarin*. Retrieved from https://www.themandarin.com.au/106572-settling-migrants-in-regional-areas-will-need-more-than-a-visa-to-succeed/.

Wright, C. F., Clibborn, S., Piper, N., & Cini, N. (2016). *Economic migration and Australia in the 21st century*. Lowy Institute for International Policy. Retrieved from https://www.lowyinstitute.org/sites/default/files/wright_et_al_economic_migration_and_australia_in_the_21st_century_0_0.pdf.

Margaret Kettle is an Associate Professor, lecturer and researcher in TESOL at the Faculty of Education, Queensland University of Technology, Australia. She teaches second language education and sociolinguistics, and supervises doctoral students in areas including English for Specific Purposes (ESP), trans-languaging, and international education. Her research interests are second language teaching and learning in schools, universities and communities, especially in regional and rural areas. Currently she is leading a project on the use of home languages in secondary education for migrant students in rural schools. Her book *International student engagement in higher education: Transforming practices, pedagogies and participation* (2017) was published by leading TESOL publisher Multilingual Matters.

Chapter 7
Thriving School Enrichment Programs for Rural South African Schools

Mosebetsi Mokoena and Dipane Hlalele

Abstract This chapter documents conditions under which school enrichment programs at rural schools may thrive. A qualitative Participatory Action Research (PAR) was adopted in generating data. The workshops (group discussions) and prompts guided by the Free Attitude Interviews (FAI) were used to generate data from ten participants. Fairclough's Critical Discourse Analysis was used as a tool to analyse and interpret data. In this case, data was analysed at three different levels; interpretive, descriptive and explanatory. The findings indicated that an environment conducive for teaching and learning, provision of well-organised and diverse activities, the existence of effective monitoring team, the high-quality programming and staffing, and establishment of strong partnerships were identified as necessary conditions under which school enrichment programs at rural schools can thrive.

Keywords School enrichment program · Sustainable learning · Rural schools

7.1 Introduction

Despite the many interpretations throughout literature, School Enrichment Programs (SEP) are associated with concepts such as 'learning support' (Bojuwoye, Moletsane, Stoffile, Moolla, & Sylvester, 2014); extracurricular classes (Byun, Schofer, & Kim, 2012); 'supplementary tutoring' (Mogari, Coetzee, & Maritz, 2009); and 'school intervention strategies' (Department of Basic Education (DBE), 2012a). Considering the different forms that SEP can take, it is noteworthy to distinguish between private supplementary tutoring and supplementary or extra tutoring. In this case, Ireson and Rushforth (2011) argue that private supplementary tutoring is often undertaken for profit purposes while supplementary tutoring is centred on the need

M. Mokoena
Faculty of Education, University of the Free State, Qwaqwa Campus, Phuthaditjhaba, Free State, Republic of South Africa

D. Hlalele (✉)
School of Education, University of KwaZulu-Natal, Durban, KwaZulu-Natal, Republic of South Africa
e-mail: hlaleled@ukzn.ac.za

© Springer Nature Singapore Pte Ltd. 2021
S. White and J. Downey (eds.), *Rural Education Across the World*,
https://doi.org/10.1007/978-981-33-6116-4_7

to address curriculum-related issues, such as learners' academic underperformance. This chapter focuses on the latter form of SEP. Supplementary tutoring involves extended learning opportunities that learners are exposed to after the 'normal' school hours or during the vacations or problem-solving classes (Mogari et al., 2009). In a more broad definition of SEP, the Western Cape Department of Education (DBE) (2012b) includes both curricular and extracurricular aspects of these programs. For Bojuwoye et al. (2014), SEP can be summarised as '…education support services directed to learners' (p. 45).

The need for these programs in rural schools is initiated by various reasons. For example, SEP are seen to be effective means of addressing a number of challenges. These range from curriculum overload, lack of financial resources to educational corruption (Mogari et al., 2009). Secondly, schools have resorted to these programs to compensate time demands exerted by the use of learner-centred teaching and learning (Bray, 2012). This is particularly true in a country such as South Africa where learner-centred teaching and methods are at the centre of curriculum delivery. Lastly, SEP are used as a way to compensate for limited number of qualified teachers (Bradley, 2012; Mogari et al., 2009). This is particularly true in the rural areas where it has been observed that young qualified teachers are reluctant to work (Easton, Gereluk, Dressler, & Becker, 2017; Hlalele, 2013; Kline, White, & Lock, 2013).

In addition to the reasons discussed above, SEP have also been effective in many areas. These include addressing the needs relating to youth development, school-age childcare and expanded learning programs (Afterschool Alliance, 2014). Moreover, these programs result in high levels of intrinsic motivation and positive moods (Afterschool Alliance, 2014; Shernoff & Vandell, 2007; Zhang & Byrd, 2013). Furthermore, it was found that the SEP in Great Britain benefited learners from disadvantaged backgrounds (Mogari et al., 2009). Similarly, Hof (2014) states that a study by De Paola and Scoppa in 2014 using regression-discontinuity design, reported an improvement in academic performance among Italian learners.

7.2 South African Rural Schools in Context

The limited, and somewhat poor implementation of policies by the DBE continues to subject many rural schools to the conditions of dysfunctionality and deprivation. According to Ndandani (2001), educationally deplorable conditions have been 'normalised' in and around rural schools. These include inadequate resources, teacher shortages, high learner-drop-out rate and poverty (John, 2019; Mafora, 2013), among others. Nearly thirty years into democracy, there are rural communities which are still plagued by poor school infrastructure. For example, the 2018 reports estimate that many schools across South Africa are built with illegal material such as mud and asbestos (Equal Education, 2018b). These reports further reveal that the rural province of Eastern Cape counted almost 80% of these poorly built schools. In its progress report on Norms and Standards, the rural province of KwaZulu Natal is said to have 908 schools built with inappropriate material (KZNDoE, 2018).

In other instances, these schools have serious constructional and structural defects (Mafora, 2013). In its report, Equal Education (2018a) makes a similar observation about the poor workmanship that was done in many ablution facilities in poor public school around Gauteng. This resulted in over 90% of these facilities being unsafe for learners and teachers. Furthermore, the report indicates that in some schools 100 learners share one sanitary facility. The 2018 cross-country audit done by the DBE about the state of sanitation in schools across the nine provinces indicates that a total of 1598 schools had plain pit latrines. In this case, the rural province of Limpopo accounts for 765 of these cases (LDoE, 2018). The 2019 *National Educational Infrastructure Management System* (NEIMS) report indicates that there are about 3710 schools across South Africa that are using pit latrines as ablution facilities (DBE, Republic of South Africa, 2019). Once again, schools in the rural provinces such as Limpopo, KwaZulu Natal, Free State, and Eastern Cape have higher number of these facilities.

Apart from the poor state of the infrastructure, rural schools lack basic services such as electricity and water (Du Plessis & Mestry, 2019). The 2017 progress report by the Department of education in Limpopo points to a total of 6 schools without electricity (LDoE, 2017). In the same vein, the recent 2019 NEIMS states that 169 schools lack access to electricity in the two rural provinces of Eastern Cape and KwaZulu Natal (DBE, 2019). Moreover, this report highlights a total number of 484 schools using generators as an alternative form of electricity supply in these two rural provinces. In this regard, we are yet to establish how the noise generated from these generators affects the quality of teaching and learning in these schools. Similarly, the health hazards resulting from inhaling the poisonous gases from these machines cannot be ignored.

Closely related to access to electricity is having access to internet and Information Technology. While they do have limited access to the former, many rural schools still face challenges pertaining to the latter (Mihai, 2017). For example, according to NEIMS 2019 report, 87% of schools in the rural province of Eastern Cape do not have computer centres, 83% of schools in Limpopo and 63% of schools in KwaZulu Natal lack access to the internet. Consequently, Ndandani (2001) points to this as a contributory factor to low enrolments of students in the ICTs programs around the country's universities.

While limited access to information technology impacts negatively on the quality of teaching and learning, the systems of communication are also affected. As recent as 2019, almost 75 schools in the Eastern Cape are without any form of system of communication. Other rural provinces such as Limpopo and KwaZulu Natal have 51 and 24 schools respectively which are cut from the rest of the country in terms of communication systems (DBE, Republic of South Africa, 2019). While it is true that this situation cuts off the communication between the schools and parents, it further sets the schools far apart from the 'outside' world.

This situation is worsened by the fact that many of these schools are located in geographically inaccessible areas. In some instances, the poor state of road infrastructure and mountainous areas exacerbate the situation. In other instances, as is often the case with farm schools, learners need to travel long distances to school. In this regard, Ndandani (2001) states that these learners are often absent from school because their parents cannot fund their transportation to and from school. In recent years, however, the DBE has introduced the scholar transport for learners to address this challenge. These learners are ferried to and from schools.

With regard to water supply, the rural schools in South Africa still face a challenge. The recent report by the Council for Scientific and Industrial Research (CSIR) indicates that eight schools lack access to water in Limpopo province (LDoE, 2016). Contrastingly, the 2019 NEIMS states that all schools across the country have access to water. However, a high number of schools in rural provinces such as the Eastern Cape, Limpopo, KwaZulu Natal and Free State depend on rain-water harvesting as a form of water supply (DBE, Republic of South Africa, 2019). In this case, there is still a need to establish the sustainability of this form of water supply in these schools.

In addition to the state of dilapidation, deprivation and lack of safety in and around rural schools (Mestry & Khumalo, 2012), the quality of teaching and learning is negatively affected. Over-crowding is a common occurrence in rural classrooms (Hannaway, Govender, Marais, & Meier, 2019; Mafora, 2013). Consequently, many teachers in rural schools engage in multi-grade teaching (Hannaway et al., 2019). Among other things, multi-grade teaching is characterised by confining learners of different grades into one classroom and teaching them different subjects simultaneously (Du Plessis & Mestry, 2019). According to Blease and Condy (2015), at least 30% of primary schools in South Africa engage in multi-grade teaching. A large proportion of these schools are located in commercial farms and former homelands (Brown, 2010; Jacobs, Stals, & Leroy, 2016). Although farm schools constitute less than 6% of schooling in South Africa, they remain underdeveloped and underresourced (Bantwini & Feza, 2017). These authors further posit that dwindling population density in and around farms as well as high failure rate among learners in these schools are some of the contributory factors to this practice. Moreover, the failure to attract and retain qualified teachers in rural schools adds to this problem (Hannaway et al., 2019; Mafora, 2013; Ndandani, 2001).

While there is an exodus of teachers from farm schools in particular, the monetary incentive (rural allowance), however, seems to have succeeded in retaining some teachers in these schools. This is a monthly amount of money that teachers in farm schools receive as a form of an incentive. However, there still remains uncertainty around the sustainability of this form of compensation as well as its ability to attract young and recently qualified graduates to work in farm schools across the country. It would, perhaps be useful for policy makers to consider additional strategies that would '…enact teacher education curriculum with a consciousness of and attention to the concept of place' (White & Reid, 2008, p. 1).

Another factor compromising the quality of teaching involves lack of physical resources such as laboratories, and libraries (Blease & Condy, 2015; Jacobs et al., 2016). In most cases, the quality of teaching and learning in rural schools is hampered by the limited resources available (Ndandani, 2001). The 2019 NEIMS standard report indicates that over 80% of schools surveyed across South Africa do not have laboratories. It is noteworthy to indicate that majority of these schools are located in both rural and farm schools. As a direct result of this situation, in recent years there has been a decline in the enrolment of rural learners in Science related programs in the universities across the country. This report further reveals that only less than 8% of the surveyed schools in the rural province of Eastern Cape have a library. This is in comparison with 16 and 26% of schools with libraries in other rural provinces of KwaZulu Natal and Limpopo, respectively. Schools with libraries also face challenges which include teachers not using school libraries because they are unable to provide relevant information services due to a lack of space; out-dated and inadequate information collections; uncatalogued and poorly organised books; inaccessible opening hours; and a lack of funds and networked computers (Shandu, Evans, & Mostert, 2014).

South Africa still faces the challenges of underperformance of learners in rural schools. In 2008 the pass rate was 62.5% (Moloi, Dzvimbo, Potgieter, Wolhuter, & van der Walt, 2010). In the same year, the Mail & Guardian (2008) reported that 50% of grade 12 learners in the Eastern Cape failed in the final examinations. Brown (2011) adds that 28.7% of grade 12 learners in the Free State failed the final examinations between 2007 and 2009. Furthermore, in 2011 only 24.3% of learners exiting the education system qualified for university entrance (Mail & Guardian, 2012). In addition, less than a third of 562,112 full-time learners who wrote the National Senior Certificate examinations in 2013 qualified to progress towards a bachelor's qualification at university.

The Parliamentary Monitoring Group (PMG) (2015) indicated that rural education was a huge part of South Africa's history and in recognising the progress the country had made, not enough attention had been given to rural education and this needed to change. South Africa has 11,252 schools in rural areas across the country and of these, 3,060 were secondary schools and 8,192 were primary schools. The majority of these schools are in the rural provinces of Eastern Cape, KwaZulu-Natal and Limpopo. The country had a total of 5,153 multi-grade schools in the rural areas. Some rural schools also have residence facilities to help support learning in rural schools (Hlalele, 2019). A notable attempt to address the situation in South Africa is the Rural Education Policy (REP) (Department of Basic Education, 2018). The REP proposes:

> Rural education provisioning that capitalises on resources available in rural communities. The provision of quality education in rural schools requires not only targeted fiscal, but also civic agency, with the OBE working in collaboration with rural communities to mobilise resources (including socio- cultural, agricultural and natural resources, as well as indigenous knowledge systems). (p. 13)

Although the school under discussion has been implementing SEP for several years now, the school has failed to achieve the desired and sustainable academic performance of learners. While many studies on SEP have been carried out in the USA and other countries, there still remains the need to explore these programs in South Africa (Bradley, 2012; Taylor, Shindler, du Toit, & Mosselson, 2010) including rural schools. More specifically, with many studies focusing on evaluating the quality, successes and extent of SEP (Byun et al., 2012; Mogari et al., 2009; Toson, 2011), we are of the view that there are limited scientific studies which have focused on how these programs can be enhanced at rural schools. Specifically, the research on the circumstances under which such enhancement may thrive in rural schools is limited.

White (2015) advocates for the addition of 'rural' to all matters relating to 'education'. However, the concept 'rural' still remains nebulous as there is no universally accepted definition in the literature (Chigbu, 2013; Hlalele, 2012). In defining this concept, Miller (1993, as cited in Barter 2008) states that rural refers to '…any place where residents live in an unincorporated area or town of less than twenty-five thousand people and over thirty miles from an urban centre' (p. 470). In addition, McSwan et al. (1995, cited in Barter, 2008) define rural in terms of the four dimensions, namely, size, geographic location, culture and the services to which only urban people have access. For Kline et al. (2013) rural is often characterised by highly restricted access to essential community services. Moreover, Ward and Brown (2009, as cited in Chigbu, 2013) define rural as '…places of tradition rather than modernity, of agriculture rather than industry, of nature rather than culture, and of changelessness rather than dynamism' (p. 830). In some instances, researchers define rural along the racial lines (Sierk, 2017). For instance, in the South African context, rural was, and continues to be, associated with being black, poor and underdeveloped. This view was rationalised and shaped by the political discourses and apartheid policies of the late 1940s. In this chapter, 'rural' is understood as an area characterised by low economic status, plagued by poor infrastructure, poor delivery of essential services such as water, electricity and limited access to information communications technologies (Hlalele, 2013).

7.3 School Enrichment Programs Conceptualised

School enrichment programs have been conceptualised as:

> Quality community-driven, expanded learning opportunities that support developmentally appropriate cognitive, social, physical, and emotional outcomes. In addition, these programs offer a balanced program of academic support, arts and cultural enrichment, recreation, and nutrition. After-school programs can run directly after school, or during evenings, weekends, summer vacations, and holidays. (Chung, Gannett, & de KanterLaPerla, 2000, as cited in Bradley, 2012, p. 7)

Adding to the development and learning issues that characterise SEP, Puvirajah, Verma, and Martin-Hansen (2014) state that SEP extend to cover issues related to opportunity for enrichment and play, training and problem-solving activities. Zhang, Lam, Smith, Fleming, and Connaughton (2006) further argue that SEP can also be understood in terms of their intention to assist in areas of scholastic development, social behaviour, the provision of a caring environment and personal inspiration. These programs are not only confined to schools, but they can also be administered in many public places (Zhang et al., 2006). While this may be a wider practice in other countries, it is not the case in South Africa where these programs are widely administered in schools. In this case, Taylor et al. (2010) distinguish between enrichment programs and placement programs. In the enrichment programs learners receive extra tutoring in their schools after school hours, over the weekend or during the school vacations. Learners in the placement programs are removed from their ill-resourced schools and taken to other well-performing and better-equipped schools to be taught by tutors or teachers from these schools.

Haglund and Anderson (2009) point to the transformation in the definition and functions of SEP. Initially, SEP were designated as places for keeping children safe while parents were at work. Later, the educational demands propelled a change in the functions of these programs resulting in them being tailored to assist children to learn and improve their academic performance (Haglund & Anderson, 2009). Currently, without discarding the purpose of responding to learners' academic challenges, SEP are seen as school-based and community-based programs in which learners engage in many curricular and extracurricular activities. Despite this transformation, there is, however, a consensus that the successful SEP share the following characteristics:

- They combine academic, recreational, physical and artistic elements in the curriculum to engage learners in a variety of supervised and structured activities (Zhang et al., 2006).
- They have well-prepared staff members.
- They form strong partnerships with other stakeholders (Little, Wimer, & Heather, 2007).

The effect of SEP on academic performance of learners is well documented in the international and national literature (Afterschool Alliance, 2014; Bradley, 2012; Prinsloo, 2008; Shernoff & Vandell, 2007; WCED, n.d.). In some instances, SEP assist in addressing curriculum overload (Mogari et al., 2009). In others, schools have resorted to these programs to compensate time demands exerted by the use of learner-centred teaching and learning (Bray, 2012). They also play a role in promoting wellness among children. Little et al. (2007) note that SEP contributed to improving the self-esteem and self-concepts of learners.

With so many advantages provided by the carefully structured and organised SEP we were curious as to why learners in the school were not performing optimally. This curiosity rose from the inconsistencies that we observed in the academic performance of learners at this school across all grades. This unsustainable and poor academic performance is a sharp contrast to the many hours and more resources that the school spends on SEP. This chapter therefore arose from the need to investigate the conditions under which SEP may flourish in order to attain improved academic performance and sustainable learning not only at this school, but possibly for other rural schools.

7.4 Theoretical Framework

The current chapter adopted Critical Emancipatory Research (CER) as a theoretical lens. The genesis of CER can be traced to the works of Adorno, Habermas and the Frankfurt Schools in the early 1920s (Mahlomaholo, 2009). At the centre of CER is the notion of empowerment and emancipation of the marginalised voices in the society (Mahlomaholo & Nkoane, 2002). In positioning the researcher and the researched, CER emphasises a relationship based on equality and partnership between these stakeholders in the quest to construct knowledge. While aimed at striking a balance between roles played by the researcher and the researched, this kind of relationship further enhances self-liberation and emancipation by the marginalised people (Mahlomaholo & Nkoane, 2002). Additionally, such positioning removes from the researcher the sole responsibility of emancipating the marginalised communities (Cohen, Manion, & Morrison, 2013). As a result, the researched are recognised as co-researchers with meaningful participation rather than objects at the researcher's disposal to *use* and construct knowledge *for*.

At the school under study, learners are excluded from the process of designing and implementing SEP. This means the design and implementation of the programs is based on the assumptions of the educators rather than the needs of the learners, who are often marginalised as they are not included in decision-making processes. This includes identification of circumstances under which SEP may thrive. In addition to challenging the status quo, the adoption of CER in this chapter ensured equal participation and collaborative decision-making which eliminated the predominant one-sided way of viewing and addressing issues. By advocating for the use of dialogical methods (Chilisa, 2012), CER benefited the co-researchers in this chapter by affording them the platform shared decision-making of CER enabled us to work together in investigating the circumstances under which SEP may thrive.

In addition to the emancipatory, communitarian and agentic attributes that CER brings to framing research, we undertook a study to tap into lenses that see rural schools as part of social spaces to explore innovative programs (SEP). Embedded in this chapter are some elements of the rural social spaces model (see Green, 2008; Reid et al., 2010). The rural social space model takes into account issues such as economy, geography and demography and their role in changing the deficit narrative around innovative programs in rural spaces, similar to CER, this model discourages the persistent and deficit view of rural communities and their abilities to solve their problems. In this regard, as argued by White, Bloomfield, & Le Cornu (2010), rural spaces can be 'rethought and represented' in more emancipated ways through the innovative programs such as SEP (2011, p. 4). In doing so, a more holistic and inclusive approach is necessary in changing the status quo and amongst others, adding rural schools to prominent national and international developmental agendas.

7.5   Data Generation

Participatory Action Research (PAR) as a methodology anchors this chapter due to its participatory nature. PAR operationalises CER as a theoretical lens to ensure partnership and equal participation all stakeholders such as parents, teachers, learners and other officials in the Department of Basic Education (DBE) investigating circumstances under which SEP may thrive with the ultimate aim of enhancing these programs for sustainable learning at rural schools. Moreover, engaging the participants in the workshops (discussion sessions) guided by the Free Attitude Interview (FAI) ensured not only meaningful participation, but also created a space for meaningful conversations and collaborative activities in investigating the circumstances necessary for SEP at rural schools to flourish (Sekwena, 2014).

At the centre of PAR lie the notions of transformation and emancipation. With these notions in mind, it guards against the exploitation and lack of respect (Smith, Baum, & MacDougall, 2006) for the researched in the research process. To ensure this, PAR places collaborative and mutual relationships at its centre as a way to enhance participation in the construction of knowledge (Blake, 2007; Smith et al., 2006; Tsotetsi, 2013; Ungar et al., 2015). This is done in the pursuit of social justice, collective action and social change (Loughran & McCann, 2015) in the marginalised communities. While acknowledging the involvement of all the stakeholders, PAR further promotes and considers the individual strengths of individuals in bringing about social change (Tsotetsi, 2013).

PAR recognises the experiences that participants bring to the research process and how these shape the outcomes of this process (Mokoena, 2017). It is the duty of the researchers, according to Glassman and Erdem (2014), to participate in these experiences or include in their chapter participants who have lived and undergone these experiences. In this chapter, the workshops (meetings) were held at the same school, situated in the same area in which most participants resided. In addition, during these workshops the participants spoke about the issues which they had experienced within their own contexts. By creating for them a platform to speak openly about their experiences, both the participants and researchers were able to share perspectives on the issue at hand. This also allowed us to create new knowledge based on multiple perspectives (Mahlomaholo, 2009).

In most cases, in our view, marginalised rural people are not always listened to or taken seriously, however, the use of workshops and meetings guided by FAI allowed such people to be heard and their contributions valued (Sekwena, 2014). In addition, the use of prompts guided by FAI allowed for flexibility and maximum participation, therefore, creating a group in which their opinions were valued concurs with the idea of empowering the participants as collaborators and co-researchers. The participants were both male and female Africans from one rural school, a total of ten from this school who volunteered. This group comprised one learning facilitator (LF), two heads of department (HoDs), two educators, three school learners and two members of the School Governing Body (SGB), all from a rural school.

For the purpose of preserving the participants' anonymity, they were referred to as 'LF ZM' for Learning Facilitator, 'LEARNER A (QN)', 'LEARNER B (PT)' and 'LEARNER C (JP)' for learners, respectively. For teachers, the following pseudonyms were used: 'TEACHER A (TKM)'; and 'TEACHER B (VB)' respectively. The pseudonyms 'HoD (VM)' and 'HoD (JP)' were used to refer to the respective HoDs while the parents who participated in the chapter were referred to as 'PARENT A (GM)' and 'PARENT B (MF)'. In addition, these workshops and observations were conducted in the area in which participants were able to express their views and thoughts freely and confidentially.

7.6   Data Analysis

All the participants' responses were recorded on an audio-tape device to ensure that they could be transcribed verbatim. It was necessary for us to categorise the responses, look at the patterns of the responses, identify and describe the themes prevailing. This deepened our understanding of the participants' conditions and perspectives. This chapter adopted Fairclough's Critical Discourse Analysis (CDA). In short. CDA state that is '…the study of speech beyond sentences…' (Avdi & Georgaca, 2007, p. 158). Alternatively, CDA has been defined as both theory and methodology, tasked with analysing the politically, political-economic and socially inclined discourse (Fairclough, 2013). It also focuses on understanding and addressing power relations (Le Roux & Adler, 2015).

Fairclough has developed a three-tiered framework in which analysis is performed on three different levels: interpretive, descriptive and explanatory (Bhattacharya, 2017). The first level involves the analysis of both written and spoken text. In other words, analysis focuses on the characteristics of the text (Bhattacharya, 2017). The second level involves analysis of text as discursive practice (Myende, 2014), with focus on language structures and the production, consumption and interpretation of texts by the participants. In this case, the focus is on the connection between the discursive process and the text (Bhattacharya, 2017). The third level focuses on analysing discourses as a social practice (Myende, 2014), emphasising how knowledge is perceived by those who receive it. Such explanations are aimed at critiquing, reflecting and understanding how social structures are designed and transformed the way they are (Rogers, Malancharuvil-Berkes, Mosely, Hui, & Joseph, 2005).

The emancipatory and exploratory notions advocated by both CER and CDA (Avdi & Georgaca, 2007; Liasidou, 2008; Paulus & Lester, 2015) fit well with the aims of this chapter. In this case, it successfully challenged and refuted the perceptions that rural people are unable to solve their own problems. By paying attention to power relations (Bhattacharya, 2017), CDA weakens such stereotypical and unjust discourses. Creating the spaces for discussions between researcher and the rural participants empowered them to solve their problems and led to a realisation of how dominance is maintained by those in the positions of power.

7.7 Discussion: Thriving Rural School Enrichment Programs

This section summarises the findings by adding to, corroborating and comparing existing literature on the circumstances under which school enrichment programs at rural school may thrive. The section draws strength in re-presenting rural places as a source of wealth and strength and as delicate environments that require innate stewardship (Corbett, 2015). Through our workshops and interactions, it emerged that co-researchers preferred an environment that would be conducive to teaching and learning. In this regard, the allocation of two empty classrooms proved useful as it was far away from the noise and other disturbances in the school.

The partnership between the school and the community contributes to making the environment suitable for teaching and learning (Kline et al., 2013). Firstly, the parents ensured the availability of sufficient furniture in the two classrooms. In this regard, parents who were serving in the SGB (co-researchers in this chapter) and other parents from the community had come together to repair the broken chairs and tables. Secondly, the parents played a role in ensuring the safety of their children in the program. Here, the parents serving in the SGB (co-researchers in this chapter) and the ones from the community volunteered and took turns in monitoring the safety of the learners in the program. Finally, the allocation of supervisory roles to the two HoDs played a significant part in creating a suitable environment for teaching and learning. They helped in liaison between other co-researchers and the other SMT members.

7.7.1 Provision of Well-Organised and Diverse Activities

Proper planning and aligning the programs' activities and its vision are important. In addition to leading to improved academic performance, such alignment and planning reduce drop-out rate in the programs (Afterschool Alliance, 2014; Cosden, Morrison, Gutierrez, & Brown, 2004). In this regard, it emerged that the drawing of an attendance register for both teachers and learners contributed to the provision of well-organised and diverse activities. The co-researchers in this chapter had previously stated that they preferred a register for teachers and learners as it would help with maintaining order in the program and would ensure active participation and increased accountability of everyone involved in the program. Diversifying types of activities that the participants engage in contribute positively to their development gains (Afterschool Alliance, 2014). For instance, the co-researchers felt that this register served as motivation for teachers to attend their sessions in the program. In this case, it was used as a standardised tool when teachers were paid for teaching in the program. It further enabled the principal to calculate what was due to each teacher who participated in the program.

While the attendance register was a critical condition in ensuring organisation in the program, the co-researchers indicated the use of technology would contribute to the provision of diverse activities. In this regard, the installation of an overhead projector and television set made the provision of diverse activities possible. Learners spent a minimum of four hours a week watching the educational programs on television, especially those dealing with challenging subjects such as Mathematics, Life Sciences, Physical Science and Accounting. In addition, the co-researchers felt that use of an overhead projector in program contributed to the provision of diverse activities. Through its use, teachers were able to project the phenomena on a screen to a rather large number of learners in a classroom, thus minimising disruptions during the lessons in the program.

In addition to the use of technology in the program, the findings indicated that the use of various teaching methods by teachers contributed to the provision of diverse activities. This enabled learners to engage in fun activities, such as games (chess), music (singing mathematics formulae) and role play (performing plays) in class. Complementing these findings, studies have shown that SEP whose activities were aligned with learners' needs leads to academic performance. Studies have also shown that the structured activities increase levels of attendance among learners, so the learners in these activities are less likely to drop out (Cosden et al., 2004) of school. Providing participants with diversified types of activities contributes positively to the participants' developmental gains (Afterschool Alliance, 2014). The findings of a longitudinal study of three SEP indicated increased academic performance and work habits (Afterschool Alliance, 2014).

7.7.2 Establishment of an Effective Monitoring Team

Supervision is central to the success of school enrichment programs (Little et al., 2007). Additionally, Cosden et al. (2004) reported on the success that resulted from learning under the structured time and adult supervised location. In this chapter, a mutual working partnership between school and community also contributed to the establishment of an effective monitoring team. In this regard, the parents' willingness to volunteer in the program to ensure safety of the learners played a significant role. Adding to this was the professionalism with which the HoDs undertook a role of supervision of learning and teaching in the program. Here, the two HoDs made sure that every teacher had necessary teaching material and resources handy. In addition, they were also tasked with recording the attendance of both teachers and learners. Similar findings were achieved in the study by Prinsloo (2008) under the auspices of the Shuttleworth Foundation which reported that the tutors were given information about their roles and responsibilities before the commencement of the intervention program in the Western Cape. In addition, the tutors were also briefed about the teaching material they would use in the program.

7.7.3 Circumstances that Made the High-Quality Programming and Staffing Thrive

The creation of positive relationships among the co-researchers made it possible for high-quality programming and staffing successful. According to White et al. (2011), it is important to guard against the predominant metro-centric model of addressing issues confronting rural spaces. In this regard, equal participation of all co-researchers in the program improved a sense of ownership of the program and the strategies aimed at enhancing it. The development of the programs' vision and mission was another factor that contributed to the successful intentional programming. For Neiva and Pepe (2012), the involvement of all stakeholders in the discussion around the vision, goals and mission of the programs offers a sense of continuity and reinforces the importance of learning. In this regard, the inclusion of all stakeholders in the program made this possible as it contributed to the realisation that the program belonged to all stakeholders involved.

Motivation of all staff members is another factor that contributes to the successful intentional programming. This motivation of staff members can take different forms. These include monetary rewards, civic and religious obligations and consistent communication (Halpern, 2002; Neiva & Pepe, 2012; Vogt, 2006). In this chapter, the motivation was mainly channelled to both learners and the staff members. The emphasis was on the need for all staff members to model positive behaviour at all time and for all learners to take their school work seriously.

7.7.4 Establishment of Strong Partnerships

Studies have also reported the positive impact of the supportive partnerships between communities and SEP. According to Jones and Deutsch (2013), the roles of the partnerships among the stakeholders are significant for a successful design and implementation of SEP. In their study, Oh, Osgood, and Smith (2014) argue that the strength of partnerships is what distinguishes dysfunctional programs from well-designed and highly effective ones. In addition, Brigham and Nahas (2008), under the auspices of HFRP stated that these partnerships need to take place at different levels, including partnerships within schools and at district level (HFRP, 2010).

It emerged during the discussions that forming strong partnerships between the school and the business people in the community was an important condition in adherence to the notion of rural schools 'as complex social spaces' (Reid et al., 2010, p. 262). The conversations that made rounds in the community resulted in one of the co-researchers convincing one local business person to sponsor the program. This had a snowball effect because other local business made donations to the school.

Another factor that contributed to the successful formation of positive partnership was the close working relationships which the HoDs (co-researchers) and teachers (co-researchers) had with other teachers and HoDs from the nearby school. This resulted in these schools sharing resources such as discs and books, and in learners exchanging information with learners from the other school. In addition, the positive working relationship between the principals of the two schools facilitated the success of the partnership. As White and Corbett (2012) posit, the gaze shifts to positive outcomes for those who live in rural communities.

7.8   Conclusion

In this chapter, while illuminating the integral, meaningful and impactful conceptualisation and application of SEP, we are also attempting to elucidate the fact that the circumstances leading to the successful enhancement of school enrichment programs at rural school need serious scrutiny. Furthermore, we caution against the uniform application of these conditions due to various challenges specific to rural schools. On the contrary, we advise for the adaptation and tailoring of these conditions to enable thriving school enrichment programs at rural schools.

References

Afterschool Alliance. (2014). *Taking a deeper dive into after school: Positive outcomes and promising practices.* Washington, DC. Accessed 24 July 2016.

Avdi, E., & Georgaca, E. (2007). Discourse analysis and psychotherapy: A critical review. *European Journal Psychotherapy and Counselling, 9*(2), 157–176.

Bantwini, B. D., & Feza, N. N. (2017). Left behind in a democratic society: A case study of some farm school primary school teachers of natural science in South Africa. *International Journal of Leadership in Education, 20*(3), 312–327.

Barter, B. (2008). Rural education: Learning to be rural teachers. *Journal of Workplace Learning, 20*(7/8), 468–479.

Bhattacharya, S. (2017). Gender representations in English textbooks used in Grade Eight under national and state boards, India. *Language in India, 17*(6), 410–432.

Blake, M. K. (2007). Formality and friendship: Research ethics review and participatory action research. *An International E-Journal for Critical Geographies, 6*(3), 411–421.

Blease, B., & Condy, J. (2015). Teaching of writing in two rural multi-grade classes in the Western Cape. *Reading and Writing, 6*(1), 1–9.

Bojuwoye, O., Moletsane, M., Stofile, S., Moolla, N., & Sylvester, F. (2014). Learners' experiences of learning support in selected Western Cape schools. *South African Journal of Education, 34*(1), 1–15.

Bradley, D. (2012). *What effect does an after-school science, maths and English enhancement program have on grade 10 to 12 students' learning physical science?* Unpublished master's dissertation, University of KwaZulu-Natal, Pinetown.

Bray, M. (2006). Private Supplementary tutoring: Comparative perspectives on patterns and implications. *Journal of Comparative and International Education, 36*(4), 515–530.

Bray, M. (2012). Out-of-school supplementary tutoring. *Childhood Education, 77*(6), 360–366.

Brigham, R. A., & Nahas, J. (2008). *Children's Aid Society/ Carrerra Integrated School Model: Documentation of early implementation in four schools.* Cambridge, MA: Brigham Nahas Research Associates.

Brown, B. A. (2010). Teachers' accounts of the usefulness of multi-grade teaching in promoting sustainable human-development related outcomes in rural South Africa. *Journal of Southern African Studies, 36*(1), 189–207.

Brown, S. P. (2011). *Assessment in the further education and training school sector: A quality assurance perspective.* Unpublished master's dissertation, University of the Free State, Bloemfontein.

Byun, S., Schofer, E., & Kim, K. (2012). Revisiting the role of cultural capital in East Asian educational system: The case of Korea. *Sociology of Education* [Online] *85,* 219. Available at: http://soe.sagepub.com/cotent/85/3/219. Accessed 6 Feb 2014.

Chigbu, U. E. (2013). Rurality as a choice: Towards ruralising rural areas in sub-Saharan African Countries. *Development Southern Africa, 30*(6), 812–825.

Chilisa, B. (2012). *Indigenous research methodologies.* London: Sage.

Cohen, L., Manion, L., & Morrison, K. (2013). *Research methods in education* (7th ed.). London: Routledge.

Corbett, M. (2015). Rural education: Some sociological provocations for the field. *Australian and International Journal of Rural Education, 25*(3), 9–25.

Cosden, M., Morrison, G., Gutierrez, L., & Brown, M. (2004). The effects of homework programs and after-school activities on school success. *Theory into Practice, 43*(3), 220–226.

DBE (Department of Basic Education). (2011). *National curriculum statement: Curriculum assessment policy statement. Guidelines for responding to learner diversity in the classroom through curriculum and assessment policy statement.* Pretoria, Republic of South Africa.

DBE (Department of Basic Education). (2012a). *National policy pertaining to the program and promotion requirements of the national curriculum statement: Grades R-12.* Pretoria: Government Printer.

DBE (Department of Basic Education). (2012b). *National protocol for assessment: Grades R-12.* Pretoria: Government Printer.

DBE (Department of Basic Education). (2017). *Rural education draft policy. Government gazette,* 630(41321).

DBE (Department of Basic Education). (2018). *Rural Education Policy* (p. 36). Pretoria: Government Notices, No.

DBE (Department of Basic Education). (2019). *National education infrastructure management systems standard report August 2019. Pretoria: Government Printers.*

DBE (Department of Basic Education). (n.d.). *Questions & answer booklet: For the advocacy of the implementation of the national curriculum statement (NCS): Grades R-12.* Pretoria: Government Printer.

Du Plessis, P., & Mestry, R. (2019). Teachers for rural schools-a challenge for South Africa. *South African Journal of Education, 39*(1), S1–S9.

Easton, E.S., Gereluk, D., Dressler, R., & Becker, S. (2017). *A rural education teacher preparation program: Course design, student support ad engagement.* In AERA Conference, San Antonio, TX (pp. 1–15).

Equal Education. (2018a). *Breaking the cycle: Uncovering persistent sanitation challenges in Gauteng schools.* Available at: https://equaleducation.org.za/wp-content/uploads/2018/11/Equal-Education-GP-Sanitation-Audit-Report-2018.pdf. Accessed 18 Jan 2020.

Equal Education. (2018b). *Implementing agents: The middlemen in charge of building schools.* Available at: https://equaleducation.org.za/wp-content/uploads/2018/11/Equal-Education-Implementing-Agents-Report-November-2018.pdf. Accessed 18 Jan 2020.

Fairclough, N. (2013). Critical discourse analysis and critical policy studies. *Critical Policy Studies, 7*(2), 177–197.

Glassman, M., & Erdem, G. (2014). Participatory action research and its meanings: Vivencia, praxis, conscientization. *Adult Education Quarterly, 64*(3), 206–221.

Green, B. (2008). *Rural social space* (Working Paper for TERRAnova Project). Bathurst: Charles Sturt University.

Mail & Guardian. (2008, December 30). Half of Eastern Cape Matrics fail. *Mail & Guardian* [Online]. Available at: http://mg.co.za/article/2008-12-30-half-of-eastern-cape-matrics-fail. Accessed 7 Feb 2014.

Mail & Guardian. (2012, January 6). Matric pass rate may be deceiving. *Mail & Guardian* [Online]. Available at: www.mg.co.za. Accessed 7 Feb 2014.

Mail & Guardian. (2013). Maths teaching in SA adds up to multiplying class divisions. *Mail & Guardian* [Online]. Available at: http://mg.co.za/article/2013-10-24-maths-teaching-in-sa-adds-up-to-multiplying-class-divisions. Accessed 7 Feb 2014.

Haglund, B., & Anderson, S. (2009). After school programs and leisure-time centers: Arenas for learning and leisure. *World Leisure Journal, 12*(5), 116–129.

Halpern, R. (2002). A different kind of child development institution: The history of after-school programs for low-income children. *Teachers College Record, 104*(2), 178–211.

Hannaway, D., Govender, P., Marais, P., & Meier, C. (2019). Growing early childhood education teachers in rural areas. *Africa Education Review, 16*(3), 36–53.

Harvard Family Research Project (HFRP). (2010). *Partnerships for learning: Promising practices in integrating school and out-of-school time program supports.* Cambridge, MA: Harvard Family Research Project.

Hlalele, D. (2012). Social justice and rural education in South Africa. *Perspectives in Education, 30*(1), 111–118.

Hlalele, D. (2013). Sustainable learning ecologies—A prolegomenon traversing transcendence of discursive notions of sustainability, social justice, development and food sovereignty. *TD The Journal for Transdisciplinary Research in Southern Africa, 9*(3), 561–580.

Hlalele, D. J. (2019). Indigenous knowledge systems and sustainable learning in rural South Africa. *Australian and International Journal of Rural Education, 29*(1), 88–100.

Hof, S. (2014). Does private tuition works: The effectiveness of private tutoring: Nonparametric bound analysis. *Education Economics.* https://doi.org/10.1080/09645292.2014.908165.

Ireson, J., & Rushforth, K. (2011). Private tutoring at transition points in the English education system: Its nature, extent and purpose. *Research Papers in Education, 26*(1), 1–9.

Jacobs, L., Stals, E., & Leroy, L. (2016). Providing books to rural school through mobile libraries. *Comparing Perspectives from Around the World BCES Conference Books, 14*(1), 58–64.

John, M. (2019). Physical sciences teaching and learning in Eastern Cape rural schools: Reflections of pre-service teachers. *South African Journal of Education, 39*(1), S1–S12.

Jones, J. N., & Deutsch, N. L. (2013). Social and identity development in after-school program: Changing experiences and shifting adolescent needs. *Journal of Early Adolescence, 33*(1), 17–43.

Kline, J., White, S., & Lock, G. (2013). The rural practicum: Preparing a quality teacher workforce for rural and regional Australia. *Journal of Research in Rural Education, 28*(3), 1–13. Retrieved from http://jrre.psu.edu/articles/28-3.pdf.

KwaZulu Natal Department of Education (KZNDoE). (2018). *Report on progress made towards meeting the requirements of norms and standards: Report 3.* Government Printers.

Le Roux, K., & Adler, J. (2015). A critical discourse analysis of practical problems in a foundation mathematics course at a South African university. *Educational Studies in Mathematics, 91,* 227–246.

Liasidou, A. (2008). Critical discourse analysis and inclusive educational policies: The power to exclude. *Journal of Education Policy, 23*(5), 483–500.

Limpopo Department of Education (LDoE). (2016). *Infrastructure norms & standards report November 2016.* Polokwane: Governement Printers.

Limpopo Department of Education (LDoE). (2017). *Norms and standards report, 2017.* Polokwane: Government Printers.

Limpopo Department of Education (LDoE). (2018). *Infrastructure, norms and standards report, 2018.* Polokwane: Government Printers.

Little, P. M. D., Wimer, C., & Heather, B. (2007). After-school programs in the 21st century: Their potential and what it takes to achieve it. *Havard Family Research Project, 10,* 1–12.

Loughran, H., & McCann, M. E. (2015). Employing community participative research methods to advance service user. *Collaboration in Social Work Research, 45,* 705–723.

Mafora, P. (2013). Managing teacher retention in a rural school district in South Africa. *Australian Educational Researcher, 40,* 227–240.

Mahlomaholo, S. (2009). Critical emancipatory research and academic identity. *Africa Education Review, 6*(2), 224–237.

Mahlomaholo, M. G., & Nkoane, M. M. (2002). The case for an emancipatory qualitative research: Reflection on assessment of quality. *Education as Change, 6*(1), 89–105.

Mestry, R., & Khumalo, J. (2012). Governing bodies and learner discipline: Managing rural schools in South Africa through a code of conduct. *South African Journal of Education, 32,* 97–110.

Mihai, M. A. (2017). Success factors and challenges of an information communication technology network in rural schools. *Africa Education Review, 14*(1), 155–170.

Mogari, D., Coetzee, H., & Maritz, R. (2009). Investigating the status of supplementary tuition in the teaching and learning of mathematics. *Pythagoras, 69,* 36–45.

Mokoena, M. S. (2017). *Enhancing a school enrichment program for sustainable learning at a rural high school.* Unpublished master's dissertation, University of Free State, Bloemfontein.

Moloi, K. C., Dzvimbo, K. P., Potgieter, F. J., Wolhuter, C. C., & van der Walt, J. L. (2010). Learners' perceptions as to what contributes to their school success: A case chapter. *South African Journal of Education, 30,* 475–490.

Myende, P. E. (2014). *Enhancing academic performance through an asset-based approach.* Unpublished doctoral thesis, University of the Free State. Bloemfontein.

Ndandani, M. (2001). Rural schools and educational technology: A case study of rural schools in the Molopo district, Mafikeng. *Development Southern Africa, 18*(3), 377–393.

Neiva, B. M., & Pepe, D. (2012). Time well spent: Designing dynamic and profitable after-school programs. *Independent School, 72*(1), n1.

Oh, Y., Osgood, D. W., & Smith, E. P. (2014). Measuring after-school program quality using setting-level observational approaches. *Journal of Early Adolescence, 35,* 11–33.

Paulus, T. M., & Lester, J. N. (2015). ATLAS.ti for conversation and discourse analysis studies. *International Journal of Social Research Methodology.* Available at: http://dx.doi.org/10.1080/13645579.2015.1021949.

Prinsloo, C. H. (2008). *Extra classes, extra marks? Report on the plus time project. Research chapter for the Western Cape Education Department by the Shuttleworth Foundation.* Cape Town: HSRC.

Puvirajah, A., Verma, G., Li, H., & Martin-Hansen, L. (2014). Influence of a science-focused after-school program on under-represented high-school students' science attitudes and trajectory: A survey validation chapter. *International Journal of Science Education, 5*(3), 250–270.

Reid, J.-A., Green, B., Cooper, M., Hastings, W., Lock, G., & White, S. (2010). Regenerating rural social space? Teacher education for rural-regional sustainability. *Australian Journal of Education, 54*(3), 262–276.

Rogers, R., Malancharuvil-Berkes, E., Mosely, M., Hui, D., & Joseph, G. O. (2005). Critical discourse analysis in education: A review of the literature. *Review of Educational Research, 75*(3), 365–416.

Sekwena, G. L. (2014). *Active learning in a high school economics class: A framework for learner engagement.* Unpublished master's dissertation, University of the Free State, Bloemfontein.

Shandu, L., Evans, N., & Mostert, J. (2014). Challenges in the provision of school library services in Katlehong secondary schools. *Mousaion: South African Journal of Information Studies, 32*(4), 13–28.

Shernoff, D. J., & Vandell, D. L. (2007). Engagement in the after-school activities: Quality of experience from perspective of participants. *Journal of Youth and Adolescence, 36,* 891–903.

Sierk, J. (2017). Redefining rurality: Cosmopolitanism, whiteness and the New Latino Diaspora. *Discourse Studies in the Cultural Politics of Education, 38*(3), 342–353.

Smith, D., Baum, F., & MacDougall, P. (2006). Participatory action research. *Journal of Epidemiology and Community Health, 60*(10), 854–857.

Taylor, N., Shindler. J., du Toit, R., & Mosselson, M. (2010). *Building what works in educa-tion: Options for talented learners from disadvantaged backgrounds.* Johannesburg: Centre for Development and Enterprise.

Toson, A. L. M. (2011). Show me the money: The benefits of for—Profit Charter Schools (EMOS). *Education and Urban Society* [Online], *45*(6), 658–667. Available at: www.sagepublications. com. Accessed 6 Feb 2014.

Tsotetsi, C. T. (2013). *The implementation of professional teacher development policies: A continuing education perspective.* Unpublished doctoral thesis, University of the Free State: Bloemfontein.

Ungar, M., McGrath, P., Black, D., Sketris, I., Whitman, S., & Liebenberg, L. (2015). Contribution of participatory action research to knowledge mobilization in mental health services for children and families. *Qualitative Social Work, 0*(00), 1–7.

Vogt, D. A. (2006). *Effectiveness of "Building a better me" after-school enrichment program for the enhancement of communication skills.* Unpublished master's dissertation, Miami University, Oxford.

White, S. (2015). Extending the knowledge base for (rural) teacher educators. *Australian and International Journal of Rural Education, 25*(3), 50–61.

White, S., Bloomfield, D., & Le Cornu, R. (2010). Professional experience in new times: Issues and responses to a changing education landscapes. *Asia Pacific Journal of Teacher Education, 38*(3), 181–193.

White, S., & Corbett, M. (2012). *Doing educational research in rural communities: Methodological issues, international perspectives and practical solutions.* London: Routledge.

White, S., Lock, G., Hastings, W., Cooper, M., Reid, J., & Green, B. (2011). Investing in sustainable and resilient rural social space: Lessons for teacher education. *Education in Rural Australia, 21*(1), 67–78. Available at: https://ro.ecu.edu.au/ecuworks2011/339.

White, S., & Reid, J. (2008). Placing teachers? Sustaining rural schooling through place conscious-ness in teacher education. *Journal of Research in Rural Education, 23*(7). Retrieved from http:// jrre.psu.edu/articles/23-7.pdf.

Zhang, J. J., & Byrd, C. E. (2013). Successful after-school programs. *Journal of Physical Education, Recreation and Dance, 77*(8), 3–12.

Zhang, J. J., Lam, T. C., Smith, D. W., Fleming, D. S., & Connaughton, D. P. (2006). Development of scale for programs facilitators to access the effectiveness of after-school achievement programs. *Measurement in Physical Education and Exercise Science, 10*(3), 151–167.

Mosebetsi Mokoena holds a Ph.D. in Curriculum Studies from University of the Free State (UFS), Qwaqwa Campus. He used to work as a teacher at Esizibeni secondary school situated in the deep rural northern part of the Free State province, South Africa. This is where his interest for working with rural communities and schools in rural spaces was ignited. Currently, Mokoena is a lecturer at the University of the Free State in the School of Social Sciences and Language Education (SSSLE) and he supervises postgraduate research. His research interests include school enrichment programs, rurality, and participatory action research in rural spaces.

Dipane Hlalele is a Professor in the School of Education at the University of KwaZulu-Natal, South Africa. Before this, he was an assistant dean and senior lecturer at the University of the Free State, a college of education lecturer and a high school deputy principal and teacher. He was a principal- and co-investigator in the *Community engagement in rural contexts: A relational leadership strategy* (2017–2019) and *Sustainable urban-rural learning connections* (2017–2018), National Research Foundation (NRF)-funded projects. Prior to this, he was a principal investigator in NRF funded projects: *Sustainable rural learning ecologies: Sustainable futures for the people of the Afromontane*; and a co-investigator in the *Adaptive leadership in community engagement and service learning.*

Part IV
Principles and Practices to Inspire the Future of Rural Education

Chapter 8
Insights to Process and Practice in Rural Education: Rural Education in the Context of Rapid (Urban) Development

Philip Roberts, Peter Bodycott, Yiting Li, and Xuyang Qian

Abstract This chapter examines issues in the preparation and practice of rural teachers in China within a comparative reference to rural education in Australia. The chapter provides a background to education in rural areas of China, along with a discussion of rurality in the context of rapid urbanisation in China. Against this backdrop policies and practices in teacher education and teacher professional development in China, and particularly those focusing upon rural schools, are examined. Overall, this chapter highlights the unique insights available from examining education in rural areas in China through a comparative perspective.

Keywords China · Policy · Teacher professional development · Comparative perspective

8.1 Introduction

In the context of rapid development and rural-urban migration, China's rural areas have experienced a significant disparity in educational achievement (Young & Hannum, 2018). While this achievement disparity is similar to educational inequality between rural and urban areas in many parts of the world, it has, in China, been a comparatively recent phenomenon. This recency affords us a unique opportunity to examine the processes, such as staffing, resourcing and outcomes that are believed to create rural-urban differences, rather than working to remedy the consequences after they have occurred. By better understanding these processes, we can also develop insights into the potential interventions needed in different contexts. Furthermore,

P. Roberts (✉) · P. Bodycott
Faculty of Education, University of Canberra, Canberra, ACT, Australia
e-mail: philip.roberts@canberra.edu.au

Y. Li
School of Education, Shaanxi Normal University, Xian, China

X. Qian
School of Education, Hangzhou Normal University, Hangzhou, China

© Springer Nature Singapore Pte Ltd. 2021
S. White and J. Downey (eds.), *Rural Education Across the World*,
https://doi.org/10.1007/978-981-33-6116-4_8

the experiences of rural China aid the examination of rurality in the modern (urban) world through comparison with the broader rural education literature, in this instance, primarily the example of Australia. Such a broadly comparative approach enables the processes of positioning the rural contra the urban to be examined outside of national cultural contexts, and as such, provides insights for other nations undergoing rapid urban development.

In this chapter, we also explore issues about policies and practices in China that are aimed towards supporting education in rural areas. Such explorations provide insights into rurality and urbanisation in modernity. In writing about China, with Chinese colleagues, yet from an Australian viewpoint, we are informed by comparative education and its rationale of providing understandings into policy and practice (Crossley & Watson, 2011). To this end, the chapter references two nations with similar geographic size and geography, but distinctly different national histories, cultures and populations in comparison.

This chapter builds on the work of Roberts and Hannum (2018) and Kong et al. (2021) who provided a background to issues in rural education in China, and is informed by rural studies and the different understandings of the term, rural (Woods, 2011). In this context, the chapter examines what it is to be rural in China and Australia, within the modern (urban) global world to seek insights into how the rural is positioned and the implications this has for the work, and role, of teachers. For example, teachers' work can be seen to either help overcome or to erase rurality in pursuit of a modernist urban citizenship. Alternatively, it can work as an actor to value and preserve rurality as a component of national identity. We consider rural policy, in the context of the rural revitalisation strategy, as policies can influence the attitude towards rurality and rural identity enormously, and influence teachers' practice relating to the preservation or erasure of rurality.

The threads running through this chapter provide a rare insight into the processes implicated in constructing the rural. As such they provide a lens through which to evaluate policies and practices that have evolved in response to an assumed rural deficit. Our analysis highlights potential issues and concerns for future practice in many national contexts confronted by rapid urbanisation.

8.2 Equity and Rurality in China

In the context of rapid urbanisation, China has had to balance equity and economic development. To date, economic development has progressed at a faster rate than equity and China has therefore become more unequal, as indicated by a Gini coefficient of 0.73 (Chen et al., 2016). The Gini coefficient is a standardised means for measuring levels of inequality on a scale of zero to one, where zero denotes absolute equality and one signifies absolute inequality. However, equity is an increasing policy focus today—as we will show in this chapter.

The official designation of urban and rural in China is related to official criteria pertaining, primarily, to demographics and economic activity. This is a little different from Australia and the USA, which tend to denote classifications based on accessibility and distance to major services and demographic concentrations. Since the establishment of the Peoples Republic of China (PRC) in 1949, the urban population had grown steadily from 10.6% to 17.4% at the initiation of the Reform and Opening Up policies in 1976. There has subsequently been an exponential growth to 52.6% in 2012 (Mu & Jia, 2014). This figure needs to be tempered by an awareness of the household registration system (hukou) in China, though, where people may be registered to a rural region while residing in an urban one. The hukou is an important element of understanding rural China, as one's registration is what determines the available services one has access to. For instance, a person with a rural hukou who moves to the city does not have access to government services in the city such as education for their children. Consequently, there are millions of children left behind in rural regions by parents who have left for work in the cities, due to the lower levels of economic activity in rural regions. One recent population survey found that there were approximately 22,900,000 left-behind children, most of whom were concentrated in the more impoverished middle-Western regions. Of those surveyed 56.4% resided with a single parent, while 32.3% were being raised by grandparents (Yiu & Yun, 2017). This context of many children in rural China is a critical context through which to understand the equity challenges in rural schooling in China.

8.3 Fei Xiaotong

In understanding how rurality is theoretically constructed as distinct in China, the work of Fei Xiaotong is seminal. Fei Xiaotong is a famous Chinese sociologist and anthropologist. His 1947 (Translated 1992) work, translated as "From the Soil" with the subtitle "the foundations of Chinese society", is often regarded as the foundation of Chinese sociology (Xiaotong, 2012). This work develops an account of Chinese society and its moral and ethical foundations, as distinctly situated and emergent from rural culture, and also in contrast with western society (Fei's graduate studies were at the London School of Economics). While this, and Fei's other work, captures Chinese society just before the revolution, it remains a foundational text for studying this society and understanding the values that define it. In this way, Fei's work is akin to authors including Durkheim, Foucault and Bourdieu in the western tradition.

While Fei Xiaotong posits Chinese society as "from the soil" he does not, as critics may claim, position the rural in an antiquarian manner. Instead, this characterisation is related to foundational values that the rural represents—perhaps akin to the "bush myth" in Australia as foundational to Australian values. Fei creates a description on various planes of social relations about kinship and social obligations to those closest to oneself. In this understanding, social relations are grounded on respect, tradition and self-management. That is, values and good character come from inside an individual, not external regulation. Indeed, in many ways, the individual does not exist; they only exist in relation to others to whom they have an obligation. Power exists in, and through, the community observing these values (Xiaotong, 2012). While one may observe that such values are akin to the socialist values of the current nation, they are, however, at odds with the individualistic capitalism of western modernity. How this relates to China's global urban cities and evolving economic policies is something that is still unfolding.

In the current context of rapid modernisation and urbanisation "From the Soil" remains integral as a foundation of distinct Chinese values and traditions. For our chapter, the work also illustrates the distinct rural values of traditional society as both distinct within modernity, and to how rurality is conceptualised elsewhere in the world. That Fei understood rural society as valuable and not as backward or ignorant, as much modernist research does, enabled him to access the depths of insight that his many works illustrate. It also helps us, for this chapter, recognise that rural society is understood in China as distinct from urban society while also holding a key place as the crucible of national values. Modern education then needs to value this past while ensuring greater equity in the present and future. This could also suggest that urban China has an obligation to rural China due to social networks pre- and post-migration from the country to the city.

Importantly, while the imperative for urbanisation and economic development has resulted in massive rural-urban inequities, it does not mean that Fei's work has lost currency. Indeed, Fei was an engaged social scientist who had a prominent role advising on rural industrialisation for many decades. The values, traditions and ideas Fei outlined provide a basis for development to occur, while also being maintained by them, to give Chinese society its distinct characteristic. This is true even in times of global economic integration. We suggest that without an understanding of these values and the place of rural society in China, foreigners will never understand Chinese society. However, such an appreciation also enables us to observe the unfolding dynamics, tensions and challenges, of a society shifting to the notion of modernity based upon urbanisation. We can observe here how modernity is fundamentally challenging these very foundations of the distinct Chinese society as described by Fei Xiaotong in redefining the national character—something we have only been able to do in hindsight in contexts such as Australia. Modernity, going back to Durkheim, has been synonymous with the move to the city, which still drives rural out migrations today.

8.4 Teacher Education in the People's Republic of China

The Cultural Revolution in the People's Republic of China (PRC) which lasted from May 1966 to 1976 was led by its Chairman, Mao Zedong. Mao at the time saw the revolution as one way to reinvigorate his views of communism by strengthening ideology. It also proved, in practice, an expedient way of identifying and removing his political opponents.

> Our objective is to struggle against and crush those persons in authority who are taking the capitalist road to criticize and repudiate the reactionary bourgeois academic "authorities" and the ideology of the bourgeoisie and all other exploiting classes and transform education, literature, and art and all other parts of the superstructure that do not correspond to the socialist economic base, to facilitate the consolidation and development of the socialist system, so as to facilitate the consolidation and development of the socialist system. (de Bary, 2008, p. 758)

The revolution saw schools and universities closed, and churches, shrines, libraries, shops and private homes destroyed. "The bourgeoisie" including political opponents, Party officials, teachers and intellectuals were publicly humiliated, beaten and in some cases murdered or driven to suicide after vicious "struggle sessions" (Dikotter, 2016).

In 1968 Mao ordered millions of urban students, many who had completed only elementary education, to be sent to the countryside for "re-education" by poor peasants. Much of this re-education involved imprisonment in labour camps, from which many would never return. At the same time, he ordered the army to restore order. This, according to Dikotter (2016), effectively transformed China into a military dictatorship, which lasted until around 1971. The Cultural Revolution came to an end on Mao's death at the age of 82.

8.4.1   Following the Cultural Revolution

Following the end of the Cultural Revolution in 1976, the challenge facing China's provincial education system was how to provide the significant and sudden number of qualified teachers needed for the schools that were being re-opened. Related problems included the work of re-opening teachers' colleges, which was to take several years, and the level of training of the teachers who had survived the Cultural Revolution.

Fronting up to these challenges, the Shanghai provincial government, for example, decided to introduce in-service training programs to upgrade the skills of the teachers already in the classrooms, and to rethink the way teachers were trained. The training included full-time and part-time training, via television, lectures on special topics and lesson preparation by subject. The government also introduced new honorary titles to commend outstanding teaching. "Such incentives were directed at improving teaching and enhancing the status of teachers in the community's eyes" (Li, 2012, p. 97).

By the mid-1980s, the PRC government had decentralised school management. Decentralisation helped reorient schools that were seen to be centrally controlled and focused on national exams. Decentralisation was also a direct response to Chairman Deng Xiaoping's declaration that education should be oriented towards the needs of modernisation, the world and the future. The shift towards decentralisation meant that schools had new levels of independence. They could decide how and what to teach. However, it also meant they had to rethink and redefine the school organisation and the different responsibilities of principals and teachers (Zhang et al., 2016). Along with decentralised management came a new national curriculum. This

> expanded learning areas to include language and literature, mathematics, natural sciences, social sciences, technology, and sports and fitness it also focused on ethics and character development, development of cognitive and learning skills such as problem-solving, physical education, arts and culture, and social learning, which meant community service and learning about the community (Zhang et al., 2016, p. 9).

These broad initiatives in the PRC tied education to advancing the economic and social goals of the nation.

National educational reforms such as decentralisation and a new national curriculum-posed significant challenges for teacher education. In response, the MOE and provincial governments gradually began steps towards change in teacher education. Nationally, five-year plans for education began in the 1990s, and with these, the creation of the high-performing education and teacher education system that now exists.

8.4.2   Teacher Education in China Today

In the PRC, teaching is viewed as a long-term career. This contrasts with other education systems that suffer from the significant issue of teacher attrition (Zhou, 2015). While not always the first choice of secondary school students, the competitive nature of the PRC higher education market means students of high calibre and skill elect to study education. These pre-service teachers mainly enter their training program via their Gaokao (高考) (college entrance examination) score.

From 1986, all students in the PRC are required by law to complete 9 years of compulsory education. This includes six years of primary school education and three years of secondary education. Students may choose to continue their education in the hope of entering university; this usually requires them to complete a further 3 years of senior secondary school. The culmination of these studies being the Gaokao examination. A student's Gaokao result is the sole criteria for admission to Chinese universities (Guo et al., 2019).

The "Gaokao" includes tests of Chinese literature, mathematics and a foreign language which in most cases is English. Students who choose to specialise in the liberal arts take tests related to history, politics and geography, whereas, students who choose a science stream, take physics, chemistry and biology tests (Wu, 2019).

8.4.3   Content of Pre-Service Teacher Education Programs

Over the last 20 years, increasing the rigour of initial qualification and training of teachers has been a consistent priority for education reform. In 2001, following piloting, the PRC government introduced the Regulations on Teachers' Professional Qualification. These regulations require that teachers at all levels have a 4-year bachelor's degree or above; the exception being primary school teachers, who were initially permitted to have a two- or three-year Associate degree. However, most provinces are gradually moving towards primary school teachers needing a bachelor's degree, and for senior secondary teachers to have a master's degree (Zhang et al., 2016).

In the PRC, the Ministry of Education (MOE) licenses teacher education programs. However, questions remain about the responsibility of educating teachers. Should it be Normal (teacher education) universities, comprehensive universities or other institutions such as normal colleges or upper secondary schools (Hu & Verdugo, 2015).

At this time, teachers in China are formally educated in one of the three-type of schools. The first is Normal schools which are selected secondary schools that provide a two or three-year education program for pre-service teachers for primary, kindergartens or nursery schoolteachers. Second, Junior Normal colleges that offer a three-year Associate or sub-degree programs are for pre-service teachers wanting to teach junior secondary school students. The third and most popular teacher education option, a three to four-year bachelor's degree programs, is offered by Normal universities (Hayhoe & Li, 2010). These programs train teachers for kindergarten, primary and upper secondary schools (Li, 2012).

For pre-service teachers, a typical 4-year bachelor teacher education program consists of subject content knowledge, and general education subjects such as pedagogy, psychology, learning theory, human development and language study including English. Commonly, in-school teaching practice or school placements of two-three months, are held in the final year of study.

Apart from curriculum subject teaching for their specified level of teaching, i.e., kindergarten, primary or secondary, there is no systematic distinction made in the preparation of pre-service teachers to teach in rural or urban schools. However, in some universities, for example, the Hangzhou Normal University pre-service primary teacher program provides training to teach in rural areas for all subject teachers.

8.4.4 The National Teacher Certification Examination

All students, having completed their diploma, associate degree or bachelor's degree, must then apply for certification. This is a two-step process involving a national professional qualification exam or national "Teacher Certification Examination". "The Teacher Certificate Examination is intended to ensure that applicants have the ethics, knowledge and skills the profession requires" (Zhang et al., 2016, p. 12). One goal of this examination is to increase the status of teachers by developing rigorous qualification requirements. Such requirements ensure the profession and the public will view teachers among the most highly skilled members of society.

The national Teacher Certification Examination requires all applicants for teacher certificates (kindergarten, primary or senior secondary school) to pass the national Chinese Proficiency Test. Applicants must also pass three different types of written examination that focus on their knowledge and skills in the areas of educational knowledge, psychology, teaching methods, and teaching ability. Topics covered include knowledge of learning and human development, pedagogy, work ethics and relevant education laws and regulations.

One of the three tests will include a 20-minute interview that focuses on the applicant's professional merits, including ethics, manners and speaking ability, and the applicant's basic teaching "know-how". The "know-how" component may involve a teaching-scene simulation (Shanghai Municipal Education Commission, 2012), or micro-teaching where the applicant shows and discusses their teaching skills and techniques such as questioning, or designing, carrying out and evaluating a classroom session (Hu & Verdugo, 2015; Shanghai Municipal Education Commission, 2012; Zhang et al., 2016).

A key point to note is that pre-service teacher education degree holders are not the only applicants for the National Teacher certificate examinations. Any university graduate student with a bachelor's degree can sit this examination. If successful, like their education degree holders, they too will gain national teacher certification. Therefore, new teachers entering the teaching profession in the PRC will, in all likelihood, have a varied educational, subject knowledge and pedagogy backgrounds; some have little or no knowledge of teaching pedagogy.

8.4.5 Ongoing Professional Development

Given the focus on subject content knowledge and their limited or no pedagogical training, new teachers entering the profession are seen as "apprentices" and are supported by the schools as such. Hiring schools assign each beginning teacher to an experienced teacher who takes on the role of mentor. The provision of mentors can be difficult in rural areas where there are often smaller schools and less experienced staff.

Beginning teacher mentoring involves support and development of understanding about all aspects of being a professional teacher and work in schools, including aspects such as teaching rules and regulation, pastoral care, the preparation of teaching materials, lesson observation and critique, teaching and evaluation methods, exam preparation and marking and career advancement. In most provinces, the mentor and the beginning teacher are both held responsible for the progress made in the first 1–3 years (CIEB, n.d).

The hiring schools also must take responsibility for supporting and training these beginning teachers through an intensive 120-hour in-service professional development program. For example, the Shanghai province runs a compulsory one-year 120-hour beginning teacher induction program. The program has four parts: professional standards and ethics; teaching practice and classroom experience; classroom management and moral education; and teaching research and professional development (Zhang et al., 2016). Again, in rural areas funding, and distance, impose barriers to genuinely accessing this training.

Following success in this one-year "apprenticeship" or "induction" programme, new teachers, like their teaching colleagues, must go on to complete 360 hours of in-service training and professional development over the next 5 years (Hu & Verdugo, 2015; Zhang et al., 2016). In the PRC, teacher certification is for a period of 5 years. The 360 hours of continuing professional development is a requirement for re-certification.

The continuing professional development of teachers in the PRC is a major priority of the Ministry of Education. The provincial programs of development are designed according to the local context, the local teacher's professional responsibilities and national priorities. For example, in 2010, the National Teacher Training Programme for Teachers in Kindergarten, Primary and Secondary Schools implemented by the MOE was designed to provide projects and professional development activities to help improve the quality of teaching in rural primary and secondary schools (OECD, 2016). Such large-scale national project initiatives and local provincial or district professional development initiatives play a significant role in ensuring that teachers in the PRC meet the needs of the profession and individual teacher progression along their career path.

8.5 Rural Schools

The difference in China's rural areas compared to its modern global cities is rather extreme (Kong et al., 2021). Rural areas are often unattractive locations for teachers due to their lower levels of economic development, poorer infrastructure (technology, roads, transport), lack of services, limited cultural resources and general youth outmigration resulting in ageing communities (Cui, 2020; Zhou, 2015). Geographic isolation from global cities, mostly on the east coast, is also a significant problem. However, recent moves to incentivise the population to move to inland cities such as Xi'an and Chengdu may have an impact in time as these become attractive global cities in closer proximity, though other situated inequities will likely remain to some degree. These internal immigration incentives, bearing in mind the hukou system of household registration, enable anyone with a bachelor's degree or higher to immigrate without any age restriction (Zhou, 2015). Those with a Zhongzhuan diploma (junior vocational education qualification) or Dazhuan diploma (senior vocational education qualification) under the age of 45 years old are also able to immigrate.

Similar to countries such as Australia, the social context of many rural areas manifests in making rural areas unattractive for many teachers, and can impact the social context in which teachers work. With the large-scale outmigration from rural areas, and issues pertaining to the hukou system and access to schooling, millions of children are left behind in rural regions (Kong et al., 2021; Cui, 2020). At the same time, their parents work in major cities. As noted above, these children then live with grandparents or extended family, who often have limited education and, typical of grandparents the world over, spoil their grandchildren and impose limited discipline. The resultant social circumstances, in-home and the community, do not create an atmosphere conducive to academic study, with less academic competition compared to the highly competitive city environment that drives standards higher (Pang & Han, 2006).

The significant lack of a younger generation also impacts upon the English language skills of a community. English is a compulsory subject in Chinese education, and in major cities people with a knowledge of English are relatively easy to come across. However, this is not the case in rural areas, meaning there are few people for both students and teachers to practise English with (Cui, 2020). This in turn influences results in the Gaokao, the university entry exam, and consequently the reputation of the teacher (Wu & Shi, 2011). We should also note here that due to the general lack of desirability of rural schools it is often teachers with lower English scores who have been recruited initially.

In general, the salary of rural teachers is lower than in the cities, with fewer school resources and infrastructure (Zhou, 2015). As rural areas are often poorer, and Chinese farmers are often comparatively poor, communities often cannot afford school fees. Furthermore, school is mainly funded from regional budgets meaning the constrained economic base means the proportion of funding available for schools is less than wealthier regions with significant economic growth. As a consequence, schools have a more limited resource based upon which to operate (Tan, 2003). This impacts upon recruitment, and ultimately outcomes. The perception of poor quality that is then holstered upon teachers limits their opportunity for advancement and mobility. Ultimately staffing is impacted further as the unattractive conditions often mean the less qualified teachers or less skilled teachers are the only ones that can be recruited in these schools, continuing the spiral of disadvantage.

8.6   Approaches to Staffing Schools

As in many international contexts, the challenges facing rural schools in China are perhaps more related to the social and economic conditions of their communities than schools themselves. However, as in other international contexts, too, the main policy approach has aimed to attract higher quality teachers as they in turn should improve student outcomes.

Unlike countries such as Australia and the USA, where teacher education *for* rural communities has been popular, there is no similar scheme of significance in China. That is, the dominant discourse in pre-service education in China is one of quality as determined by examination results (MOE, 1995). However, in Australia and the USA, teacher education programs *for* rural communities often have programs that begin from the perspective that rural schools and communities are different and as such, require distinct approaches. Excellence in China, though, links to the whole system as there are two main curriculum tracks in schooling, meaning teacher supply in subject areas is not as big an issue as in other countries.

When it comes to the entrance examination for teaching in China, no specific pre-service degree is required. Prospective teachers only need to pass a test on moral, professional and psychological knowledge. They can do any degree, e.g., a Bachelor of History, and then pass the related qualification exam, in this case, history. High ranking schools typically have additional requirements for teachers, such as a degree from a Normal University, whereas harder-to-staff rural schools are not as selective. An explicit limitation is different standards of entry to the teaching profession. Another is that entry to the profession is examination driven. Prospective teachers may have the subject knowledge, but there is no requirement for professional or pedagogical knowledge or skills (Pang & Han, 2006). Compared to Australia and the USA, there is limited pedagogical training for prospective teachers, even when studying for a teaching degree.

In facilitating access to university and reducing the financial costs involved students at Normal universities have pathways whereby they may not need to pay tuition fees (MOE, 2007, 2018a). One pathway is as a free student, which requires high grades in the university entry exam, the Gaokao. Entering a teaching degree at a rural university is comparatively more achievable than being accepted to a university on the Eastern seaboard. Other approaches are similar to university loan repayments in Australia for rural teachers. In some Chinese provinces, students can have university fees reimbursed if they choose to return to a rural school. That is, provided they agree to stay and teach for a designated period, e.g., 6 years. Such arrangements are common and are naturally attractive in areas where the general economic conditions make paying university fees a significant financial burden on families.

We have noted that salaries for rural teachers are lower than those of teachers on the East coast. In general, salaries are set by local authorities and are dependent on the funds available at the local government or provincial level. Such an approach is more akin to the system of school districts in the USA than the broader state-based awards in Australia where all teachers receive the same pay regardless of location. Such an approach can make rural schools less attractive places for teachers to work, especially after having met the conditions for having their tuition debts paid. One approach to counter this is to provide salary increases for teachers, other than those on the 6-year agreements, after they have stayed for three years. Graduate studies are increasingly popular and are increasing becoming the expected level for a professional teacher in China. Therefore, free students can, post-graduation, apply to do a Master's Degree, after which they have to return to the school where they previously worked (MOE, 2018a). The perceived benefit is that teachers do not need to take the entrance exam to enter the degree.

There are a number of local approaches to try to improve the employment conditions in Chinese rural schools. There has been a deliberate approach to give local provincial authorities more autonomy over local education matters. However, and perhaps linked to the national focus on improving outcomes and economic development in rural regions and to improve related social conditions, the central government has been increasingly getting involved. As part of a national ethos, the notion of doing good work for the nation by raising communities out of poverty is promoted as a way o f encouraging graduates to work in rural regions. However, this does not seem to motivate all. Instead the central government provides extra in-service training for teachers in rural areas which is paid for by the Central government (MOE, 2010b). Another approach involves increased national subsidies for rural teachers' salaries to make them more attractive than city locations (MOE, 2014a). This approach is used in emerging areas of high minority populations in China. Furthermore, incentives for example, the payment by provincial governments of medical, insurance and legal access are emerging. Similar incentives such as cash bonuses and housing subsidies are provided by Australian State governments.

Recognising the importance of school leadership, there is a Chinese national plan for rural school principals (MOE, 2014b). This plan involves government support for school principals to spend time in outstanding city schools to enhance their management skills and broaden their experience. There is also a principal and teacher rotation and exchange plan, whereby 10–20% of exceptional teachers and principals are rotated through rural areas (MOE, 2018b). For example, in some provinces, rural school principals must rotate after 8 years. Other programs also exist where city schools help rural schools by sending their principals to support schools for two years before they return to their (previous) school.

8.7 Policy

8.7.1 Policy for Equity

There is a phrase in China about the "cask effect"—meaning that the capacity of a wooden bucket is dependent upon the shortest board—that has become a common reference for the notion that the quality of education for the nation as a whole is dependent upon the quality of rural education. Such notions link into the emerging policy architecture that is developing within the last few years in the interests of enhancing equity and social development. Two such policies are "balanced development of compulsory education" (MOE, 2005) and "modernization of education 2035" (MOE, 2019), each of which seeks to integrate rural and urban areas. The "modernization of education 2035" is a systematic strategy which refers to eight fields of education: constructing a lifelong learning education system; universal preschool education; balancing quality compulsory education; access to senior school education (including vocational education) for every student; raising the competences of vocational education; increasing competition of higher education; construct improved inclusive education; and promote development of education governance.

The policy approach to integrate rural and urban education is aimed at closing the gap between rural and urban schools by integrating design, development, institutions, policy, finance, teacher resource, school construction and education quality. There is no discernible definition of balancing development between urban and rural. There is, however, a general consensus about balancing the distribution of education resources and rural student access, opportunity and outcomes in the schools. It appears the notion of integration is founded in economic thinking about resources and outcomes, and is aimed more at breaking dualistic thinking about urban and rural. Language such as balancing, however, connotes more sociological overtones and provides space for sociological theory to be engaged.

Such policies are informed by a perspective that rural schools are disadvantaged, and as such the state should help them to develop to be equal to city schools. This is the perennial issue of rural schooling across the world; how to address disadvantage. However, such issues are consistently framed in a metro-centric notion of the city as being the basis of comparison and itself the arbiter of the standard to be achieved (Roberts & Green, 2013). Here we see the tension of modernity unfolding before us, a struggle between the foundational values captured by Fei Xiaotong, and a need to equalise rural spaces with the areas that have rapidly expanded into globalised cities within the last generation. How this can be achieved, in a manner that integrates with Fei Xiaotong's values, while providing services expected in modernity is, one may suggest, an unachievable challenge. Instead, we may be observing the mechanisms through which modernity works to erase rurality through the discourse of equity that assumes the values of the city.

These discourses of disadvantage facilitate the phenomena of some parents moving to the city to access better education—where they must pay if they do not have the relevant hukou. This accelerates the marginalisation of rural spaces in a declining spiral—only leaving an aging population, fewer students, typically the less mobile due to pre-existing economic hardship. Consequently, the community is in decline and is even less attractive for teachers, regardless of the increasing resourcing level. This cycle can be observed in Australia in nearly the exact same manner.

8.7.2   Policy for Revitalisation

Beyond the pragmatics of staffing schools, the social and economic context is a critical influence on what happens in these communities and schools. To this end, major policy reforms have been underway such as the "Rural Revitalization Strategy". Here the revitalisation of rural education in China has recently been identified as the key to social and economic development. This is subtle yet significant, semantic reorientation. The language here is not one of integration or balance, but positioning education as an active driver of development. Indeed, this is one of the top priorities among current Chinese development strategies. As such, this comparative analysis allows examination of both the process of rural decline and large-scale initiatives to redevelop the rural sector in a modern economy. This is a reorientation that is yet to occur in Australia in any significant manner. Though we should caution such an approach may orientate again towards economic outcomes in its current form, so the concern about valuing the social aspects of rurality as per Fei Xiaotong's values remain an ongoing development to follow closely.

The "Rural Revitalization Strategic Plan" (2018–2022) (CPC Central Committee and the State Council, 2018) and "Education Informatization 2.0 Action Plan" (MOE, 2018b) are two national strategies that provide significant policy support for rural education development in contemporary China. At the 19th National Congress of the Communist Party of China in 2017, Chinese President Xi Jinping put forward the idea of "implementing the strategy of rural revitalization", aimed at the overall development of the country. Notably, in this chapter, we have chosen to address the changing characteristics of urban–rural relations during the process of modernisation and the national goal of seeking a better life. The strategy's overall goals are directed at building rural areas with thriving businesses, pleasant living environments, social mores and civility, effective governance and prosperity.

Perhaps echoing Fei Xiaotong, this plan notes the significant role the rural plays in the development of Chinese society, including its complex natural, social and economic characteristics; its multiple functions for productivity, living, ecology and culture; and its mutual promotion and coexistence with the urban. Hence, the country can only be prosperous if the rural is prosperous; the country can only be weak if the rural is weak. In this sense, the implementation of the rural revitalisation strategy is the fundamental basis of the entire Chinese economic system, traditional culture, ecological development, social governance and people's well-being. In line with our concern above, it would seem the balance of measures to be achieved are themselves founded in the modernity of the new urban society. Within this mutuality of rural-urban, there are echoes of what Judith Brett (2011), in the Australian context calls, the trade-off between the city and country. Here for a long time, the city accepted its role in supporting the rural as they were interdependent, however under new economic policies of the 1990s this compact was broken as the perspective shifted to individualism and paying one's own way (Brett, 2011). Within this, we suggest, there are a number of the causes of accelerated rural inequity in Australia. It would appear that China is making moves to develop such a compact in the interests of national development.

Under the rural revitalisation strategy, several related (equity) policies exist as noted above, aimed at improving the quality of teachers, access to resources and access to education. Indeed, the strategy contains a specific chapter on "The Development of Rural Education" such that the development of rural education has once again been placed in the priority position of national ideals and national strategic development (Zhu et al., 2019).

A second related policy here is the "Education Informatization 2.0 Action Plan" (MOE, 2018b), which aims "to accelerate the modernization of education and the construction of a strong country in education", and to "promote the development of information technology in the new era and foster a new engine for innovation and drive development". While this plan does not explicitly refer to rural education, it does aim to promote development through improving the quality of the population. This is to be achieved through approaches including supporting the development of education informatisation in deep poverty areas with a focus on three districts and three states,[1] and improving quality, equity and equality in education. This again relates to the policies mentioned above, for improving teacher and leader quality through professional development. However, a specific focus of this plan is related to cloud classrooms in the national open universities, information technology-based teaching equipment, the development of high-quality digital education shared resources and related educational information services. This will include partnerships between high achieving and struggling schools, joint online teaching and professional networks of teachers. To make this happen the provision of balanced technology resources is central to the strategy, to eradicate the digital divide in education.

Central to these policies is the notion that improving the educational access and achievement of rural students is not only an equity issue but also a fundamental pre-condition for national economic development. Furthermore, enhancing social outcomes is itself linked with economic development *and* this is the responsibility of government. This is striking on two fronts. Firstly, in many "developed western' nations", responsibility for economic advancement has been shifted to the individual, from the state. Secondly, the explicit recognition that to make rural places more attractive for professionals, and to enhance educational achievement, there is an interrelationship between the social-economic context and education. In contrast, in many other contexts, the focus has shifted towards teacher quality and remediating the individual teacher based on student outcomes divorced from their school context. While there are insights here for international contexts about how to re-consider the relationship between education and rural spaces, the question remains, on what values will this development proceed, and how will rurality, a fundamental component of Chinese national identity and values, fare in the transition.

The recent history of rural areas, and rural education, in China, provides insights into ways of positioning the rural that are distinct from the experiences of many nations. In the example of China, we see the recent development of many of the historical rural-urban inequities that are unfortunately common. However, in its recentness, we can see these inequities have developed as a consequence of modernity and economic development, themselves framed in an urban-centred metro-normative imaginary. However, we also see recent policy interventions that honour the foundational values of Fei Xiaotong and position the enhancement of education in rural areas as implicitly interwoven with the revitalisation of rural regions—socially, culturally and economically. This appears distinct from much international experience and as such, provides a vital trial that rural-related scholars will watch with great interest. Finally, the evolving policy associated interventions and practices aimed at improving the education of rural communities are also supported by significant national investment. Such a level of commitment may well reflect what many in the international community would hope for in their own contexts. Again, we watch with interest.

---

[1] Note: "Three Districts and Three States" are the deep poverty areas at the national level in China. The "Three Districts" refer to Tibet, four regions in Southern Xinjiang and The Tibetan in the four provinces, namely Qinghai, Sichuan, Yunnan and Gansu provinces other than the Tibet Autonomous Region, where Tibetans and other ethnic groups live together; "Three States" refer to Linxia state of Gansu province, Liangshan state of Sichuan province and Nujiang state of Yunnan province.

References

Brett, J. (2011). Fair share: Country and city in Australia. *Quarterly Essay, No. 42.* Black Inc.

Center on International Education Benchmarking (CIEB). (n.d.). *Shanghi-china overview.* Retrieved from http://ncee.org/what-we-do/center-on-international-education-benchmarking/top-performing-countries/shanghai-china/.

Chen, G., Glasmeier, A. K., Zhang, M., & Shao, Y. (2016). Urbanization and income inequality in post-reform China: A causal analysis based on time series data. *PLoS ONE, 11*(7), e0158826. https://doi.org/10.1371/journal.pone.0158826.

CPC Central Committee and the State Council. (2018, Sept. 26). *Central Committee of the Communist Party of China issued the Rural Revitalization Strategic Plan (2018–2022).* Retrieved from: http://www.gov.cn/gongbao/content/2018/content_5331958.htm.

Crossley, M., & Watson, K. (2011). Comparative and international education: Policy transfer, context sensitivity and professional development. In J. Furlong & M. Lawn (Eds.), *Disciplines of education: their role in the future of education research* (pp. 103–121). Routledge.

Cui, B. (2020). *Teacher wellbeing in rural China: An appreciative mixed-methods study in Jilin province.* Ph.D. Dissertation, University of Adelaide.

de Bary, T. (2008). The Mao regime. In T. de Bary, (Ed.), *Sources of East asian tradition: The modern period, Volume two.* (pp. 747–761). Columbia University Press.

Dikotter, F. (2016). *The cultural revolution: A people's history, 1962–1976.* New York, NY: Bloomsbury Press.

Guo, L., Huang, J., & Zhang, Y. (2019). Education development in China: Education return, quality and equity. *Sustainability, 11*(13), 3750. https://doi.org/10.3390/su11133750.

Hayhoe, R., & Li, J. (2010). The idea of a normal university in the 21st century. *Frontiers of Education in China, 5*(1), 74–103.

Hu, A., & Verdugo, R. R. (2015). An analysis of teacher education policies in China. *International Journal of Education Reform, 24*(1), 37–53.

Kong, P. A., Hannum, E., & Postiglione, G. A. (2021). *Rural education in China's social transition.* New York: Routledge.

Li, J. (2012). The Chinese model of teacher education. *Frontiers of Education in China, 7*(3), 417–442.

MOE. (1995, Dec, 12). Teacher qualification regulations. Retrieved from http://www.moe.gov.cn/s78/A02/zfs__left/s5911/moe_620/tnull_3178.html.

MOE. (2005, May, 25). Ministry of education issued on further promoting the balanced development of compulsory education. Retrieved from http://www.moe.gov.cn/srcsite/A06/s3321/200505/t20050525_81809.html.

MOE. (2007, 11). Trial implementation about charge free for students in six normal university under administration of the ministry of education. Retrieved from https://baike.baidu.com/item//15482786?fr=aladdin.(Discardalready).

MOE. (2010a, Jul, 29). Plan for national medium-term and long-term development 2010–2020. Retrieved from http://old.moe.gov.cn/publicfiles/business/htmlfiles/moe/info_list/201407/xxgk_171904.html.

MOE. (2010b, Feb, 22). National training plan for preschool, primary and secondary teachers. Retrieved from http://www.moe.gov.cn/srcsite/A10/s7034/201803/t20180313_329820.html.

MOE. (2014a, Jun, 11).Ministry of education notification about national plan for primary and secondary principles. Retrieved from http://www.moe.gov.cn/srcsite/A10/s7034/201406/t20140611_170727.html.

MOE. (2014b, Aug, 15). Ministry of education issued promoting principals and teachers in compulsory education schools exchange within county (District) region. Retrieved from http://www.moe.gov.cn/srcsite/A10/s7151/201408/t20140815_174493.html.

MOE. (2018a, July, 30). Notification about change free to expenses of students in six normal university under administration of ministry of education. Retrieved from http://www.gov.cn/zhengce/content/2018-08/10/content_5313008.htm.

MOE. (2018b, Apr, 13). Ministry of education issued education informationization 2.0 Action Plan. Retrieved from http://www.moe.gov.cn/srcsite/A16/s3342/201804/t20180425_334188.html.

MOE. (2019, Feb, 23). Modernization of education 2035 Strategy. Retrieved from http://www.moe.gov.cn/jyb_xwfb/s6052/moe_838/201902/t20190223_370857.html.

Mu, G. M., & Jia, N. (2014). Rural dispositions of floating children within the field of Beijing schools: Can disadvantaged rural habitus turn into recognised cultural capital? *British Journal of Sociology of Education, 37*(3), 408–426.

OECD. (2016). Education in China: A snapshot. *Organisation for economic co-operation and development.* Retrieved from https://www.oecd.org/china/Education-in-China-a-snapshot.pdf.

Pang, L., & Han, X. (2006). Problems and countermeasures on rural compulsory educational teachers' team in China. *Educational Research, 9,* 47–53.

Roberts, P., & Green, B. (2013). Researching rural place(s): On social justice and rural education. *Qualitative Inquiry, 19*(10), 765–774.

Roberts, P., & Hannum, E. (2018). Education and equity in rural China: A critical introduction for the rural education field. *Australian and International Journal of Rural Education, 28*(2), 1–13.

Shanghai Municipal Education Commission. (2012). *Education statistics 2012 report.* Shanghai Education.

Tan, S. (2003). Status quo, difficulties and countermeasures of the development of rural education in China. *Peking University Education Review, 1*(1), 99–103.

Woods, M. (2011). *Rural.* London: Routledge.

Wu, Z., & Shi, Ni. (2011). The trends and policy issues for rural school layout and adjustment in the last decade in China. *Educational Research, 7,* 22–30.

Wu, C. (2019). Everything you need to know about the Gaokao. Retrieved from http://www.thatsmags.com/china/post/13965/explainer-gaokao.

Xiaotong, F. & 费孝通 & Han, Geli, (translator.) & Wang, Zheng, (author.) & 韩格理, (translator.) et al. (2012). Xiang tu Zhongguo: Han Ying dui zhao = From the soil: the foundations of Chinese society.

Yiu, L., & Yun, L. (2017). China's rural education: Chinese migrant children and left-behind children. *Chinese Education & Society, 50*(4), 307–314.

Young, N., & Hannum, H. (2018). Childhood inequality in China: Evidence from recent survey data (2012–2014). *The China Quarterly* pp. 1–25.

Zhang, M., Ding, X., & Xu, J. (2016). *Developing Shanghai's teachers.* Washington, DC: National Centre on Education and the Economy.

Zhou, J. (2015). The mobility and attrition of teachers in rural schools in China: A review of literature. *Teacher Education Research, 27*(1), 60–67.

Zhu, C., Yan, G., & Zhu, D. (2019). Rural construction and rural education: Integrated model of accurate poverty alleviation for vocational education and rural revitalization strategy. *Journal of East China Normal University (Educational Science Edition), 37*(02), 127–135.

Philip Roberts is an Associate Professor in Curriculum Inquiry and Rural Education in the Faculty of Education at the University of Canberra and Adjunct Professor in the Institute for Education Research in Western China, Shaanxi Normal University, China. He is the research leader of the Rural Education and Communities Research Group in the Centre for Sustainable Communities at the University of Canberra. Philip's ongoing research focuses on place and the sustainability of rural communities and his work is situated within rural sociology, the sociology of knowledge, educational sociology and social justice. Dr. Roberts has served as the national convener of the Rural Education Special Interest Group of the Australian Association for Research in Education 2015-18 and as co-convenor 2013-15.

Peter Bodycott is Professor of Teacher and International Education in the Faculty of Education at the University of Canberra, Australia. His teaching and research specialisations include: English literacy teaching and learning; comparative and international education; the internationalisation of education; intercultural communication, and; teaching English as a second or foreign language. His most recent published works explore the internationalisation of the curriculum and the socio-cultural and psychological effects of study abroad on international students and educational policy and practice.

Yiting Li is a PhD student in comparative education at Shaanxi Normal University, Xian, China. Ms Li is researching place-based rural teacher development and rural vocational education. She has participated in research projects on vocational education for technical workers and research projects on strategies for promoting international education and culture exchanges between China and other international countries. Ms Li holds a Masters of TESOL from Monash University, Australia, and a Bachelor of English in literature from Lanzhou University, China.

Xuyang Qian is an Associate Professor of the School of Education at Hangzhou Normal University and a visiting scholar at Harvard Graduate School of Education. Her research interests include integrated curriculum studies, place-based learning, and embodied understanding. She has participated in various research projects including developing the National Curriculum Guideline for an Integrated Curriculum of Practical Activity, classroom culture change in the digital age and evaluation of teachers' professional development. She is currently conducting funded studies to assess teachers' TPACK, explore place-based learning approach for ecological literacy cultivation, and Chinese children's identity shifts in the digital age. She serves as a committee member at the International Association for the Advancement of Curriculum Studies (IAACS) and the Curriculum Reform Committee of Basic Education in Zhejiang Province, China.

Chapter 9
Structures of Feeling and the Problem of Place in Rural Education

Michael Corbett

Abstract In this chapter I argue that settler societies contain multiple sociocultural creation stories that serve to generate powerful emotional landscapes, or what Raymond Williams called "structures of feeling". These can be inclusive, respectful and generous, or alternatively narrow, xenophobic, nativist, racist and otherwise exclusionary. Drawing on ideas from the critical sociology of education and contemporary work in rural education, I offer a theoretical approach to rural teacher education that imagines schooling as a relational enterprise where stories connect rather than diverge, supporting a movement of the field of rural education into productive conversation with the culturally responsive pedagogy movement and Indigenous scholarship. This involves, I argue, a careful analysis of the idea of the rural along with its attendant emotional and spatial dimensions.

Keywords Teacher education · Structure of feelings · Rural education · Place · Space · Nova Scotia · Emotion · Tourism

9.1 Introduction

Until recently, the field of rural education has operated largely without theory. It has been a field in search of itself, trading on key tropes such as community (Corbett, 2014) and place (Corbett, 2020; Nespor, 2008), generating research that focuses either on the particularity of distinct and allegedly insular communities, or as part of larger comparative work in which rural appears as a variable among a range of others (Coladarci, 2007). To illustrate the latter approach, I point to quantitative studies that compare the "performance" or rural to urban students on some form of standardized metric (Echazarra & Radinger, 2019; Nugent, Kunz, Sheridan, Glover, & Knoche, 2017).

What is needed, in my opinion, is an approach to innovative or best practices that is connected to coherent theoretical understandings of the uses and misuses of the idea

M. Corbett (✉)
School of Education, Acadia University, Wolfville, NS, Canada
e-mail: michael.corbett@acadiau.ca

© Springer Nature Singapore Pte Ltd. 2021
S. White and J. Downey (eds.), *Rural Education Across the World*,
https://doi.org/10.1007/978-981-33-6116-4_9

of rurality itself. Too much work in the field of rural education is disconnected from the main currents of social science thinking, too often imagining rural communities as though they were isolated from modernity and capitalism, and/or as spaces apart containing people who are implied to be somehow different from the mainstream of (urban) society. Rural is not a primordial space apart from capitalism, but rather a crucial part of what Henri Lefebvre (1992) called the production of space under capitalism. It is transformed, by global economic activity ranging from more or less mechanized and automated primary production, through established and emerging forms of manufacturing and by the world's largest industry which is tourism. As such, rural places, like cities, are crucially shaped by what Andreas Malm (2016) calls "fossil capital" which is predicated on the European colonial enterprise that is alive and well today, slicing and dicing the globe, fundamentally altering natural processes, and rendering considerable parts of the non-metropolitan earth "dead" (Sassen, 2014).

More theoretically attuned work is appearing as emerging scholars apply contemporary social and political theory to problems in rural education. Much of this work is animated by spatial theory under the intellectual leadership of Bill Green in Australia (Green, 2008, 2013; Green & Letts, 2007; Reid et al., 2010). An example is Jason Cervone's (2017) analysis of the corporatization of rural education that draws heavily on Lefebvrian social geography. Another is Wendy Geller's (2015) feminist geography of education and mobility. Kim Donehower and colleagues (2007, 2011) have initiated a subfield within literacy studies that takes up the meanings of rurality in literacy practices. Other recent work draws on political theory (Cuervo, 2016; Roberts, 2016; Roberts & Green, 2013), cultural and critical race theory (Pini and Bhopal, 2017; Tieken, 2014); critical rural development theory and comparative education (Wu, 2016), and curriculum theory (Reynolds, 2017a). These are all book-length treatments of rural education issues that explicitly draw on contemporary social, spatial, curriculum and political theory to develop rich analytic understandings of educational phenomena and the way that rurality and education mutually refract in practice.

The challenge at this stage is not to retreat into some form of place-based educational practices that celebrate the insularity, particularity and even exceptionalism of particular rural places. Rather, what is needed is a scholarly recognition of the politics, histories of violence and exploitation and uneven development that have characterized the development of settler societies particularly, but also the development of the global concentration of power and privilege in the equally unevenly resourced and structured "global cities" (Sassen, 1991). The production of space also moves bodies in and out of places and while the central dynamic of industrial and post-industrial capitalism has been shifting populations out of the countryside and into cities, other dynamics reshape non-metropolitan areas as corporate farms, ex-mountain slag-heaps, coastal playgrounds and genteel retreats for middle-class urbanites. Rurality also contains juxtapositions of rich, heritage sites and protected wilderness areas for tourist consumption, and low-cost housing ghettos for the urban poor removed for neighbourhood gentrification. Rural places may represent "close-knit" communitarian dreams, just as a city neighbourhood can, but questions about who is missing from these comfortable spaces haunt the dream. On the other hand, rural places can be considerably "loose-knit" and as impersonal and functional as a stereotypical disconnected urban locale where families "hunker down" in their enclaves (Putnam, 2007).

One way to answer the question concerning why rural matters in education is to attend to the amount of attention paid to the real and imagined role that the rural United States is alleged to have played in the election of Donald Trump. The social conditions that led to this situation are often considered to be the direct result of educational deficits which are themselves easily layered on established rustic stereotypes that position rural social subjects as uneducated, crude, rustic, xenophobic, resentful and racist (Ching & Creed, 1996). This imagery is played out both in contemporary liberal political discourse as well as in American cinema, television and social media on a daily basis (Beech & Guy, 2017; Reynolds, 2017b). As more nuanced commentary demonstrates, rural Americans have been systematically marginalized by the neoliberal shift in education policy and resourcing providing youth little choice other than to stay and take what is available in marginalized rural communities or leave (Hall & Biddle, 2017). In this reading, a lack of education is not the cause of rural resentment and angst, it is the effect of a system that offers little hope to rural areas.

What has emerged is an expanding slate of rural biographies (Vance, 2016; Westover, 2018) and social analysis (Cramer, 2016; Hochschild, 2016; Wuthnow, 2018) that seek to explain what is going on in rural America in the wake of the 2016 presidential election. It is demonstrably the case that rural America voted strongly for Donald Trump, while in the city centres (including in heavily republican states), voters just as heavily supported Hillary Clinton (Bloch, Buchanan, Katz, & Quealy, 2018; Tavernise, Gebeloff, & Lee, 2019). As Kai Schafft put it when he was interviewed by the *New York Times*—an exceedingly rare event for a rural education scholar— "all of a sudden rural is on everyone's mind" (Pappano, 2017).

What motivates this current drift and how does rural imagery play into it? Rurality has a particular structure of feeling (Williams, 1983) which is evoked by the images that spring to mind when the word rural is uttered. These structures of feeling take perhaps a distinct shape in settler society contexts where the exploitation of the land was engineered as part of colonial projects over a relatively short span of historical time. The "opening up" or settlement of the land by European antecedents is a living memory for some rural Canadians today. For many others, rural roots go back only a generation or two. The same is true for Australia, New Zealand and the United States. This rural structure of feeling which evolves and moves in ways our fiction and scholarship struggle to capture has become significant as liberals and contemporary social analysts and journalists attempt to understand the emerging political landscape of authoritarian populism. It is easy to find scapegoats for such phenomena and rural citizens, the disenfranchised working class, and those lacking higher education credentials are easy targets. The analysis of blame though both simplifies a complex problem and generates increased misunderstanding and entrenchment of sociopolitical armies living behind what Arlie Russell Hochschild (2016) cogently calls an "empathy wall". Here we move into emotional territory and the tension produced in what Lauren Berlant (2011) calls "cruel optimism" for an object of desire (in this case, often taking the form of a nostalgic longing for an imagined rural past) which is not only beyond reach, but which itself becomes pathological (see also Kelly, 2009, 2013).

9.2 Structures of Feeling

In the mid-1950s Raymond Williams (1958/1983) developed the concept of "structure of feeling" to express how, at any given moment in history, there are not so much particular epochal ways of thinking, but rather, competing ways of feeling that emerge from the inevitable contestations and tensions that co-exist in any given time and place. Williams sympathetically critiqued the idea that dominant structures of feeling articulate theoretically in Marx's ideology, or in Gramsci's idea of hegemony. Williams' idea points to the depth and automaticity represented by the idea of feeling building on Heidegger's (1927/2010) *dasein* with its attention to place (being-there). Trumpism, for instance, is clearly not a thoughtful movement, but rather, one that is shot through with feeling. In Williams' idea, there are multiple ways we experience the world as things change and emerge/evolve. As he put it elsewhere, culture always contains residual and emergent cultural forms which interact in social space at a given moment. Structural conditions do not create foreclosures or structurally predictable responses, but affective orientations that inflect but never determine agency.

Williams work was a seminal part of a larger movement in social science theorizing that has generated what might be considered a complex, relational vision of the social that integrates time and space and that seems to problematize and even transcend categorical conceptual binaries and boundaries that have generated and limited established ways of conceptualizing what the social sciences are about. This includes both broad poststructural critiques as well as the idea that the social sciences have not really come to grips with developments in continental philosophy in the twentieth century (Giddens, 1971, 1976, 1979). With his use of the idea of structured feeling, Williams illustrates both the emergence of structural phenomena and how practice is grounded in everyday emotional landscapes. These structured emotional landscapes not only bring objects into view, they shape how we interpret and interact with them. To use the contemporary theoretical language of the new materialism, our concepts do not reflect reality, they refract and change how reality is constructed.

If ever there was an established and problematic binary, it is that of rural and urban space. This binary has been employed in the central narrative of colonial modernity in the story of a movement from the country to the city (another of Williams' preoccupations in both his fiction and prose, cf. Williams, 1960, 1974), the transition from agricultural to industrial societies, from traditional knowledge forms to scientific inquiry, from lives based on what Talcott Parsons (1950) juxtaposed as "ascription" orientations to those defined in terms of "achievement", and the list goes on.

The rural/urban binary sits as the heart of how contemporary subjects understand progress, development, themselves, geography and history. In other words, many cotemporary structures of feeling relate in one way or another to this binary. For instance, the *Ginn Basic* elementary school readers (Ousley, 1961) I encountered as a school child in the mid-1960s had as its central boyhood prototype a light-skinned boy named Tom who lived in a leafy suburban or small town neighbourhood. Tom's father arrived at home wearing a suit and carrying a briefcase to meals prepared by his mother. Apart from the rather obvious gender, racial and social class subjectivization at play here, in one of the readers, Tom goes to visit his grandparents who are farmers and this book moves from town to the country with its rolling hills, farm machinery and men who work in overalls. Often, when I give talks on rural education topics, I will be approached by audience members (including academics) who want to share some nostalgic story about their relationship with rural work experience, forebears and geographies. Sometimes, when I describe my work to colleagues, they will assume I work in developing countries. For the modern subject, rural is elsewhere in time and space. Like a ghost, it remains on the fringes until an event like the 2016 United States presidential election provides the conditions out of which the unlikely spectre emerges, far from dead.

9.3 Spectrology

While rural structures of feeling remain prominent for many of us, much of this sentiment is confined to the margins of history, memory or other places. But of course, even in the most advanced capitalist societies, at least one in five people's lives in a space that is somehow defined as rural.[1] In 2006, I wrote a piece in the *Alberta Journal of Educational Research* that used Jacques Derrida's (1994) notion of a new discipline he called "spectrology" or "hauntology" (Corbett, 2006). Derrida's text, *Spectres of Marx: The State of the Debt, The Work of Mourning and the New International* was originally published in French in the early 1990s when a rapid change was sweeping Europe with the fall of the Berlin Wall, the dissolution of the Soviet Union and the emergence of new state configurations in the wake of these change. As Francis Fukuyama (1992) famously put it, state communism lay in ruins, liberal democracy was globally ascendant, and history was at an end. It was a time of optimism, globalization with a smiling face and the apparent realization of Adam Smith's dreamscape of peaceful free trade, harmony and a real sharing of the wealth of nations. There seemed to be, at the time, a sense of an emergent unified structure of feeling that articulated with liberal democratic values, ubiquitous and instantaneous communication that would promote ever-increasing understanding, a diminution of armed struggle and warfare and a post-nationalist globalization of

---

[1]There are of course exceptions like modern city states such as Macao and Hong Kong. What is and is not counted as rural is also a persistent and intractable problem. Thus, any definition or boundary making is problematic which again illustrates how the rural/urban binary serves ideological, symbolic and political more than descriptive purposes. Yet, critique notwithstanding, the structures of feeling around the rural render the concept resilient and emotionally meaningful.

trade and commerce. This sensibity of the end of history was similar to the idea that rurality is similarly at an end, replaced by ascendant urbanization.

What has transpired since then if of course, something entirely different and Derrida saw it coming. What Derrida suggested in *Spectres of Marx*, with his characteristic deconstructive flair, is that any grand social dream is troubled or haunted by ghosts. These ghosts are neither living nor dead, present or absent, but rather they exist beneath the surface of totalizing tales refusing to fade away. They reappear like the ghost of Hamlet's father or Marx's spectre of communism to appear in shadowy form raising questions about the nature of present reality itself. Both Shakespeare and Marx illustrate the crucial power of these spectres in the spectacular bloodbath at the conclusion of Hamlet and in the eventual emergence of ordinary workers as the central agents of history in Marx. The same might be said of Jesus Christ's inscription of the reversal of the social order in the afterlife where the last shall be first, and in the presence of a holy spirit (Holy Ghost in my 1960s Catholic education) as part of a divine masculine trinity. Obviously, other spectres have emerged, unearthing passions, practices and ideas that seem to overturn the enlightenment and catapult to power leaders who seem to have little interest in the liberal values Fukuyama invoked. Quite the opposite, and for many of them rurality is a potent emotional weapon.

I argued in my 2006 article that education theorizing tends to be caught in an urbanizing imaginary in which education itself is conflated with the metropolis. Not only is education in rural areas typically understood to be fundamentally about increasing the "options" and mobilities available to youth, in the process, rural places are ignored, denigrated and/or consigned to the past in a way that is not dissimilar from the approach taken in the Ginn Basic readers in the 1950s and 60s. The very purpose of education then is to accomplish the work of elevating the rural subject out of what Ching and Creed (1996) called rusticity. Indeed, the term rural, as it is situated in the Oxford English Dictionary, plays on a set of definitions that elaborate this cultural theme. Because of this marginal framing, the spatial logic of schooling in rural areas has tended to obscure if not erase serious consideration of place and space in curriculum and pedagogy. What followed from this metrocentric approach to the business of schooling are a series of interlocking erasures of rural geographies and practices and what I have termed "learning to leave" (Corbett, 2007). With this imagery of escape, I was gesturing towards a largely subliminal subtext of rural schooling in which rural culture recedes and urbanization advances and where the central purpose of schooling is to mobilize the modern educational subject towards the city and modernity.

The problem that has been noted for at least a century though, is that rural people and places have never disappeared. Some leave, but many return and local institutions and services do not always die easily, particularly as select rural communities are transformed into service centres, tourist centres and at least partially gentrified real estate markets. The rural school is defended by community activists unconvinced that the large centralized operation up the road will educate their children better is a rather obvious example. But so too are those more or less "resistant" children and youth who retain emotional engagement with place and rural cultural and social practice and have little desire to escape to a bigger place. These figures haunt the modernizing impulses of centralization and consolidation and confound the linear myth of transition from the rural to the urban.

9.4   The Production of Place

Binary rural/urban framing creates illusion that rural and urban are entirely different sorts of places. The rural represents a residual culture in terms of attitudes and values as Williams pointed out nearly fifty years ago. What carries on is a vestige of these "older ways" somehow isolated in "pockets" that have managed to remain outside modernity in sometimes splendid but more often, squalid exceptionalist isolation. This view was promoted by a generation of cultural intellectuals who combed North America principally to discover what they imagined were "pure" forms of European folk music and story freeze-dried in the isolated hollows of Appalachian United States and the coastal communities of Nova Scotia, Canada (McKay, 1994; McKay & Bates, 2010). This imagery plays nicely into the province's tourism promotion strategy which has long constructed Nova Scotia as a Eurocentric enclave representing a therapeutic retreat (Kelly, 2013) to a space that sits outside modernity waiting quietly for stressed urbanites to come and "unwind".[2]

Canadian historian Ian McKay argues that in the case of Nova Scotia, a coterie of cultural intellectuals from the 1920s and 30s developed an image of the "folk" who inhabited rural and coastal communities carrying on cultural practices that represented foundational ethno-racial (both terms were used to describe cultural groups) "types" that could still be found on the back roads. In a series of travel books authored in the 1950s Will R. Bird (1950, 1956, 1959) produced guides for motor tourists who could use the newly paved highways of the province to access the unspoiled seldom-seen beauty of rural areas and spend time with the ethno-racial types who continued to inhabit out-of-the-way places. Bird worked for the provincial government in tourist promotion from the early 1933 until his retirement in 1966.

From the 1930s, key Nova Scotian cultural intellectuals including Bird, music collector Helen Creighton, artist Mary E. Black and provincial premier Angus L. Macdonald[3], worked systematically to produce an image of Nova Scotia that has

---

[2] An iconic verse in Alister MacGillvary's folk song *Song for the Mira* (https://www.youtube.com/watch?v=3as9K3CSJvg) illustrates this sensibility.

> Out on the Mira, the people are kind
>
> They'll treat you to homebrew and help you unwind
>
> And if you come broken, they'll see that you mend.

[3] Macdonald (1890–1954) served separate two lengthy terms as provincial premier (1933–1940 and 1945–1954), dying in office. His Liberal party won the 1940 election, but Macdonald was summoned to Ottawa for federal war service in which he oversaw the expansion and development of Canada's wartime navy (Henderson, 2007). Macdonald spoke Gaelic and was an influential

as its central motor, the fabricated idea of a rural quintessence of isolation, "pure" European tradition kept alive by people living in isolation. This was the height of what Niergarth (2018) calls Canada's "heyday of public commemoration" which featured the establishment of parks and monuments to colonial history dovetailing with the work of cultural intellectuals to construct the image of the "real" Nova Scotia in which Indigenous and people of African descent get scarcely a mention. In Bird's travelogues, each rural region of the province is home to Scottish (Northern Nova Scotia and Cape Breton), German (South Shore), French (Clare, Argyle southern Cape Breton), Irish and British "types" that tourists can meet sampling food and enjoying traditional song and story.

Little changed until relatively recently when critics raised questions about exclusively monochrome, Eurocentric images in provincial tourism literature. Recent provincial reports and academic analysis stimulated more by racialized minority critique than by historical scholarship have also highlighted the need for cultural change and a recognition of the historic, yet lingering, colonial imaginary (Hollingshead, 2009). As yet, few Canadian scholars or public intellectuals have addressed the connection between how iconic Eurocentric imagery in settler societies is inflected by the imagined purity and isolation of rural setter values, people and places. There is almost nothing in this vein relating to education. One key exception is Joanne Tomkins' (2002) sensitive analysis of pre-service teachers in rural Nova Scotia struggling to come to grips with Indigenous education and recognizing the blind spots created by their rural upbringings. One of McKay's (1994) key points is that many of the most committed consumers of the myth of Nova Scotia are Nova Scotians themselves who still proudly perform Tartanism developing and extending the very structures of feeling imagined by the mid-century cultural intellectuals.

---

promoter of Scottish culture playing a key role in the development of what McKay (1994) calls "Tartanism", or the iconic association of the province, and particularly Cape Breton Island, with Scotland. Helen Creighton (1899–1989) was an amateur folklorist who collected more than 4000 folk songs travelling through rural Nova Scotia from the late 1920s to the mid 1970s. Like many other mid-century folklorists, Creighton was seeking what she considered to be pure forms of English folk songs kept alive by the isolation of rural Nova Scotia villages. She did also record the music of other ethnic groups, generally without making the same sorts of claims for the purity of form that she would for English ballads. Her work is critiqued by McKay for its promotion of an alleged quintessential rural rusticity in Nova Scotia. Mary E. Black (1895–1988) spearheaded a parallel movement to "revive" and promote the production and marketing of rural craft work, particularly textile arts. Her work included support for the 1953 design of the Nova Scotia tartan which remains prominent both as an iconic commodity in its own right as well as a ubiquitous feature in provincial tourism promotion for more than 60 years. Will R. Bird (1891–1984) was a Nova Scotia autodidactic novelist, travel writer, and amateur historian who wrote at least 27 books between 1928 and 1975. I met Bird in the early 1970s in Amherst Nova Scotia when I delivered newspapers in his neighbourhood.

9.5 Difficult Histories

In 2018, I was presented with the opportunity to address a large gathering of rural educators at the 2019 Canadian National Congress on Rural Education. The national congress has been in operation for 25 years and it is a gathering of rural school district officials, school principals, trustees and a coterie of academics, mostly connected with the educational administration unit in the College of Education at the University of Saskatchewan. This conference is generally a gathering where best practices in rural education are shared and its program tends to be very pragmatic and focussed on the professional field. It tends to look more like a professional conference than academic meetings where research is shared and discussed by those who create it. The role of the keynote address is to provide food for thought in an engaging way that is accessible and palatable to conference attendees. I wondered what I might have to say to this group that they didn't already know and that might capture the present moment.

While preparing for my talk, I read a piece in *Roar* by Max Haiven (2019) about racially motivated murders of Indigenous youth in Thunder Bay. Haiven describes the rise of industrial capitalism in the city, the dispossession of Indigenous people with the decline of the fur trade and the racial and labour struggles that followed. What remained constant through this history, he writes, is the persistent marginalization and abuse of Indigenous citizens who suffer from the highest murder and suicide rates in what he calls Canada's "most racist city". But Haiven acknowledges that these problems are not confined to Thunder Bay but represent only one example of what he calls "the dire failure of the Canadian model of liberal capitalism, corporate multiculturalism, and half-hearted 'reconciliation'". Since the publication of the Report of the Truth and Reconciliation Commission of Canada (2015), progressive Canadians of settler descent have been struggling to understand and enact reconciliation. Haiven concludes that good things are indeed happening in Thunder Bay at the grassroots level, but the bit in his piece that struck me most powerfully was his account of an encounter he and a group of non-Indigenous student activists had with an elder at a protest rally. I think it is worth quoting at some length.

> I was once part of a group of well-meaning graduate student activists who went to an Indigenous blockade near where we were going to school. We were all nervous: police and white supremacists were active in the area. Nothing at the blockade matched our understanding of order. We couldn't figure out who we were supposed to meet with and, when we did, she was busy for hours before we could talk. Some of us had classes to teach. "Go back and find your own indigenous ancestry." The elder, a protest leader, told us: "your ancestors had their land taken and that's why they came here. Now you're taking our land. Maybe you don't have to go back to those lands, but learn who your ancestors were and their struggles and then we can talk eye to eye". (Haiven, 2019)

The idea of going back and finding one's own ancestry struck me. Is this not precisely what Bird, Creighton, Black and Macdonald were doing when they invented the version of heritage and history I have described above? Macdonald was no stranger to the impact of the Highland Clearances that largely created the Scottish presence in Nova Scotia. Could stories of European diasporas be used to support reconciliation rather than retrenchment of exclusive settler mythologies that actually motivated exclusionary and racist national policies like the White Australia doctrine, the residential school system, Japanese detention camps in the Second World War or the Canadian government's refusal to accept Jewish refugees fleeing the Holocaust.

Using tools that often inform racial intolerance to confront racial intolerance is obviously difficult and dangerous business, but it is what I wanted to do with this address. Subsequently, I have encountered a similar strategy in Darryl Leroux's (2019) recent analysis of White claims to Indigenous identity through what he calls a personalized self-indigenizing "race shifting". Leroux documents the creation of ad hoc Métis organizations in eastern Canada after the Powley Decision of 1993 that gave hunting rights to Métis people who meet twelve conditions established in ruling. These conditions require that anyone claiming Métis status must prove an ongoing multigenerational relationship with established Indigenous communities and cultural practices and not just blood ancestry in the more or less distant past. Leroux shows that by using genealogical slight-of-hand, groups in Québec, New Brunswick and Nova Scotia have either established or fabricated Indigenous ancestors (mostly from the 1600s). He then deconstructs these "eastern Métis" movements, demonstrating the weakness of these claims, none of which have met the Powley Test in Canadian courts.

Leroux does not simply critique the questionable genealogical practices used by the race shifters, he also conducts a personal genealogical search, carefully tracing his own blood ancestry back to ancient Indigenous individuals. Contrary to the approach of the race shifters, he uses careful genealogical research (he also demonstrates the extreme lack of care taken by most ad hoc eastern Métis organizations) to establish his lack of geographic, cultural connection to any Indigenous communities or any living Indigenous descendants of his long-ago blood ancestors currently living in Indigenous territory. This is an example of a use of genealogical research that complicates both the notion of distant blood connections as well as reductionist mythologized heroic/victim heritage story. Among these stories are ironic claims to indigeneity by white-supremacists and others seeking benefits and access to resources documented by Leroux as well as perhaps more benign examples such as spiritual narratives of new-age self-indigenizers, established settler heritage promoters drawing similar blood connections to European and more innocent/naïve well-meaning European-descended people seeking redemption from past wrongs through what Tuck and Yang (2012) call "moves to innocence". Indeed, Tomkins (2002) did not find rural teacher education candidates who harbour overt racist attitudes; they tend to be young people who are genuinely ignorant of their own histories and social position and who default to the psycho-logic of assuming that differential educational outcomes are due to individual factors such as intelligence, engagement, self-control, and attitude. In their communities and families, it may be impolite to think otherwise (Corbett & Gereluk, 2020).

9.6   Problematizing Place

In the field of rural education, we have tended to focus on how place-based educational practices are superior to forms of education that focus principally on abstractions and what many (including me) have called placeless knowledge. The usual foes in this piece are the standardized test and the transmission curriculum which together are said to elide, ignore and even dismiss John Dewey's central theoretical tenet that education begins in the experience of the child. Dewey's psychology is often aligned with a form of rural education sociology that focuses more on particular local places rather than on structural transformation (like capitalism, globalization, contemporary communication technologies, etc.) that bring virtually all places into complex relationships with one another (Nespor, 2008). These complex relationships include colonialism and the uncomfortable and violent history that has created and continues to create existing relations of power and privilege are easy to wish away. It is eminently clear that individual choices and educational and career trajectories are complicated by ubiquitous change including pressure on the nuclear family to support young adults' protracted emotional and economic socialization journeys (Arnett, 2014; Giddens, 1993). Current social conditions also increase the centrality of reflexivity and the complexity of contemporary forms of reflection for understanding social conditions (Archer, 2012).

In recent years, the idea of place-based education has gained significant traction in rural education circles. This attention goes back to foundational American work in the field by scholar/activists Theobald (1997), Haas and Nachtigal (1998) and Shelton (2005) as well as to national rural community development initiatives such as 1995 Annenburg Rural Challenge in the United States and the establishment of the Canadian Rural Restructuring (later changed to revitalization) Foundation in 1991. This work draws on the early twentieth century progressive traditions in rural North America that can be traced to the work of John Dewey, the Country Life Movement, and in Canada, to the Antigonish Movement and Frontier College (Canniff, 1998; Welton, 1987).

While a focus on place as a foundation for rural education (and indeed, for any education) is crucial, how we situate and imagine place also needs to be considered. I think rural educators also need to problematize their very focus on place by critically interrogating established local perceptions of belonging in particular places and how those places became what they are today (Jackson, 2010). It is, I think, important to acknowledge that colonial projects are responsible for European settlement in North America/Turtle Island. We say a lot in Canadian teacher education about the necessity for teachers to confront themselves first of all, and part of this confrontation involves complicating our relationship with place (see also Corbett & Gereluk, 2020). This can be very difficult for non-indigenous, non-racialized rural teachers precisely because, for many of us, place and a sense of belonging (if not entitlement) loom large in our own family histories, affect and identities. I suggest that, following the Mi'Kmaq elder cited by Haiven, that we begin at home exploring first of all the diversity in imagined categories like whiteness, settler, *pur laine*,[4] born and bred, etc. This involves recognizing the systematic displacement of Indigenous people that the arrival of our settler ancestors represented while simultaneously interrogating the European diasporic upheavals that brought our ancestors here as foot-soldiers of empire.

9.7 Diasporic Autobiography

In my own history there are two significant European Diasporas that brought my forbears to what is now known as eastern Canada. The first of my historical and genealogical investigations derived from my maternal and paternal grandmothers (Annie LeBlanc and Mae Benoit) is the French colonial diaspora that followed the Wars of Religion through the last three decades of the sixteenth Century. This was one of the bloodiest wars in European history and it ravaged the part of France where it might be said my ancestors were indigenous. According to Naomi Griffiths (2004, p. 5), these people, who came to be called Acadians, originated in the very places where the struggle was most bitter and destructive. They escaped thirty years of pretty much continuous bloodshed, attendant property destruction, famine, plagues and other related horrors.

By the early seventeenth century French fishing expeditions routinely spent a considerable part of the year catching and salting cod and then returning to Europe. The "New World" provided lucrative opportunities. When French colonial ambitions created the possibility of emigration, it was undoubtedly attractive to many people living in plague and famine-prone, war-ravaged regions of France. Acadian escaped brutal warfare only to face an ethnic cleansing in the mid eighteenth century at the hands of the British in what is euphemistically known as the "Expulsion" of the Acadians. I am descended from the Acadians who made their way back to the areas they settled only to find that the land they formerly occupied was now in the hands of anglophone settlers from the British-held Thirteen Colonies to the south. Like the Indigenous people of the area, the Acadians were subsequently relegated to marginal lands where they came to rely principally on fishing and logging. This occupational pattern continued into my mother's youth when the family left pluri-occupational subsistence farming, fishing and logging in 1939 for wartime factory work in an Anglophone community in Nova Scotia where I grew up (Corbett, 2013).

My paternal and maternal grandfathers (John Corbett and William Fagan) emigrated from Ireland in the nineteenth century. The former emigrated in 1820, following rural market collapse, British repression and sectarian violence that followed the Napoleonic Wars, the latter in the 1840s escaping famine and colonial exploitation. The systematic starvation of the Irish people by British colonial authorities during the large famine of the 1840s (which was part of a long series of famines

---

[4]A Québecois expression for a descendent of the original French settlers explicitly translated as "pure wool" and roughly translated to mean "dyed in the wool".

that ravaged Ireland through the nineteenth century) is a relatively well-known colonial atrocity in the 800-year British occupation of Ireland. The antecedents of my paternal grandfather William Fagan settled, somewhat ironically, in a southern New Brunswick region allotted to Acadians who returned to Atlantic Canada following the mid-eighteenth century "expulsion" and despite my grandfather's Irish surname he was a monolingual Francophone for the first half of his 74 years.

What pushed William Fagan's ancestors out of Ireland is easy to understand. Less well known is the situation in southern Ireland following the Napoleonic Wars. This period of European warfare (1803–1815) was a time of prosperity for farmers in North Cork and Southern Tipperary. The English military machine needed food, and Ireland was a ready source. However, post 1815, agricultural incomes collapsed, exacerbated by the systematic dumping of English goods on the market following the war. This situation was aggravated by harvest failures in 1816 and 1821, a drought in 1818 and a major epidemic that lasted from 1816 to 1819. Through this period separatist and sectarian violence ramped up and Catholic paramilitary gangs with names such as the White Boys, The Ribbon Society, The Right Boys, The Defenders and Captain Rock generated mass instability through violence and destruction of property and livestock. This uprising was met by British colonial authorities with the deployment of 25,000 demobilized and battle-hardened British troops into Ireland in the early 1820s. Sectarian unrest was also stoked by enforced tithes to the Anglican Church and the suspension of civil liberties, the abolition of trials, mass arrests, transportation to Australia, and the imposition of curfews. My Irish ancestors (John Corbett and Mary Casey) fled chaos, colonial violence, disease and starvation in southern Ireland in 1820 landing in Malignant Cove Nova Scotia, subsequently moving to Havre Boucher where the family lived for about a century before dispersing throughout North America from my father's generation onward.

Other Diasporas would follow. My mother's family left southern New Brunswick in 1939 for factory work at the beginning of World War II in an English community in Nova Scotia. My father's antecedents spread throughout North American from the late nineteenth century when trains and merchant vessels transported many young people away from rural Nova Scotia to urban opportunity, principally in the "Boston States" (New England) but also to Ontario and throughout the United States. In the 1960s and 70s growing up in the town into which my mother's Acadian family emigrated in 1939, I came to understand that there was limited opportunity for me and that I too would have to leave home. This was a central part of my interest in geographic mobility and its connection to education in rural and small-town Atlantic Canada.

9.8 Conclusion

One of the most important activities I do with pre-service teachers is a culturally responsive pedagogy activity entitled "What's in a Name" (Stoltzfus, 2019). In the activity students, one by one, unpack their name. I begin by telling a story of my own name, how it hides the 75% of my identity associated with women in my direct ancestry and tracing the Irish and French roots of my name. The purpose of the activity is to complexify whiteness and to illustrate how each of us has multiple identities that entwine ascribed and chosen elements. The exercise illustrates how in a classroom populated principally by more or less light-skinned people of European descent there is remarkable diversity.

We explore autobiographical stories, gender, culture and ethnicity, race, language, social class and the extent to which students are aware of how they came to be sitting in a Bachelor of Education in Nova Scotia, Canada at this given moment. Some students have little knowledge of their family background while others are uncomfortable speaking about their family history for various reasons. Some are adopted which raises questions about the exercise itself. These stories tend to tap into deep structures of feeling and the autobiographic narratives that provide us with a sense of past and place. Many of these tales are proud stories of rural resilience. This activity helps pre-service teachers locate themselves in a cultural landscape while at the same time considering the ambiguity of their own identity constructions and some problematics it contains. It helps, I think, erase the normalizing myth of whiteness that many of these pre-service teachers have never considered. It can also help us to shift from simplistic established juxtaposed/binary positions of innocence and guilt to recognize a more complex and historically conscious sense of responsibility.

Finally, we come to see that most of us are all products of what Paul Gilroy has called the *Black Atlantic*. Rather than focusing on place, Gilroy (1993, 2010) suggested the importance of a focus on movement, relationality and hybridity that arises from the colonial experience which creates cultural forms that are new (see also Bhabha, 1990). It seems to me precisely the fear of the movement of the other into what is thought to be one's exclusive place that drives much rural angst in North America today, from the hysterical politics of fear at Trump's rallies and the attack on the Capitol, to the banning of religious symbols for public servants in Québec. The Heideggerian notion of dasein (being-there), for all of its analytic clout, has the potential to conflate habit, people and place. It is here that rural education can support and promote new structures of feeling for new times rather then re-embed established and exclusive rural settler narratives.

References

Archer, M. S. (2012). *The reflexive imperative in late modernity.* Cambridge University Press.

Arnett, J. J. (2014). *Emerging adulthood: The winding road from the late teens through the twenties.* Oxford University Press.

Beech, J., & Guy, M. (2017). Fat guys in the woods naked and afraid: Rural reality television as prep-school for a post-apocalyptic world. In W. M. Reynolds (Ed.), *Forgotten places: Critical studies in rural education* (pp. 45–60). International Academic Publishers: Peter Lang Inc.

Berlant, L. (2011). *Cruel optimism.* Duke University Press.

Bhabha, H. K. (1990). *The location of culture.* Routledge.

Bird, W. R. (1950). *This Is nova scotia.* Ryerson Press.

Bird, W. R. (1956). *Off-Trail in nova scotia* (1st ed.). The Ryerson Press

Bird, W. R. (1959). *These are the maritimes* (1st ed.). The Ryerson Press.

Bloch, M., Buchanan, L., Katz, J., & Quealy, K. (2018, July 25). An extremely detailed map of the 2016 presidential election. *The New York Times*. Retrieved from https://www.nytimes.com/interactive/2018/upshot/election-2016-voting-precinct-maps.html, https://www.nytimes.com/interactive/2018/upshot/election-2016-voting-precinct-maps.html.

Canniff, J. G. (1998). *On living well in our place: Earlier rural reform movements.* https://eric.ed.gov/?id=ED444792.

Cervone, J. A. (2017). *Corporatizing rural education: Neoliberal globalization and reaction in the United States*. Palgrave Macmillan.

Ching, B., & Creed, G. W. (Eds.). (1996). *Knowing your place: Rural identity and cultural hierarchy*. Routledge.

Coladarci, T. (2007). Improving the yield of rural education research: An editor's swan song. *Journal of Research in Rural Education, 22*(3), 1–9.

Corbett, M. (2006). Educating the country out of the child and educating the child out of the country: An excursion in spectrology. *Alberta Journal of Educational Research, 52*(4), 289–301.

Corbett, M. (2007) *Learning to leave: The irony of schooling in a coastal community*. Fernwood Publishing.

Corbett, M. (2013). Remembering French in English: The meditation of an assimilated Acadian. In T. Strong-Wilson, C. Mitchell, & S. Allnutt (Eds.), *Productive remembering and social agency* (pp. 89–103). Sense Publishers.

Corbett, M. (2014). The ambivalence of community: A critical analysis of rural education's oldest trope. *Peabody Journal of Education, 89*(5), 603–618.

Corbett, M. (2020). Place-based education: A critical appraisal from a rural perspective. In M. Corbett & D. Gereluk (Eds.), *Rural teacher education: connecting land and people* (pp. 279–298). Springer.

Corbett, M., & Gereluk, D. (Eds.). (2020). Rural teacher education: Connecting land and people. Springer.

Cramer, K. J. J. (2016). *The politics of resentment: Rural consciousness in Wisconsin and the rise of Scott Walker*. University of Chicago Press.

Cuervo, H. (2016). *Understanding social justice in rural education*. Palgrave Macmillan.

Derrida, J. (1994). *Spectres of Marx: The state of the debt, the work of mourning and the New International*. New York: Routledge.

Donehower, K., Hogg, C., & Schell, E. E. (2007). *Rural literacies*. SIU Press.

Donehower, K., Hogg, C., & Schell, E. E. (2011). *Reclaiming the rural: Essays on literacy, rhetoric, and pedagogy*. SIU Press.

Echazarra, A., & Radinger, T. (2019). *Learning in rural schools: Insights form PISA, TALIS and the literature* (p. 77). Organization for Economic Cooperation and Development.

Fukuyama, F. (1992). *The end of history and the last man*. Free Press.

Geller, W. (2015). *Rural young women, education, and socio-spatial mobility: Landscapes of success*. Lexington Books.

Giddens, A. (1971). *Capitalism and modern social theory*. Cambridge University Press.

Giddens, A. (1976). *New rules of sociological method: A positive critique of interpretative sociologies*. Stanford University Press.

Giddens, A. (1979). *Central problems in social theory: Action, structure and contradictions in social analysis*. University of California Press.

Giddens, A. (1993). *The transformation of intimacy: Sexuality, love and erotism in modern societies*. Stanford University Press.

Gilroy, P. (1993). *The Black Atlantic: Modernity and double consciousness*. Harvard University Press.

Gilroy, P. (2010). *Darker than blue: On the moral economies of Black Atlantic culture*. Harvard University Press.

Green, B. (2008). *Spaces and places: The NSW rural teacher education project*. Centre for Information Studies, Charles Sturt University.

Green, B. (2013). Literacy, ruralty, education: A partial mapping. In B. Green & M. Corbett (Eds.), *Rethinking rural literacies: Transnational perspectives* (pp. 17–34). Palgrave Macmillan.

Green, B., & Letts, W. (2007). Space, equity, and rural education: A "trialectical" account. In K. Gulson & C. Symes (Eds.), *Spatial theories of education: Policy and geography matters* (pp. 57–76). Routledge.

Griffiths, N. (2004). *From migrant to Acadian: A North American border people, 1604–1755.* McGill-Queens University Press.

Haas, T., & Nachtigal, P. M. (1998). *Place value: An educators' guide to good literature on rural lifeways, environments, and purposes of education.* Eric Clearinghouse on Rural.

Haiven, M. (2019). The colonial secrets of Canada's most racist city. Retrieved October 25, 2019, from *ROAR Magazine* website: https://roarmag.org/essays/colonial-secrets-canadas-racist-city/.

Hall, D., & Biddle, C. (2017, January 18). How education is failing rural America—Education week. *Education Week.* Retrieved from http://www.edweek.org/ew/articles/2017/01/18/how-education-is-failing-rural-america.html.

Heidegger, M. (1927). *Being and time.* State Univ of New York Press.

Henderson, T. S. (2007). *Angus L. Macdonald: A provincial liberal.* University of Toronto Press.

Hochschild, A. R. (2016). *Strangers in their own land: Anger and mourning on the American right.* The New Press.

Hollinshead, K. (2009). "Tourism state" cultural production: The re-making of Nova Scotia. *Tourism Geographies, 11*(4), 526–545.

Jackson, A. Y. (2010). Fields of discourse: A foucauldian analysis of schooling in a rural, U.S. Southern Town. In K. A. Schafft & A. Y. Jackson (Eds.), *Rural education for the twenty-first century: Identity, place, and community in a globalizing world.* The Pennsylvania State University Press.

Kelly, U. A. (2009). *Migration and education in a multicultural world: Culture, loss, and identity* (1st ed.). Palgrave Macmillan.

Kelly, U. A. (2013). Find yourself in Newfoundland and Labrador: Reading rurality as reparation. In B. Green & M. Corbett (Eds.), *Rethinking rural literacies: Transactional perspectives* (pp. 53–74). Palgrave Macmillan.

Lefebvre, H. (1992). *The production of space.* Wiley-Blackwell.

Leroux, D. (2019). *Distorted descent: White claims to indigenous identity.* University of Manitoba Press.

Malm, A. (2016). *Fossil capital: The rise of steam power and the roots of global warming.* Verso.

McKay, I. (1994). *The quest of the folk: Antimodernism and cultural selection in twentieth-century Nova Scotia.* McGill-Queen's University Press.

McKay, I., & Bates, R. (2010). *In the province of history: The making of the public past in twentieth-century Nova Scotia.* McGill-Queen's University Press.

Nespor, J. (2008). Education and place: A review essay. *Educational Theory, 58*(4), 475–489. https://doi.org/10.1111/j.1741-5446.2008.00301.x.

Niergarth, K. (2018). In search of authenticity: Public memory, living history, and folk art in modern Canada. *Acadiensis, 47*(1), 243–256.

Nugent, G., Kunz, G., Sheridan, S., Glover, T., & Knoche, L. (Eds.). (2017). *Rural education research in the United States.* Springer.

Ousley, O. (1961). *Ginn basic readers.* Ginn.

Pappano, L. (2017). Colleges discover the rural student. *The New York Times.* Retrieved September 17, 2019, from https://www.nytimes.com/2017/01/31/education/edlife/colleges-discover-rural-student.html.

Parsons, T. (1950). *The social system.* New York: Basic Books.

Pini, B., & Bhopal, K. (2017). Racialising rural education. *Race Ethnicity and Education, 20*(2), 192–196. https://doi.org/10.1080/13613324.2015.1115620.

Putnam, R. D. (2007). E Pluribus Unum: Diversity and community in the twenty-first century the 2006 Johan Skytte prize lecture. *Scandinavian Political Studies, 30*(2), 137–174.

Reid, J.-A., Green, B., Cooper, M., Hastings, W., Lock, G., & White, S. (2010). Regenerating rural social space? Teacher education for rural-regional sustainability. *Australian Journal of Education, 54*(3), 262–276.

Reynolds, W. M. (Ed.). (2017a). *Forgotten places: Critical studies in rural education*. International Academic Publishers: Peter Lang Inc.

Reynolds, W. M. (Ed.). (2017b). Rural place: Media, violent cartographies, and chaotic disruptions. In *Forgotten places: Critical studies in rural education* (pp. 31–44). Peter Lang.

Roberts, P. (2016). *Place, rural education and social justice: A study of rural teaching and curriculum politics* (Charles Sturt University). Retrieved from https://researchoutput.csu.edu.au/en/publications/place-rural-education-and-social-justice-a-study-of-rural-teachin-3.

Roberts, P., & Green, B. (2013). Researching rural places on social justice and rural education. *Qualitative Inquiry, 19*(10), 765–774. https://doi.org/10.1177/1077800413503795.

Sassen, S. (1991). *The Global City: New York, London, Tokyo*. Princeton University Press.

Sassen, S. (2014). *Expulsions: Brutality and complexity in the global economy*. Cambridge: Belknap Press.

Shelton, J. (2005). *Consequential learning: A public approach to better schools*. New South.

Stoltzfus, K. (2019). *What's in a name? Huda Essa on culturally responsive teaching—ASCD empower19*. Retrieved October 29, 2019, from http://empower.ascd.org/general-information/conference-daily/whats-in-a-name.aspx.

Tavernise, S., Gebeloff, R., & Lee, C. (2019, October 25). Are the suburbs turning democratic? It depends where you look. *The New York Times*. Retrieved from https://www.nytimes.com/2019/10/25/us/democrats-republicans-suburbs.html.

Theobald, P. (1997). *Teaching the commons: Place, pride, and the renewal of community*. Westview Press.

Tieken, M. C. (2014). *Why rural schools matter: Why rural schools matter*. The University of North Carolina Press.

Truth and Reconciliation Commission of Canada. (2015). *Honouring the truth, reconciling for the future: summary of the final report of the truth and reconciliation commission of canada*. http://www.trc.ca/assets/pdf/Honouring_the_Truth_Reconciling_for_the_Future_July_23_2015.pdf.

Tomkins, J. (2002). Learning to see what they can't: Decolonizing perspectives on indigenous education in the racial context of rural Nova Scotia. *McGill Journal of Education / Revue Des Sciences de l'éducation de McGill, 37*(3). Retrieved from http://mje.mcgill.ca/article/view/8646.

Tuck, E., & Yang, W. (2012). Decolonization is not a metaphor. *Decolonization: Indigeneity, Education and Society, 1*(1), 1–40.

Vance, J. D. (2016). *Hillbilly Elegy: A memoir of a family and culture in crisis*. New York: Harper.

Welton, M. R. (Ed.). (1987). *Knowledge for the people: The struggle for adult learning in english-speaking Canada, 1828–1973*. The Ontario Istitute for Studies in Education.

Westover, T. (2018). *Educated*. Toronto: HarperCollins Publishers.

Williams, R. (1958/1983). *Culture and society, 1780–1950*. Columbia University Press.

Williams, R. (1960). *Border country*. Dufour Editions.

Williams, R. (1974). *The country and the city*. Oxford University Press.

Wu, J. (2016). *Fabricating an educational miracle: Compulsory schooling meets ethnic rural development in Southwest China*. SUNY Press.

Wuthnow, R. (2018). *The left behind: Decline and rage in rural America*. Princeton University Press.

Michael Corbett works in the School of Education at Acadia University in Canada and at the University of Tasmania where he holds an adjunct research professorship in rural and regional education. He has studied youth educational decision-making, mobilities and education, the politics of educational assessment, literacies in rural contexts, improvisation and the arts in education, conceptions of space and place, the viability of small rural schools, and "wicked" policy problems and controversies in education.

Index

© Springer Nature Singapore Pte Ltd. 2021
S. White and J. Downey (eds.), *Rural Education Across the World*,
https://doi.org/10.1007/978-981-33-6116-4